MW00775498

The Theology *of* Marriage

The
Theology
of Marriage

Personalism,
Doctrine, and
Canon Law

Cormac Burke

Foreword by Janet Smith

THE CATHOLIC UNIVERSITY
OF AMERICA PRESS

Washington, DC

Library of Congress Cataloging-in-Publication Data
Burke, Cormac, 1927–
The theology of marriage : personalism, doctrine, and canon law /
Cormac Burke ; foreword by Janet Smith.
pages cm
Includes bibliographical references and index.
ISBN 978-0-8132-2685-9 (pbk. : alk. paper)
1. Marriage—Religious aspects—Catholic Church.   2. Catholic
Church—Doctrines.   3. Marriage (Canon law)   I. Title.
BX2250.B8655 2015
234'.165—dc23   2014039453

Contents

Foreword by Dr. Janet Smith   vii

Acknowledgments   xix

Introduction   xxi

Abbreviations   xxvii

1. Marriage: Sacramentality and Faith   1

2. Marriage: Sacrament and Sanctity   30

3. The Ends of Marriage: A Personalist or an Institutional Understanding?   50

4. A Further Look at the "Good of the Spouses" as an End of Marriage   71

5. Church Law and the Rights of Persons   103

6. The "Good" and the "Bad" in Marriage according to St. Augustine   125

7. The Inseparability of the Unitive and Procreative Aspects of the Conjugal Act   164

8. An R.I.P. for the *Remedium Concupiscentiae*   181

Bibliography   243

Index   251

Foreword

DR. JANET SMITH

I suspect most Catholics tend to think of canon law as the by-laws of the church or just some necessary in-house rules. Among those who know where to find canon law, some occasionally dip into it to solve some dispute, as if they could go to a canon and brandish it about. For some years now I have been carpooling with a canon lawyer and have come to realize that amateurs should tread cautiously in attempting to interpret canon law. I have also learned that canon law has a range and importance that can hardly be overestimated. Even those who know a great deal about the faith have little idea how intertwined canon law is with theological concepts, how canon law must be interpreted in light of theological principles, and how theology must be interpreted in light of canon law. In this book we see canon lawyer and theologian Monsignor Cormac Burke utilize his extensive knowledge of canon law and of theology along with his experience working with married couples to expand our understanding of the sacrament of marriage. Readers will appreciate how Monsignor Burke clearly identifies various misunderstandings of whatever subject he raises before he addresses that subject. Readers will hopefully find themselves among those who hold some of those false understandings and will also be thrilled to learn what the church really teaches about these matters.

The content of the first chapter of this volume will likely surprise most readers. It is a tightly argued defense of the position that the marriages of all who have been baptized are sacramental marriages whether or not their faith is active, as long as the parties intend to enter into the natural state of marriage. I learned a great deal from the chapter but more perhaps about the powers of the graces of baptism than about the sacrament of marriage (though I certainly learned much about the latter). Burke is very emphatic about the power of baptism to change everything about one's life and to open one to the graces that come with a sacramental marriage even if those contracting the marriage have little or no understanding of the sacrament. I found that argument to be wonderfully consoling—baptism is a powerful gift, and God does not want to let those who have been baptized fail to receive the sacramental graces he has planned for his children.

Burke also makes it perfectly clear that marriage is a sacrament that the spouses bring about through the exchange of vows: the priest only witnesses the sacrament and does not cause it. Most readers will be surprised at the minimal elements necessary for a theologically valid marriage as well as the kind of variables that juridical elements introduce. This chapter sets the stage for the rest of the book in a rather peculiar but quite fascinating way, for Burke shows that the juridical elements are bound to the natural elements and thus should not be perceived as confining but as liberating. Burke is convinced of the inherent attractiveness of the *bona*, the "goods" of natural marriage—procreation, permanence, and exclusivity. These are not negative elements of marriage, but rather the very goods that attract people to marriage. The sacramentality of Christian marriages makes these elements means of salvation as well as of worldly happiness.

Monsignor Burke urges Catholics to be more conscious of the graces conferred on them through the sacraments. He advises that we routinely call them to mind and think of them as a source for renewed and increased grace in our lives. Burke works out his ideas by wrestling with various theories that have been proposed regarding the nature of the sacrament of marriage. Few readers are likely to be familiar with the theories but will learn a great deal by following Burke as he establishes his views, such as the position that the marriage bond is a constant source of graces for the spouses. He believes that there has been a disproportionate emphasis on the sign value of the sacrament of marriage and a deficiency in theological reflection about the sanctifying effect that marriage has on the spouses, and begins to remedy that deficiency with an extended reflection on the fifth chapter of Ephesians. Burke recommends that pastors place greater emphasis on the availability of graces for assisting spouses in meeting the demands of their state in life. Many will find particularly useful his identification of the specific graces that marriage makes available to spouses in their attempts to live for the sake of the other and of the ways in which marriage can effect the sexual healing that our culture needs.

In chapter 3, Monsignor Burke revisits the vexing question of the hierarchy of goods within marriage. Refreshingly, he notes that the personalist goods of marriage, love and self-donation were not the invention of the Second Vatican Council but were prominent some thirty years earlier in *Casti Connubii*. He also shows how a personalist understanding of marriage has been incorporated into the 1983 Code. Canon law introduces the "good of the spouses" as an end of marriage. Predictably there is a great deal of controversy about the precise meaning of the phrase. Burke works to explain what the term means but more importantly to show that procreation and the good of the spouses are personalist as well as institutional ends of marriage. Remarkably, he demonstrates this claim by an analysis of the two creation accounts in Genesis, an analysis supplemented with a powerful explanation of why procreation is to be considered a personalist good. Ultimately he makes a very strong case for the wisdom of abandoning talk of a hierarchy

of ends and focusing instead on the notion that the ends are inseparable; they cannot be achieved apart from each other. Especially
notable is his explanation that it is the openness to children, not
the actual having of children, that is the good of procreation.

The precise connotation of the novel term *bonum coniugum*
is the subject of chapter 4. There Burke attempts to flesh out the
personalist meaning of the "good of the spouses." In order to do so,
he provides a fine introduction to the basics of personalist philosophy by distinguishing it from modern individualism. While both
the church's personalism and modern individualism make the
person the foundation of their philosophy, modern individualism
celebrates the singularity of the person and his right to be autono-
mous and self-actualizing whereas Christian personalism teaches
that each one must make a gift of himself to find himself.

Burke finds an innovative and illuminating expression of the
church's teaching on marriage in the new definition of consent
given in canon 1057 of the 1983 Code: "Matrimonial consent is an
act of will by which a man and a woman by an irrevocable covenant mutually give and accept one another for the purpose of establishing a marriage." While he considers that canon to be novel
and strongly personalistic, Burke also finds the roots of such an
understanding in both Augustine and Aquinas, and demonstrates
that there has always been a strong strain in church tradition that
understands marriage to be a mutually beneficial friendship. He
notes that there is an underdeveloped strain of personalism in the
tradition, especially in the value of marriage in serving to advance
spouses in holiness.

Burke interprets the *mutuum adiutorium* (mutual help) of
the tradition to be the means to the *bonum coniugum* (good of the
spouses) which is the spouses' union with God, or their sanctification. This is achieved in many ways, but one novel element emphasized by Burke is that both spouses must present and receive

each other as they really are, and that they are each inevitably imperfect. The graces of marriage are meant to confirm the spouses in their masculinity and femininity and also to order their sexual relationship. Here as elsewhere Burke stresses the importance of the spouses being aware of the graces available to them and of consciously drawing upon those graces.

Burke navigates skillfully between the traditional understanding of marriage that emphasizes procreation as the primary end of marriage and the personalist understanding that strives to delve more deeply into the spouses' experience of loving union, both physical and spiritual. He demonstrates that while personalist values were present in *Casti Connubii*, fully embraced by *Gaudium et Spes*, and dominant in the teaching of Pope John Paul II, the good of procreation has not been diminished and has come to be understood as a personalist good. Burke shows how personalist values were incorporated into the 1983 Code and also illustrates that canon law in fact advanced the personalist understanding of marriage by speaking of two ends of marriage: the good of the spouses and the procreative good. He attempts to nail down a meaning for the novel term "good of the spouses" and also to show how both ends are "institutional ends" of marriage. In doing so he engages in a fascinating analysis of the two creation accounts in Genesis which respectively emphasize one of the two ends of marriage. He also proceeds to show how the essential properties of marriage relate to its ends, and especially how fidelity, indissolubility, and procreation contribute to the maturation and perfection of the spouses. Burke also parses carefully the difference between essence and ends, driving home the point that the "good" of the *spouses*, being an end of marriage, simply cannot be categorized as a fourth essential property to be added to the traditional Augustinian triad of the "goods" of *marriage*. This portion of the book will challenge even metaphysicians but it is a very important point to work out.

Burke explains beautifully how having children and remaining faithful in an indissoluble union both assist spouses in maturing and growing in holiness. The goods of marriage are truly goods for the spouses. He also shows how a spouse's unfaithfulness or desertion does not invalidate the marriage or make it impossible for the betrayed or abandoned spouse to experience the goods of marriage—this is also one of the most salient concepts of Burke's earlier book, *Covenanted Happiness*. He concludes chapter 4 by providing canon lawyers with reflections on what bearing the "good of the spouses" has for determining the validity of a marriage.

In chapter 5, Burke acknowledges that most people seem to think of law as a restrictive element in their lives and that some favor a "pastoral approach" that tends to play fast and loose with the law. Some exalt the "charismatic gifts" and wrongly argue that they negate the dictates of law. Burke proceeds to explain the great gift that law is, in part by distinguishing individualism from personalism. He demonstrates that personalism is directed towards self-gift and the common good, and that law is an aid to those ends. He shows that the Second Vatican Council's preference for a description of the church as the "people of God" nods in the direction of stressing the necessity of law. Burke notes that "rights" language is often understood in individualistic ways whereas, in a proper understanding, rights clearly point to the need for a juridical system to protect those rights. They also point to the duties that are spelled out in canon law, as rights are correlated with duties. He then goes on to show how personalism and a respect for institutions are not only not at odds, but that institutions in fact protect persons.

Burke continues in this section with a discussion of the importance of not letting "pastoral" concerns trump the real good of the indissolubility of marriage, which is a good for the children, for

culture, and for the spouses themselves. He speaks beautifully of
the natural goodness of fidelity and the ability of the law to bring
about a justice which is healing, and also stresses the need for good
pastoral preparation for marriage and good pastoral response to
troubled and broken marriages; pastors need to help spouses grasp
the goodness of the law and its just demands. He notes that it is
much more likely that those who work through the difficulties of a
troubled marriage will ultimately find more happiness than those
who divorce.

Chapter 6 moves beyond the practical consideration of the
goodness of indissolubility to a theological consideration guided
largely by the thought of St. Augustine. Burke explains well why
Augustine is an excellent expositor of the goods of marriage. This
chapter will be very helpful for those who think that Augustine set
the church down the wrong path in its understanding of sexuality insofar as it shows that, properly understood, Augustine's three
goods of marriage are personalist goods.

Augustine's contribution to the church's understanding of
marriage is complex. He did not share our culture's worship of romance and sex but rejoiced in unions that were indissoluble, faithful, procreative, and thus deeply fulfilling. While our culture has a
largely "anything goes" mentality, Augustine, not least because of
his own susceptibility to sexual sin, understood how deeply men
and women are affected by concupiscence and thus how difficult it
is for them to order sexuality correctly. Burke patiently shows how
Augustine's thought on sexuality and concupiscence matured, il-
lustrating that we need to look at the whole of his work to grasp
his thinking rightly. Burke notes that Augustine was concerned
about the power of concupiscence within marriage to rob the act
of its selfless possibilities. In Burke's presentation one can see elements that are present in Pope John Paul II's theology of the body.
Augustine looks to Genesis to see what conjugal chastity really

looks like. Burke delves into the truths revealed to us by Genesis that correspond to feelings that we have about our sexuality. For instance, he argues that modesty is more "natural" than immodesty since it respects the goods of sexuality.

In this chapter Burke also expands on points introduced earlier—in particular, that procreation should be numbered among the personalist goods of marriage. He shows that once the procreative value is rejected, the desire for a constant sex partner becomes the foundation of marriage rather than the desire to be in a committed conjugal union with another. Neither the goods of self-giving nor the good of the healing of loneliness can really be achieved in such sexually-based relationships. He explains that Augustine tremendously valued faithful and enduring love over the ephemeral pleasures of romantic love. Augustine, like John Paul II, began his consideration of the goods of marriage not with procreation but with faithful companionship as a means of helping man and woman fulfill their natural sociability.

Burke also uses Augustine's reputation as someone who emphasized the sinful aspects of sexuality to good purpose, arguing that our culture seems to have lost altogether an understanding of the effects of original sin on our sexuality. He stresses that Augustine was neither pessimistic nor optimistic about sexuality; he was simply realistic. He did believe that concupiscence (which he distinguishes from sexual pleasure) is an evil and that it is present in all marital acts but also held the nuanced position that this does not always mean that there is personal sin in all marital sexual acts. The disorder is the result of original sin, not of our choices. Burke's explanation of these distinctions is long and careful and includes the frank acknowledgement that Augustine's views evolved and were much impacted by his struggle with his own unruly sexual desires. Concupiscence is a desire for sexual pleasure that resists the direction of the reason and will; Augustine argues that chaste spouses can "use" this concupiscence to good purposes, to develop self-mastery and to learn how to transform their sexual acts into acts of self-giving rather than selfish acts of pleasure-seeking.

Monsignor Burke's seventh chapter provides a superb explanation of why, on personalist grounds, contraception is immoral. He provides a clear exposition of the idea that the procreative meaning of the sexual-conjugal act is essential to its unitive meaning: giving the possibility of becoming a parent with another person speaks magnificently to that person of the desire to establish a life-long union. He speaks beautifully about the necessity that spouses come to know each other sexually and how contraception prevents that knowledge from coming to be.

The final chapter on *remedium concupiscentiae* (the "remedy for concupiscence") contains the most powerful reflections in the book. Burke fights strongly against the understanding that somehow marriage legitimizes lustful sex, nor does he think that marriage is any kind of remedy for concupiscence in the sense that the mere act of getting married will satisfy or remove concupiscence by providing opportunity for sexual intercourse. Rather, marriage continues to be an arena where lust and sexual disorder may exert themselves. It is not that concupiscence cannot be remedied in some true sense, but Burke maintains that it is not marriage that does the remedying but the sacramental graces available through marriage that heals our broken nature. Burke distinguishes carefully between lust, which is a selfish desire for sexual satisfaction, and sexual desire, which is perfectly compatible with respect for one's beloved and if regulated by love is often akin to tenderness. It is one of the forces that leads lovers to want to make a life-long committed union together rather than to seek simply to enjoy sexual pleasure with each other. The desire for a committed union can be precisely what fosters respect and assists those in love to avoid premarital sex, for instance. Burke has lovely things to say about the natural purity, modesty, and respect that can be found in sexually inexperienced teens, and what we can learn from their natural reticence.

Burke affirms that a contracepted act of sexual intercourse would not serve to consummate a marriage. I am not certain this is an accepted position among moralists (or even that I agree) but Burke makes a powerful case that would justify such a judgment. More importantly he speaks of how the phrase "in a human manner" refers to the need of the spouses to move beyond seeing the other as a sexual partner to understanding the sexual act as a gift of persons to each other. Monsignor Burke provides some guidelines on how spouses can avoid having their lustful tendencies insinuate themselves into the conjugal act, an act meant to be one of self-donation rather than self-satisfaction. He notes that in the past, spouses have been advised to abstain periodically as a means of purifying their passions. That is not a solution that Burke advances. Rather he advises that spouses "humanize" their conjugal acts. Here he draws upon Pope John Paul II's theology of the body and draws from that work the wisdom of preserving a healthy sense of "shame" or modesty about sexual matters. Spouses can learn from the story of Adam and Eve, reflecting on their relationship both before and after the fall. Burke also stresses the need for the spouses to reflect upon the sexual act as an opportunity for self-donation and for an opportunity to put their sexual appetites in service of affirming the other. He also recommends prayer as a means of properly ordering desire.

My primary disagreement with Burke's book concerns his view that "the hitherto prevalent evaluation of conjugal intercourse—centered almost exclusively on its procreative function and finality—is both dated and deficient." My study of the history of the church's teaching on marriage has led me to believe that there has always been an appreciation of the unitive ends of marriage and of procreation as a great good. Moreover, I suspect that many believe what Burke asserts because the opponents of the church's teaching on contraception are those who have presented a distorted vision of that teaching. Certainly, there were some advocates of the church's teaching that pressed the natural, procreative end too strongly, but I do not believe that this has been a magisterial position or even the dominant strain among moralists. Nonetheless, Monsignor Burke's knowledge of the tradition is surely deeper and more extensive than mine, so perhaps I need to revisit the question.

Those reading *The Theology of Marriage* may well experience what many who read Pope John Paul II's *Love and Responsibility* experienced; wonder that a celibate Christian could have such profound insights into the dynamics of lust and sexual passion within marriage as well as insights into how the human spirit desires precisely the goods that marriage exists to offer. Monsignor Burke brings precisely what John Paul II brought to the subject of love and marriage; extensive philosophical and theological training, a genuine and profound spirituality, and abundant experience in hearing from spouses about their married lives. They both also share a willingness to see beyond the surface of traditional formulations and to seek the deeper truths expressed in those formulations in a way that makes them accessible to our confused culture. This is a learned book, filled with fresh insights and argued carefully. It will delightfully inform many.

Acknowledgments

The ideas expressed in this book have been developed over the past thirty years. Most of the individual theses first appeared as separate studies in various academic journals. The themes now brought together have been reworked and matured so as to strengthen the overall unity of thought in the book. In almost all cases this has involved considerable modification and development.

Chapter 1 is based upon "The Sacramentality of Marriage: Theological Reflections," *Annales Theologici* 7 (1993): 47–69. Chapter 2 is drawn from "Marriage as a Sacrament of Sanctification," *Annales Theologici* 9 (1995): 71–87. Chapter 3 is an expanded version of "Marriage: A Personalist or an Institutional Understanding?" *Communio* 19 (1992): 278–304. Chapter 4 is a synthesis of various studies: "Personalism and the *bona* of Marriage," *Studia canonica* 27 (1993): 401–12; "Autorealizzazione e Dono di Sé, nel Matrimonio e nella Famiglia," *Studi Cattolici* (Feb. 1997): 84–90; and "The Object of Matrimonial Consent: A Personalist Analysis," *Forum* 9, no. 1 (1998): 39–117.

Chapter 5 is drawn from "The Pastoral Character of Church Law," *Homiletic and Pastoral Review* (March 1988); and "Marriage: A Personalist Focus on Indissolubility," *Linacre Quarterly* 61 (1994): 48–56. Chapter 6 is translated and expanded from my article "San Agustín, Matrimonio y Sexualidad," in *El pensamiento de San Agustín para el hombre de hoy* (3 vols.), edited by José Antonio Galindo Rodrigo (Valencia: Edicep, 2010), 3:601–49.

Chapter 7 was outlined in the article "Marriage and Contraception," in the official Vatican newspaper, *Osservatore Romano* (English Edition) of October 10, 1988. Finally, chapter 8 is adapted from "A Postscript to the *Remedium Concupiscentiae*," *The Thomist* 70 (2006): 481–536.

Introduction

Matrimonial themes, primarily approached from the perspective of morality, make up a large part of my writings. My reflections on marriage were partly curtailed in the early 1980s when I began to teach canon law at St. Thomas Aquinas Seminary in Nairobi, Kenya. Appointment in 1986 as judge of the Roman Rota, the High Court of the church, brought me back into the matrimonial field, although from the viewpoint of canonical theory and practice. In other times this might have led to a narrowing of horizons. My own impression is that it did not, perhaps for the accidental (or maybe providential) reason that my entrance into the practical life of a canonist coincided with the introduction of the revised Code of Canon Law in 1983. Combined with this was the disadvantage (or possibly, as someone suggested to me, the advantage) of possessing no real canonical-jurisprudential mindset formed under the old Pio-Benedictine Code.

The 1983 Code posed challenges to all canonists. For those working at the rotal level, these challenges were particularly evident in the field of matrimonial law, all the more so in that the function of rotal jurisprudence—to offer guidelines to lower tribunals—took on greatly increased importance with the introduction of the new Code.[1] It should be borne in mind that each rotal

1. In his address to the Rota some few days after the promulgation of the 1983 Code, Pope John Paul II insisted on the "decisive role" of the Rota in "the transitional phase between the old and the new canon law" and emphasized its function in the period just inaugurated, so as "to guarantee ever greater fidelity to the Church's doctrine concerning the essence and properties of marriage, which are for the rest amply

judge, in writing a sentence of which he is the *Ponens*, is free to make whatever contribution he thinks fit in the *In Iure* part of the sentence (where he reflects on background issues of the law that may be relevant to the case). Among the main elements shaping my own approach to the elaboration of a new jurisprudence in consonance with the directives of the Second Vatican Council, I would list the following: a conviction that this Council, rightly understood and implemented, was indeed a council of renewal; a particular enthusiasm for the magisterial teaching of Pope John Paul II; and a growing conviction that Christian personalism offered the answer to the issue of modern individualism.[2] To these could be added a long-standing interest in St. Augustine. Finally, as I became aware of the tendency of some post-conciliar canonists to write and theorize as if the Council warranted a turning away from and even a total jettisoning of prior ecclesial thinking (especially in the area of matrimony), I also felt the need to seek and highlight points of that development-within-continuity which marks genuine ecclesial and canonical thought.

After my first few years at the Rota, some of my colleagues on the bench of judges asked me, with the greatest tact, to consider if I was not possibly introducing too much theology into the *In Iure* part of my sentences. My reply was that it was not so much theology as anthropology that I at times introduced where I thought it helpful. I added that surely no more particular justification was needed for this than for the introduction of psychology, often inspired by secular schools, that had become so strikingly present in rotal jurisprudence since the 1970s. But of course theology came in too, although I always felt that, with regard to marriage

---

represented with theological richness in the new Code of Canon Law" (Address of February 26, 1983, in *Acta Apostolicae Sedis* [Vatican City: 1909–], 75:558 [hereafter "AAS"]).

2. This conviction led me later to write my book *Man and Values: A Personalist Anthropology* (Nairobi, Kenya: Scepter Press, 2007.)

in particular, that theological teaching would find strong support
in sound anthropology. After all, if man (male and female) is an
imago Dei, only a proper vision of man and of human realities (a
vision that is profoundly distorted today) can reflect and lead us to
God. Here of course I was simply following the lead of Pope John
Paul II. Sound theology needs sound anthropology, and sound
canonical jurisprudence needs both. It is not that I pursued theological and anthropological reflections at the Rota to the neglect
of my canonical and judicial responsibilities, or at least I hope not.
But I did feel that proper jurisprudential work, especially at the
present time, depends on a clear grasp of certain theological and
anthropological principles.

Let me comment on this and give a particular example. Not
all canon law calls for a theological analysis or needs a theological basis, but many of the core canons dealing with the sacraments
certainly do. Moreover, without an adequate theological backing,
some canonical considerations may turn out to be insufficiently
grounded. The awareness of this frequently led me to do quite a
bit of theological research before undertaking a canonical study
or exposition of a topic. A case in point concerns the issue of the
sacramentality of marriage. Certain canonical opinions of a few
decades ago seem to me to treat the theme in a theologically inadequate manner. Therefore, to equip myself to tackle such cases,
I first researched and published a study, "The Sacramentality of
Marriage: Theological Reflections," followed by a related article,
"The Sacramentality of Marriage: Canonical Reflections."[3] The
former has been developed and enlarged into the first chapter
of the present book, while the second chapter takes us one stage
further. Marriage between the baptized is always a sacrament and
hence a continuing source of grace. The current argument is that it

3. These articles are found in (respectively) *Annales Theologici* 7 (1993): 47–69;
and *Monitor Ecclesiasticus* 119 (1994): 545–65.

constitutes a divine calling in its own right, in other words, a personal vocation to sanctity. Only in recent times has this great truth begun to receive adequate attention.

It would seem to follow that the ultimate end and purpose of matrimony is the sanctification of conjugal and family life. Theology and canon law have never expressed the matter so simply, however. In both fields, a more complex formulation of the ends prevailed over many centuries. The last hundred years were to witness a split in this common thinking, which gave way to two radically opposed fields of thought: a "personalist-spouse-centered" view of the ends of marriage and an "institutional-procreative" view. Chapter 3 attempts to unravel the tangled history involved and to show how the modern magisterium is proposing a new synthesis. The key here is precisely the revised Code of Canon Law of 1983, which was the first magisterial document to describe these ends in new terms, omitting the former hierarchical order of one "primary" and two "secondary" ends and presenting the "good of the spouses" (the *bonum coniugum*) and the "procreation-education of children" as, so it seems, co-equal ends. This presentation is followed in the 1992 *Catechism of the Catholic Church* and also in the 2005 *Compendium* of the same. The introduction of such a totally new term as the *bonum coniugum*, hitherto practically never to be found in ecclesial usage, calls for justification. And so, in chapter 3, I have tried to underline its roots in Scripture (corresponding to the dual account in Genesis of the creation of the sexes) as well as tradition, and also to show how it should facilitate the defense of the true notion of marriage. This seems all the more important given the multiplicity of interpretations of the *bonum coniugum* that lack adequate depth.

Chapter 4 continues the analysis of the *bonum coniugum* in terms of Christian personalism, connecting it with the description in the 1983 Code of matrimonial consent as involving the mutual self-giving and accepting of the spouses. To my mind, many post-conciliar trends of "renewal" have been bedeviled by a sort of pseudo-personalism that, though it often invokes the concept of community, is fundamentally individualistic in nature. It breeds a spirit of habitual conflict toward church doctrine and discipline, one of its frequent claims being that the rights of the faithful are violated by the rigid "institutional" aspects or structures of the church: the magisterium, the narrowness of doctrinal declarations, the rigidity of canon law, etc. In the context of matrimony, this mindset has commonly regarded two properties of marriage—its procreativity (or openness to life) and its indissolubility—as institutional impositions inimical to the personal fulfillment of the spouses. In chapter 5, as a response to this view, I try to show that the fundamental institutions in the church are designed to protect the rights of each individual Christian to access to Christ and to foster personal growth in believers; then I set out to apply these principles to indissolubility in its purpose and effect.

The treatment here is more anthropological than theological. No doubt the same holds good for chapter 7 on the inseparability of the procreative and unitive aspects of the marital act. That contraception is a grave moral disorder by no means rests only on perennial church teaching. Human reason too can clearly show that contraception inflicts serious harm to the very nature and dignity of marriage, and also to the mutual love and respect between the spouses. Contraception nullifies true spousal self-giving and therefore contraceptive marital union is a contradiction in terms, giving a lie to the intimate nature of the conjugal relationship.

The insertion between these two chapters of a more theological study on St. Augustine is not accidental. I have always resisted the suggestion that Augustine was a pessimist regarding sex and marriage. He was in fact an optimistic realist: an optimist inasmuch as he was the first great defender of the goodness of marriage against the contempt it provoked in the Manichaeans, and a realist (in contrast to the pseudo-optimism of the Pelagians), in underlining the disorder in sexual relations caused by lust.

In the last chapter I say goodbye and good riddance to the concept that marriage serves in itself as a "remedy of concupiscence." Sexual concupiscence or lust remains in marriage as a disorder affecting both sexual appetite and conjugal sexual union. More than remedying or "legitimizing" this disorder, matrimony provides the sacramental graces to counter it, leading to a conjugal love ever more purified from self-centeredness. To my mind, the former notion of the *remedium concupiscentiae* reflected a superficial treatment of the sacramental nature of matrimony and a failure to take seriously the call to holiness that by divine will is inherent to the married state. Thus the first two chapters prepare the way for the final chapter, and so the circle of these reflections remains open rather than closed.

Abbreviations

AA   *Apostolicam Actuositatem* (Second Vatican Council, Decree on the Apostolate of Lay People)

AAS   *Acta Apostolicae Sedis*

AG   *Ad Gentes* (Second Vatican Council, Decree on the Church's Missionary Activity)

CC   *Casti Connubii* (encyclical of Pope Pius XI)

CCC   *Catechism of the Catholic Church*

CD   *Christus Dominus* (Second Vatican Council, Decree on the Pastoral Office of Bishops)

CIC   *Code of Canon Law* ("Codex Iuris Canonici")

FC   *Familiaris Consortio* (apostolic exhortation of Pope John Paul II)

GS   *Gaudium et Spes* (Second Vatican Council, Pastoral Constitution on the Church in the Modern World)

HV   *Humanae Vitae* (encyclical of Pope Paul VI)

LG   *Lumen Gentium* (Second Vatican Council, Dogmatic Constitution on the Church)

PL   *Patrologia Latina* (Migne, ed.)

PO   *Presbytorum Ordinis* (Second Vatican Council, Decree on the Ministry and Life of Priests)

TB   *Theology of the Body* (title of the first English translation of Pope John Paul II's *Catechesis on Human Love*)

The Theology *of* Marriage

I

Marriage
Sacramentality and Faith

St. Paul speaks of matrimony in terms of a great sacrament (cf. Eph 5:32), and in the next chapter we will try to draw out the splendidly positive consequences that flow from the sacramental nature of Christian marriage. However—and this of course is true of all the sacraments—it is only in the context and in the light of faith that this greatness can be understood. Hence we will begin, in this chapter, with a consideration of the intimate connection between faith and matrimony.

This seems all the more necessary since recent decades have seen considerable theological debate regarding whether "active" or "conscious" faith is necessary for a person entering into a marriage in order for the marriage to be truly sacramental. The thesis of those who hold that conscious faith is needed calls for proper evaluation. Attention should also be given to the corollary some would draw from this thesis; namely, that a marriage between Christians without active faith would be non-sacramental (although valid) and hence would not have to be considered indissoluble.

Marriage is a natural reality and a part of God's creation. At its institution, God endowed it with its essential natural character-istics: a union between one man and one woman which is exclu-sive, permanent, and open to life.[1] A union between two persons which lacks or excludes any one of these characteristics is not a true marriage in any natural sense. In the new dispensation (and therefore within a Christian theological view), marriage between baptized persons is also a supernatural reality, a sacrament. At the same time it is a part of Catholic teaching that when marriage is raised to the sacramental level, its natural or human reality is not taken away; on the contrary, sacramental marriage retains all of its natural properties.[2]

These are elementary and long-established truths. Neverthe-less, the period immediately following the Second Vatican Council saw a certain tendency to over-separate the natural and supernat-ural aspects of Christian marriage, leading to a vague suggestion that in certain cases non-practicing Christians can contract a natu-ral non-sacramental marriage which would in some way be more soluble than a sacramental marriage. Further (and this is the point we propose to study here in greater detail), the doubt was raised whether baptized persons, who lack "active" faith, can in fact con-tract a sacramental marriage; with the implicit inference that, ab-sent this "active" faith, their union would be simply a natural non-sacramental marriage and hence in some way "more" soluble.

Such notions cut at the heart of the Catholic concept of mar-riage, both in its natural and its sacramental reality. Therefore, be-fore proceeding to other topics, we wish to consider in this first chapter whether a valid sacramental marriage depends on the pos-session of a conscious and "active" Christian faith.

---

1. Gen 1:27–28 and 2:18–24. See Chapter Three below; see also *Catechism of the Catholic Church* (1992), nos. 1603–5. [hereafter "CCC"].

2. See *Gaudium et Spes*, no. 48 [hereafter "GS"], where we read (among other things): "Spouses . . . are fortified and, as it were, consecrated for the duties of their state by a special sacrament."

Sacramentality: An Element or Property of Marriage?

Sacramentality denotes the supernatural power which, by the will of Christ, accompanies certain human actions or material substances: the singular way in which divine grace works through particular natural realities, incorporating them, temporarily or permanently, into a new order; *instrumentalizing* (beyond mere "changing") them for supernatural purposes. Sacramentality therefore cannot properly be said to be an element (or property or accident) of water in baptism, of chrism in confirmation, or of the imposition of hands in ordination. It is rather an efficacy permeating these natural substances or actions, by which they become instruments of Christ's operation and productive of divine effects. The sacramental and non-sacramental use of these realities are of course clearly distinguished. Water or oil do not become "intrinsically" sacramental for the Christian, for he or she can also use them for a natural purpose without any sacramental effect or significance.

The eucharist is unique among the sacraments inasmuch as the natural realities of bread and wine used as "matter" are not just endowed with supernatural efficacy *in usu*, but are actually changed. Nothing of the former natural reality remains except the appearances: the substance has become totally other. Matrimony is closer to the eucharist and differs from the other sacraments in that the sacrament consists not in a passing action but in a resulting reality that is permanently sacramentalized.[3] While sacramentalized, it is not substantially changed; and in this way it differs

3. That is, the bond. Some thinkers would apply sacramentality to the moment of consent alone. According to St. Thomas, not just matrimonial consent, but the *bond* established by it, is the sacrament of matrimony (*Supplementum* q. 42, a. 3, ad 2) [hereafter "Suppl."].

fundamentally from the eucharist. While in the case of the eucharist the natural substance does not remain, in the case of marriage, it does—as a natural reality endowed with supernatural signification and efficacy.

Sacramentality, as applied to marriage, nevertheless escapes easy classification. At times it is referred to as if it were a "component" of matrimony, some sort of "spiritual thing" added to marriage to make it Christian, but this is not the case. Nor is it an element or property, however essential, of matrimony. It is rather a supernatural force that permeates and vivifies each and every one of the natural elements and properties of marriage, raising them to the order of supernatural meaning and efficacy. It coincides with marriage itself, which by the fact of baptism has been inserted into the economy of salvation.[4]

Sacramentality refers to the special ontological configuration of the marriage between two baptized persons. Each sacrament has its distinctive nature and efficacy. If, for instance, we compare eucharist and matrimony (each being a sacrament of "communion"), it is helpful to note that in the case of the eucharist, the bread and wine are changed into the body and blood of Christ, into a sacramental reality, but it is not really accurate to say that matrimony "becomes" a sacrament, or is "changed" into a sacrament. Again, one does not speak of bread and wine being "raised" to sacramental dignity or efficacy. Yet that is exactly what one says of marriage; and in being raised to the dignity of a sacrament, it becomes operative on a new level.

In the eucharist, nothing remains of the natural reality of the bread and wine except the appearance. The reality is no lon-

---

4. "It is the teaching of the Catholic Church that the Sacrament is not an accidental quality added to the contract, but is essential to matrimony itself" (Letter of Pope Pius IX to the King of Sardinia, Sept. 9, 1852, in *Acta SS.D.N. Pii PP. IX ex quibus excerptus est Syllabus* [Rome, 1865], 105).

ger what it seems: what appears on the outside is no more than the "sign." In matrimony, on the contrary, the natural reality—the marital bond or relationship—remains intact, but it is endowed with grace and a new significance which are not externally evident.[5]

It is perhaps more important than it might appear at first to avoid saying that the matrimonial covenant "becomes" a sacrament, for this appears to imply that in the case of each marriage that is sacramentally celebrated a "passage" occurs from one reality to another (as in the case of the eucharist). If this were so, then one could begin to hypothesize about what "remains" if and when sacramentality is excluded. And it would become possible to suggest that, just as there can be a non-sacramental eucharist where the bread and wine remain in their natural reality, so there can be a marriage between Christians that is complete in its natural reality even though sacramentality has been excluded.

Baptism: The Basis for the Sacramentality of Marriage

Behind the sacramentality of each sacrament always stands the will of Christ, wishing to incorporate the human person and her or his life into the supernatural order. Baptism is the gate to the other sacraments. Those baptized are "in" Christ; their lives henceforth bear this ineffaceable stamp or character—that of a daughter or son of God. Baptism is not merely the gate to matrimony as a sacrament but is also its key in the sense that, given the positive institutional will of Christ, baptism causes marriage to be sacramental.

If Christians marry sacramentally, this is in virtue of their being "in Christ" through baptism. "By means of baptism, man and

5. See Eph 5:32.

woman are definitively placed within the new and eternal covenant, in the spousal covenant of Christ with the Church. And it is because of this indestructible insertion that the intimate community of conjugal life and love, founded by the Creator, is elevated and assumed into the spousal charity of Christ, sustained and enriched by his redeeming power."[6] It is not simply the expression of marital consent (which in no way differs from the expression of consent to natural marriage), but the fact that the consent is *expressed by baptized persons*, that brings about the sacrament. We are moving here on the level not of juridical effects, but of ontological realities.

Baptism gives a person a new ontological relationship with God. Marriage gives a man and a woman a new human relationship to each other. If they freely choose to establish this relationship between themselves, it is also affected by their already existing ontological relation with God. What occurs here eludes the power of their will. In fact the only way that two Christians who truly marry could exclude sacramentality would be by ceasing to be Christians—but this does not lie in their power.[7] The human will, which is not omnipotent, does not have the power to change the order of being established by Christ, but must work within it.

The Rite of Sacramental Marriage

The old axiom that "God produces grace by means of the sacramental rite" needs to be properly understood in its application to marriage. The "sacramental rite" of matrimony does *not* refer to any liturgical ceremony or religious setting or church celebration. The sacramental *rite* is simply the valid exchange of consent between two Christians: their "yes" to accepting each other as hus-

---

6. Pope John Paul II, *Familiaris Consortio* (1981), no. 13 [hereafter "FC"].
7. T. Rincón-Pérez: "Fe y sacramentalidad del matrimonio," in AA.VV. *Cuestiones fundamentales sobre matrimonio y familia* (Pamplona: 1980), 193.

band and wife, in mutual conjugal self-donation. Valid Christian marital consent is therefore always a sacramental rite even if no external "religious" ceremony is performed.[8]

It is in virtue of their baptism, as we have noted, that two Christians marry "in Christ." To marry in Christ is to marry "in the church." From a theological viewpoint, therefore, one can never say that a valid marriage between two Christians, no matter how it was instituted, is a "private" contract. Christian matrimony is always a "church event," and therefore, theologically considered, public. Marriage between Christians is always celebrated "in the church," even if it is not celebrated "in church" or "in a church."[9]

Before the Council of Trent, when clandestine marriages were frequent and valid, many people entering such marriages probably had no sense or intention of performing a religious rite, but such marriages were nevertheless true sacramental marriages.[10] In modern times, getting married "in church" has become such a frequent phrase that spouses may easily be convinced that the religious rite *is* the sacrament. Here we could add that the attitude of many non-practicing or "non-believing" baptized persons is that they

8. St. Robert Bellarmine, commenting on the teaching of the Council of Trent (Session XXIV, 970, in H. Denzinger, *Enchiridion Symbolorum* [Freiburg: Herder, 1937], hereafter "Denz."), makes the point that the difference between matrimony in the Old versus the New Testament lies not in the rite (which in essence remains the same), but in the simple fact that matrimony in the New Testament is a cause of grace, and in the Old Testament was not. "The Council does not acknowledge any difference between Matrimony in ancient times, whether before or after the sin of Adam, and Matrimony as it is a Sacrament of the new law, insofar as concerns the rite. It places the distinction in that the latter is a cause of grace, while the former was not. According to the Council of Trent therefore, the matter, form and minister of the Sacrament of Matrimony are the same as they were in the Marriages of the ancients, which were not Sacraments" (Robert Bellarmine, *De Sacramento Matrimonii* [Venice: 1721], chap. 7).

9. If one says that the requirement of canonical form has the effect of making the marriage a public event, one is speaking in ecclesio-sociological terms, but not theologically.

10. St. Thomas Aquinas, *In IV Sententiarum Libros* [hereafter "*In IV Sent.*"], dist. 28, q. unica, art. 3; Bellarmine, *De Sacramento Matrimonii*, chap. 6.

simply do not care whether their marriage is a sacrament or not, but they do have objections to a "church celebration." This is what they dislike having "imposed" on them. It is going to a church that causes difficulty, in the sense either of the supposed hypocrisy which some of these non-believers may read into what is asked of them, or of the scandal which some believers may take when they see notorious non-practicers having a "church wedding."

That is why the expression "religious marriage" needs to be used with circumspection. Every valid marriage between Christians has full religious value, in that it involves "marrying in Christ." The marriage of two Protestants who exchange valid natural consent before a civil registrar is a religious marriage and a sacrament. Hence, while one can draw a contrast between "Christian" and "natural" marriage, one cannot in all propriety do so between "religious" and "civil" marriage—nor are "religious" and "sacramental" marriage necessarily the same thing. Common parlance may understandably fall into looseness of expression in these points, but theological or canonical discourse should avoid it.

To suggest that, without the presence of witnesses, there is no sacrament because there is no essential reference to the church is to mistake the theological nature of marriage.[11] I therefore cannot agree that "the presence of the priest and of the community in the celebration of marriage is the expression and the cause of the very presence and action of Christ," on the ground that while the spouses are ministers, they are not such "independently of the apostolic function that links them to the risen Savior, nor separate from the fraternity into which they have been incorporated."[12] To

---

11. Indeed this holds good for the other sacraments. Would one maintain that there is no "essential reference" to the church in the case of baptism administered in an emergency by a hospital nurse?

12. S. Maggiolini, *Sessualità umana e vocazione cristiana* (Brescia, 1970), 140 (cited in P. Barberi, *La celebrazione del matrimonio cristiano* [Rome, 1982], 57).

posit that the presence of the Christian community—represented at least by the witnesses and by the officiating priest—is necessary in order to achieve the "complete sacramental structure" of matrimony is an attempt to develop a theological thesis based on an accidental juridic requirement.

In short, then, with regard to marriage of Christians, one must distinguish between canonical (or liturgical) form, and sacramental form. The sacramental form is the same as in natural marriage (the expression of consent),[13] as is the essential rite (matter and form combined). Bellarmine criticizes Melchor Cano's error in this respect, which was precisely to claim that "if matrimony is truly a sacrament, then, besides the civil contract, it should have some sacred form, as well as an ecclesiastical minister."[14] It is important to realize that the question of canonical form is completely irrelevant to the theological consideration of marriage and concretely of its sacramentality. Much of the confusion concerning this matter that has developed over the past few decades must be attributed to theologians allowing the question of form to be invoked as if it had theological relevance.

At times it has been suggested that the church should drop the requirement of canonical form and simply recognize marriages celebrated according to civil law. While there are significant difficulties to this suggestion,[15] they are of a merely socio-juridical or pastoral-practical nature. There are, in other words, no theological difficulties to be advanced against the possible legislation of such a change. Marriages thus celebrated between two Christians would be just as sacramental as those celebrated "in church." More accurately, to insist on what we have said, such civil marriages would—

---

13. Aquinas, *In IV Sent.*, d. 26, q. 2, a. 1, ad 1.

14. Bellarmine, *De Sacramento Matrimonii*, cap. 8.

15. See those proposed by Corecco, Navarrete, Tomko, and others in Barberi, *La celebrazione*, 242–43, 394–95, 489, 527, and 535.

in the theological, though not in the merely human-social sense—be celebrated "in church."

While the church has competence over the form or social expression of matrimony, the concrete way chosen to exercise this competence is a canonical-legal issue, which leaves unaddressed the theological principle that it is not any church intervention but rather the ontological status of baptized persons that makes every valid marriage between Christians sacramental. Careless thinking here leads to proposals which run into insuperable theological difficulties, as in the frequent suggestion that those baptized persons who do not want a sacramental marriage should be allowed to contract a valid (canonical or purely civil) non-sacramental marriage, which, if they so wished and if they had developed the appropriate dispositions of faith, etc., could later—through a liturgical celebration—acquire the deeper sacramental dimension.

Ministers and Recipients

Certain canonists and churchmen have consistently and energetically defended the church's right to "marry Christians." Theologically speaking, of course, the expression is inexact. The church does not really *marry* or *join* its members in marriage; it is they who marry one another. Again, while spouses tend psychologically to consider themselves simply as recipients of marriage, the theological fact is that they are both ministers and recipients. In the Eastern Orthodox churches, it has been generally held that the essence of matrimony consists in the "crowning" or "nuptial blessing," and therefore the priest is the real minister of the sacrament. The Catholic church, in contrast to the Orthodox position, has been constant in teaching that the spouses are the ministers.[16]

---

16. "The wedding-blessing given by the priests is not of the essence of matrimony; it is a simple sacramental" (*Suppl.*, q. 42, a. 1). The Decree for the Armenians laid down that the exchange of consent and not the blessing of the priest is the effective cause of the sacrament (Denz., 702); see CCC, no. 1623.

Modern efforts to show that the priest's intervention is essential, while no doubt moved by a laudable ecumenical desire, have produced no real theological basis for the thesis. It should be added that these efforts represent in effect an attempt to clericalize what is in practice an essentially lay-administered sacrament. While in pre-conciliar times matrimonial consent was given in the form of a reply to a question put by the priest, this question-and-answer form has been replaced in the 1969 *Ordo Celebrandi Matrimonium* by a simple declaration of acceptance ("*Ego accipio te . . .*"), made by one spouse to the other. This is obviously intended to put clearer theological emphasis on the role of the spouses.[17]

The Intention Required

One striking difference between matrimony and other sacraments should be noted. In other sacraments (apart from infant baptism), a specific sacramental intention is needed for their reception. In matrimony, the intention of receiving the sacrament is not required; it is enough if one intends the natural reality. Not even a religious intention is needed—rather, simply the intention to marry. If this is the parties' intention, both being in Christ, they receive what they intended, raised (perhaps without their realizing it) to the sacramental and supernatural level, enriched and transformed by grace. What is needed is not a sacramental intention—not even implicitly[18]—but a *matrimonial* intention. Regarding marriage itself, then, the parties must have full personal intention to marry; regarding sacramentality, no further intention is required of them.

---

17. See Barberi, *La celebrazione*, 206.

18. It is therefore not necessary to posit the difficulty, as J. M. Aubert does, that "it seems difficult to allow that the general intention of truly marrying must automatically be considered as including the implicit intention of receiving the sacrament of marriage, if one does not believe in it" ("Foi et sacrement dans le mariage," *La Maison-Dieu* 104 [1970]: 130).

These statements tend to provoke difficulties, but I would suggest that they are of a psychological, not a theological, nature. Is it so hard (as some seem to find it) to accept that the simple human act of consent to marriage can be so radically transformed by the "mere" fact of a person having been baptized?[19] The clear ontological root of this transformation is to be found in the Christian sacrament of baptism. No person is the same in any of his acts once he has received the baptismal character, and so comes to "be in Christ." The problem here—apart from an underevaluation of the effects of baptism itself—would appear to be one of confusing the ontological and the psychological planes, in other words, reality and intentionality.

The Intention of Doing What the Church Does/Intends

The Council of Trent decreed that, for the validity of a sacrament, the minister conferring it must have the intention of doing what the church does.[20] Below we study certain ambiguous statements in two 1977 documents of the International Theological Commission which seem to provide a basis for holding that the dogmatic principle laid down by Trent could be applied to matrimony in the same way that it is applied to the other sacraments. This is mistaken for a reason that is both clear and striking: the *church*, as such, "does" *nothing* in the conferral of the sacrament of matrimony. The church has enacted legislation on a series of points that affect the valid celebration of marriage, but these dispositions of positive ecclesiastical law do not take away from the fact that, by divine law, matrimony is the one sacrament in which the church has nothing to *do* for its confection, as the church does not really "celebrate" the sacrament of matrimony. It provides no distinctive

19. See Barberi, *La celebrazione*, 312.
20. Denz., 854; Session VII, c. 11.

liturgical or ecclesiastical ceremony that is, strictly speaking, theologically essential to the sacrament.

We repeat: there is no church rite that converts marriage into a sacrament. A valid marriage between Christians is a sacrament, with or without the church's intervention. The church has never made any particular religious rite a condition of validity; it simply requires (as does the civil authority) that marriage be contracted according to certain formalities designed to establish externally the fact of mutual consent; but these formalities need not necessarily include any specifically religious rite whatsoever.[21] It is for social or communitarian reasons that the church has made its action in "receiving" the consent of the spouses a requirement for validity, but the significance of this measure is purely disciplinary, not theological.

The practical application of the principle, "doing what the church does," is that the minister must have the internal will of fulfilling the external sacramental rite prescribed by the church. However, what is the distinctive external *sacramental* rite of matrimony prescribed by the church? There is none. The religious rite that Catholics usually follow when marrying is simply the canonical form which, under present discipline, is required for validity, but that is *not* the sacramental rite.[22] Consequently, the principle of "doing what the church does" is either inapplicable to the sacrament of matrimony, or—due to the particular nature of this sacrament—must be understood in a very different way regarding how it applies in the case of the other sacraments.

Nothing is "done" by the church to "confect" the sacrament of marriage; all is done by the spouses. If we wish, we can say that in the moment of matrimonial consent, the spouses *are* the church.

---

21. See *Codex Iuris Canonici* (Rome: Libreria Editrice Vaticana, 1983), c. 1116 [hereafter "CIC"]. "CIC" is used for both the 1983 and the earlier 1917 Codes. Without specification it always refers to the present (1983) Code.

22. This, as we have seen, is simply the valid exchange of consent between the spouses.

Insofar as "a presence" of the church is necessary for the confection of the sacraments, this presence—in the case of marriage—is supplied by the spouses and not by the priest. That is why statements like the following appear to be essentially flawed: "The canonical-liturgical form required at present for the sacrament-sign causes the marital consent expressed in this context to objectively have the meaning indicated by the economy of salvation, that is, the meaning of the sacramental sign."[23] The canonical form currently required for the validity of marriage is something introduced by positive ecclesiastical law; it is theologically unacceptable to see in it the cause or explanation of the sacramental sign.

A passage from Pope John Paul II's Apostolic Exhortation *Familiaris Consortio* applies here: "When in spite of all efforts, engaged couples show that they reject explicitly and formally *what the Church intends* when the marriage of baptized persons is celebrated, the pastor of souls cannot admit them to the celebration of marriage."[24] John Paul II does not use the phrase "what the Church does" ("*quod facit Ecclesia*") but rather he speaks of what it *intends* ("*quod Ecclesia intendit*"). This indeed seems the only accurate way to refer to the matter. While the church "does" nothing in this sacrament, it (insofar as it is present or aware of a marriage taking place) no doubt intends something—that two Christians marry. It intends, in other words, a marriage between two persons who are "in Christ." The question is this: do the spouses intend what the church intends? Do the spouses intend to marry in Christ? If they intend to marry, they do, because—in virtue of their baptism—they are in Christ. They intend what the church intends[25]

23. Barberi, *La celebrazione*, 429.

24. "Cum . . . nuptias facturi aperte et expresse id quod Ecclesia intendit, cum matrimonium baptizatorum celebratur, se respuere fatentur" (FC, no. 68); in AAS 74 (1982): 165.

25. See Susan Wood, "The Marriage of Baptized Nonbelievers: Faith, Contract, and Sacrament," *Theological Studies* 48 (1987): 292.

(just as the church intends what they intend) and so they have a sufficient sacramental intention.[26] It would not be accurate to say that the church wants them to be married "as" Christians, for they *are* Christians, though one could say the church wants them to be married so as to receive help to be *better* Christians.

Contrary to Barberi, therefore, the person marrying does not have to "do" what the church does (the church, I repeat, "does" nothing), but he or she does have to intend what the church intends: that is, a valid marriage between two persons who are baptized.[27] It is important to distinguish what the church intends in matrimony from the theological significance of matrimony. It is required that the spouses intend what the church intends, but it cannot reasonably be required, for validity, that they have a full theological understanding of all that the church reads into the sign value of matrimony. It would be excessive to make a grasp of the church's theological understanding of matrimony a condition for the valid reception of the sacrament.[28] What is asked of the contracting parties is simply an *intention*. However desirable it may be that this intention be theologically informed and consciously sacramental, this is not required for validity. For validity, the intention required is simply the intention to marry on the natural plane.

26. "The minister of a sacrament acts in the person of the whole Church, whose minister he is. In the words spoken the intention of the Church is expressed—which is sufficient for the fullness of the sacrament, unless something is exteriorly expressed on the part of the minister and the recipient of the sacrament" (*Summa Theologiae* III, q. 64, a. 8, ad 2). "When a sacrament is celebrated in conformity with the intention of the Church, the power of Christ and of his Spirit acts in and through it, independently of the personal holiness of the minister" (CCC, no. 1128).

27. Barberi, *La celebrazione*, 431.

28. "What is required then is to do what the Church does, not to understand what the Church understands—the conjugal covenant as a sacrament. No minimum of faith therefore is required" (Denis Baudot, *L'inséparabilité entre le contrat et le sacrement de mariage: la discussion après le Concile Vatican II* [Rome: Pontifica Università Gregoriana, 1987], 358). This is expressed well, though I would prefer "intend" rather than "do."

In order to bring about a sacramental marriage, then, just two elements are needed: baptism and a natural matrimonial intention. Given genuine intention and capacity, it is the fact of baptism that sacramentalizes matrimony. To the question therefore whether there can be a valid marriage between Christians which is not sacramental, the answer is "no," because (to repeat the fundamental reason) sacramentality simply means the special ontological configuration of the marriage of those who are baptized. The dignity of sacramentality is of the essence of marriage between Christians.[29]

The Importance of Faith

In recent decades, there has been a revival and development of the thesis according to which the sacramentalization of marriage depends not on the objective factor of baptism but on the subjective personal faith of the contracting parties: that is, if they lack faith, they do not and cannot validly enter into sacramental matrimony. In other words—and this is presented as a theological principle—actively and consciously held faith is necessary for marriage to be sacramental.[30] Is this principle theologically sound?

It is obvious that conscious and active faith is necessary for a particular marriage to be fully *fruitful* in all of its possibilities for the Christian maturing of spouses and children. The point at issue, however, is not fruitfulness but validity: that is, whether some degree of active faith is necessary for the *valid* reception of the sacrament. It is important here not to confuse "faith" and "intention." A very specific intention is required in order to receive the sacrament (but this, we repeat, is a marital intention and not necessarily a sacramental intention). Faith in the sacrament, however, is not

29. Denz., 1766 and 1773.
30. See Michael G. Lawler: "Faith, Contract, and Sacrament in Christian Marriage: A Theological Approach," *Theological Studies* 52, no. 4 (1991): 721.

required for its valid reception. I can see no theological grounds to support the thesis that the absence of personally professed faith impedes the valid sacramental reception of matrimony. Protestants, after all, who do not believe that matrimony is a sacrament, nevertheless receive the sacrament when they marry.

The matrimony of those who lack faith poses pastoral but not theological problems. In 1970 the French Episcopal Committee for the Family, noting that "lack of faith does not affect the validity of the sacrament," added: "the total absence of faith in those marrying undermines the authenticity of their step in the actual celebration of marriage."[31] This is a fair expression of the problem. It is pastorally important to help Christians have a personally coherent, "authentic" approach to the religious celebration of marriage, but even if this is not achieved, their lack of faith does not affect the sacramental validity of their marriage.

The thesis that lack of conscious faith invalidates the matrimony of baptized persons poses formidable doctrinal difficulties which, to my mind, have been brushed over rather than resolved. Our considerations so far highlight one of these difficulties: the effective denial or at least ignoring of the ontological consequences of baptism for the person. Yet more difficulties arise if one holds that faith as a habit or infused virtue is required for validity.[32] How can one gauge the "quantity" of faith required?[33] How can one quantify faith? Is it an absolute loss of faith that alone impedes sacramentality? Or is a person's marriage sacramental if he or she retains a "minimum" of faith? One can suffer *degrees* of loss of faith. How can one calculate when such a loss becomes total, so that not the least "*vestigium*" is left?

31. Barberi, *La celebrazione*, 359.
32. Wood, "Marriage," 294.
33. See Rincón-Pérez, *Cuestiones fundamentales*, 192; and O. Fumagalli Carulli, "La dimensione spirituale del matrimonio e la sua traduzione giuridica," *Ius* 27 (1980): 45.

Determining the minimum of faith required is not the only difficulty. One would need to further specify what *type* of faith is necessary for validity: christological faith, which admits the divinity of Christ; ecclesial faith, which accepts the institution and authority of the church; sacramental faith; or merely matrimonial faith, which accepts the nature of marriage as proposed by the church. Then one would need to decide whether the required faith is to be explicit or implicit, etc.[34] The practical difficulties do not end here. Is a non-practicing Christian to be always excluded from marrying in church? Who is to be assigned the invidious task of "classifying" Catholics according to the "acceptability" or otherwise of their degree of faith, deciding that a person does not have faith, or has not "enough" faith? Some priests would be more liberal in this task, others more conservative. The danger of discrimination and of violating the fundamental right to marry is readily apparent, as is the risk of fostering "elitism."[35]

Here I would add that the suggested exclusion of *"infideles baptizatos"* from the broad category of *"Christifideles"*[36] seems to me not only theologically unacceptable, but also runs the grave danger of being elitist. The Second Vatican Council, in broad but specific terms, described *Christifideles* as those who are "incorporated into Christ through baptism."[37] It is not the *Catholic* faith, but the fact of baptism, that causes a person to be a member of the people of God. Working from this fact, various degrees of incorporation into Christ and his church can be distinguished.[38] What

34. See Baudot, *L'inséparabilité*, 362–63.
35. See FC, no. 68, para. 6.
36. See R. C. Finn, "Faith and the Sacrament of Marriage," in *Marriage Studies*, vol. III (Washington, D.C., 1985), 104–5; and Lawler, "Faith, Contract," 728. Lawler goes on in fact to say that "baptized nonbelievers have no right to be equated with Christian believers" (729). If this affirmation is intended to carry pastoral weight, it may be acceptable, but is it sound theologically?
37. *Ad Gentes*, 15 [hereafter "AG"].
38. See *Lumen Gentium*, no. 14 [hereafter "LG"]; and CIC, cc. 204–5.

degree of incorporation are we demanding? Are only those "perfectly" incorporated into Christ to be included?

Faith and Fruitfulness

It is not theologically certain that all the sacraments require conscious faith (for example, infant baptism does not), but it is certain that they all foster it. It is arguably those with weak faith who stand in most need of the graces deriving from the sacrament of marriage. The task of pastors is to instruct them so that they understand the power of these graces, and it would show unreasonable pastoral impatience to expect such a task to be completed in the few weeks that pre-marriage instruction normally covers. A marriage "in church" may mark the *beginning* of a long and fruitful process of catechizing those who are notoriously weak in faith, and may also ensure the possibility of the Catholic education of their children. Refusal of a "church marriage" may preclude both. Is there not a certain (unconsciously) penal character to the thesis that baptized nonbelievers cannot enter a valid sacramental marriage? It leaves people deprived of divine resources for turning toward Christ.[39]

It has been suggested that married people without faith cannot signify the union of Christ and the church, but this is to confuse sign and testimony. Every Christian marriage signifies the Christ-church relationship even though some couples fail to *testify* to a loving and faithful union. However, this failure cannot be taken as an invalidating defect in the sacrament; it is simply the spouses' failure to respond to sacramental grace.

On reading that "the lack of faith is an obstacle to the assumption of the commitments of marriage deriving from the fact of the sacrament,"[40] one asks: what are these "commitments" be-

---

39. FC, no. 68, para. 5.
40. S. Gherro, *Diritto matrimoniale canonico* (Padua, 1985), 237.

yond those of non-sacramental marriage? One readily admits that the lack of faith is an obstacle to truly grace-assisted *fulfillment* of these commitments, but not to their assumption. Here once again there is perhaps an unconscious passage from the ascetical-pastoral to the theological-juridical sphere, as well as an idea that lack of faith can be taken as a safeguard against having to assume duties and is not seen as a hindrance to the reception of benefits.

Absence of faith may hinder the fruitful reception of the sac-rament (that is, the fruitful operation of sacramental grace, within marriage *in facto esse*) but does not hinder the actual reception of the sacrament in the moment of consent (marriage *in fieri*). A failure to note this distinction can facilitate equivocal statements such as the following: "The profound unity between the human reality and its sacramentality in the case of baptized partners is not realized in the absence of faith. While remaining ordered to a sac-ramental state by the baptismal character, their unbelief prevents the actualization of this state."[41] Even as regards the fruitfulness of the sacrament of marriage, it is by no means certain that lack of faith absolutely impedes baptized persons from achieving that fruitfulness. Sacramentality offers them an extra strength of su-pernatural efficacy (of which the couple may be unaware) to live a more dedicated love for their partner and children. The lack of faith of two Protestants who marry does not necessarily prevent them from receiving the sacramental graces of their matrimony.

Those who advocate a non-sacramental valid marriage for Catholics seem to pass lightly over the fact that the sacramentality of matrimony confers graces—advantages—even upon those who are unaware of them. This explains the repeated directives of the

41. Finn, *Marriage Studies*, 3:106. This article, incidentally, is not alone in ad-vancing the claim that St. Albert, St. Thomas, St. Bonaventure, etc., all teach the need of active faith for the *reception* of marriage; whereas, as a simple reading of the Latin texts included in the article shows, they posit faith as necessary for the efficacy of the sacrament (once constituted) but not for its valid constitution.

Holy See, under the 1917 Code, insisting that while every effort must be made to instruct those who are ignorant of Catholic doctrine, spouses who refuse this instruction should not be denied the celebration of marriage.[42] If the whole conjugal covenant between the spouses becomes a source of grace, then Christian spouses are always "in" a sacramental state, even if one or other, or both, are not personally in a "state of grace." The grace of matrimony makes it easier for them in fact to "return" to a state of grace if they have lost it. It would also seem to follow that those Christians with little or apparently no faith who enter into a sacramental marriage will have more grace for the finding or restoration of their faith than if they had entered a non-sacramental union.[43] The sacramental state of marriage reconfirms or relocates people "in" Christ even if they are unaware of the nature and extent of this benefit. Pastors need to overcome the tendency to analyze sociologically what is essentially a theological reality, a "great mystery in Christ," where the power of redemption is always—however hiddenly—at work. The ecumenical implications of these considerations need to be carefully weighed. If it became accepted doctrine that active faith and/or a positive sacramental intention are needed for the valid reception of matrimony, then the vast majority of the marriages of

42. See Barberi, *La celebrazione*, 351–54. The 1983 Code remains in the line of these directives (cc. 1063–72), as does FC, no. 68.

43. Strong faith strengthens Christian couples in their resolve to keep their marriage together. Weak and uninformed faith, on the other hand, deprives them of the power they should be able to turn to in the inevitable moments of crisis that occur in every marriage. The following words of Pope Benedict XVI are very much to the point: "Marriage is linked to faith, but not in a general way. Marriage, as a union of faithful and indissoluble love, is based upon the grace that comes from the triune God, who in Christ loved us with a faithful love, even to the Cross. Today we ought to grasp the full truth of this statement, in contrast to the painful reality of many marriages which, unhappily, end badly. *There is a clear link between the crisis in faith and the crisis in marriage*," Homily, Oct 7, 2012 (http://www.vatican.va/holy_father/benedict_xvi/homilies/2012/documents/hf_ben-xvi_hom_20121007_apertura-sinodo_en.html) (emphasis added).

our separated brethren would need to be considered invalid by the Catholic church.[44]

The 1977 Documents of the International Theological Commission

We must not omit a reference to a pair of documents formulated by the International Theological Commission in 1977: "The Sacramentality of Christian marriage" and *"Foedus matrimoniale."*[45] The traditional doctrine of the inseparability of covenant and sacrament is clearly presented in passages such as the following: "As between two baptized persons, matrimony, as an institution willed by God the Creator, cannot be separated from marriage as a sacrament, since sacramentality does not constitute an accidental element of marriage between the baptized (which might or might not be present in it), but is so bound to its essence that it cannot be separated from it."[46] "For the Church, as between two baptized persons, there exists no natural marriage separate from the sacrament, but only a natural marriage raised to the dignity of sacrament."[47]

However, there are other passages which are less clear and are quoted at times in support of the view that conscious and active faith is essential to the validity of sacramental marriage, or that the possibility of a valid non-sacramental union should be allowed for Christians. It is stated, for instance:

[The matrimonial covenant] becomes a sacrament only if the future spouses agree to enter conjugal life by passing through Christ to whom they are incorporated through Baptism. Their free adhesion to the mystery of Christ is so essential to the nature of the sacrament that the

44. FC, no. 68, para. 6.
45. *Enchiridion Vaticanum,* Edizioni Dehoniane (Bologna, 1992–), 352–97.
46. Ibid., 385, no. 495.
47. Ibid., 389, no. 498.

Church wishes, by means of the ministry of the priest, to be assured of the Christian authenticity of their commitment. The human conjugal covenant therefore does not become a sacrament in virtue of a juridic statute that would be efficacious of itself independently of any freely given adhesion to Baptism. It becomes such in virtue rather of the publicly Christian character which their mutual commitment intimately implies.[48]

Such a statement can hardly be called a model of clarity. What is meant by this "passing through Christ," which (so it seems to be implied) was not effected by their being incorporated into Christ by baptism? The spouses have *already* passed "through" Christ, and are ontologically *in* him in virtue of their baptism—this is why they marry in Christ. No theological reasons are given to support or explain the suggestion that some further "passing through Christ" is necessary in order that their matrimony may "become" a sacrament. (Further, the phrase "*so* essential" is both puzzling and imprecise, as essentiality does not admit of degrees—something is essential or it is not.) Presumably the sense is that "adhesion to mystery of Christ" is *important* to the fruitfulness of the sacrament (rather than essential to its constitution); a point we agree with, but which should have been stated more precisely.[49]

Regarding the priest's intervention—which is simply that of a qualified witness—it is doubtful that it can properly be called a "ministry." We would further note that what the church wishes to ensure through the priest's or other qualified witness's presence, rather than (the very woolly idea of) the "Christian authenticity of the spouses' commitment," is their intention of exchanging genuine matrimonial consent. Therefore, as the *Ordo Celebrandi*

48. Ibid., 363, no. 471.
49. The Commission itself, in contradiction to what it suggests here, seems later to acknowledge this point: "Faith is presupposed as a *causa dispositiva* of the fruitful effect of the sacrament; the validity of matrimony, however, does not necessarily imply that it be fruitful" (ibid., 383, no. 492).

Matrimonium states, the priest questions the spouses about "their freedom, their intention of mutual fidelity and of accepting and educating offspring."[50] Contrary to what the Commission seems to suggest, no questions relating to "free adhesion to the mystery of Christ" are to be found in the *Ordo*. The second document, "*Foedus matrimoniale*," states:

In the last analysis, true intention is born of living faith and nourished by it. Therefore where there is no trace of faith as such, the practical doubt arises whether or not there exists the aforesaid general and truly sacramental intention, and whether the marriage contracted is valid or not. As pointed out, the personal faith of the contracting parties does not of itself constitute the sacramentality of marriage; but in the total absence of personal faith, the very validity of the sacrament would be undermined.[51]

Once more we must note the imprecision of language. What is a "trace of faith"? What is the unacceptable minimum? When does faith become utterly extinguished? Besides, while some take the last phrase (that in the total absence of faith, the very validity of the sacrament "would be undermined") as the conclusion of the passage, one must ask what sure conclusion can be drawn from a *doubt* ("the doubt arises"). The text in fact continues: "This gives rise to new problems for which a satisfactory solution has not yet been found, and imposes grave pastoral responsibilities regarding Christian marriage." Theological and pastoral considerations are mixed together in these documents. The theological opinions rather obscurely advanced[52] have received no support from the

50. *Ordo Celebrandi Matrimonium* (Rome: Libreria Editrice Vaticana, 1970), cap. I, no. 24.
51. *Enchiridion Vaticanum,* 383, no. 492.
52. A particularly obscure passage concerns the case of malformed Catholics who consider that they can contract matrimony even though they exclude the sacrament. The Commission weighs, on the one hand, their lack both of faith and of the intention of doing what the church "does," which makes them "incapable of contracting

subsequent magisterium; the clear pastoral concerns expressed have been dealt with in detail by Pope John Paul II in *Familiaris Consortio*.

The International Theological Commission is an advisory body to the Congregation for the Doctrine of the Faith, and is not in any way an organ of the magisterium. Since it is composed of papally appointed theologians, its views should be studied with particular attention. It is clear however that they carry no more weight than their intrinsic worth. The intrinsic theological worth of the documents referred to here (also in view of their many internal ambiguities or contradictions) is questionable. For the purpose of the subject under discussion, it is evident that they carry no magisterial authority.

Separability

According to the theory of "separability," marriage can in certain cases exist as a valid natural alliance or contract between Christians, without its being a sacrament. The theory rests on the view mentioned earlier: that if spouses lack faith, they do not and cannot validly receive sacramental matrimony. Out of respect for their human rights, the thesis goes on, it should be acknowledged that in such a case, despite their baptism, they can and do receive valid marriage in its natural entity "alone." In other words, such persons, according to their circumstances, can validly contract either a sacramental marriage or else a simple "natural" marriage. The theory is frequently proposed today, although it so far remains out of harmony with official church teaching.[53]

---

a valid sacramental marriage," and on the other, their "natural right to contract marriage." It continues: "In such circumstances they are capable of giving and accepting each other as spouses" and yet concludes that "such a relationship, even though it may offer the characteristics of matrimony, can in no way be recognized by the Church as a conjugal society, even in a non-sacramental form" (ibid., 387–89, no. 498).

53. The inseparability of sacrament and contract has been held to be "fidei

In passing I confess to not being very happy with the use of the term "contract" in discussing this subject (as if it were tied up necessarily with "contractualist" theories of marriage). The more precise expression of the issue is whether marriage itself is divisible into two realities for Christians: a valid, natural, non-sacramental marriage, on the one hand, and a sacramental marriage, on the other. More importantly, I find that "separability" (or "inseparability") is an inappropriate working term. It suggests two elements or "components" of Christian marriage, whereas in fact, as we have tried to show, there is simply one indivisible reality. One can indeed debate whether the reality of marriage exists inside or outside the sacramental order, but the solution of this question depends not on constitutional principles of marriage but on the ontological condition of the spouses.

The separability theory would grant the person marrying the power to dissect Christian marriage: to separate and exclude its specific Christian aspect (which is its sacramentality), while retaining its valid natural aspect. This is a power which he or she does not have, any more than a person has the power to "separate" Christ from the consecrated Host. It is as if a person were to think: "I will receive the host as a memorial meal; but I will not receive the true body and blood of Christ," but this is an impossibility.

According to the church's understanding, if a person goes through the actions of any other sacrament but excludes the supernatural efficacy which the church sees in it, the sacramental aspect is lost but the natural aspect remains. If the minister of baptism excludes the intention of conferring a sacrament, no sacrament is in fact conferred, but the natural action of pouring water—a natural ablution—remains. Is it not logical to say that the same can happen

---

proxima" (P. Palazzini, "Il Sacramento del Matrimonio," in *I Sacramenti* [Rome, 1959], 756). For a list of magisterial documents, see Barberi, *La celebrazione*, 412n174.

in the case of marriage, that a person can simply contract marriage in its natural sense, while excluding the supernatural significance the church attaches to it? If the answer once again is "no," it is for a reason which underlines the uniqueness of matrimony among the sacraments, and explains why the analogy does not hold. God did not will that every ablution of Christians be a sacrament; but this is exactly what he *did* will for every marriage between Christians.[54] Sacramentality is a consequence not of their will, but of their condition as Christians incorporated into the economy of salvation.[55]

Here we could refer to the rather striking conclusion of an article by Michael Lawler, a conclusion which, he says, "is evident and needs no further elaboration": that "if the marriages of nonbelievers, including baptized nonbelievers, are nonsacramental, then they are also dissoluble according to the norms of canon 1143."[56] Since the dissolution of a marriage under canon 1143 requires as a *sine qua non* condition that the marriage be between two nonbaptized persons, it is not clear how one would elaborate this conclusion in reference to our subject. Surely Susan Wood is right when she states that the proponents of a possible non-sacramental valid marriage for baptized nonbelievers also insist that it would be indissoluble.[57] The common theological opinion has been that the marriage of a baptized person to one non-baptized is not sacramental. Yet such marriages (entered by the Catholic party with a dispensation from the impediment of disparity of cult) are considered no less indissoluble than a marriage between two Catholics.

---

54. Palazzini, "Il Sacramento," 756.

55. In the Encyclical *Arcanum*, Leo XIII taught it is false to hold that "the sacrament is a certain added ornament, or outward endowment, which can be separated and torn away from the contract at the caprice of men" (*Acta Sanctae Sedis* [Vatican City: 1865–1904], XII.394).

56. Lawler, "Faith, Contract," 731.

57. Wood, "Marriage," 295–96.

Conclusion

To my mind, certain views advanced in the "separability" debate show not only a defective appreciation of the beauty, dignity, and purpose of the sacrament of marriage itself, but (perhaps paradoxically) also a devalued concept of marriage considered on the natural level as well. One notes a tendency to see the properties of the conjugal covenant (procreativity, exclusiveness, permanence) in a negative rather than a positive light. In this context, I believe that certain pastoral and canonical views of marriage have become hampered by a one-sided understanding of these properties, emphasizing the obligations they involve rather than the basic goodness they represent. We need a revived appreciation of St. Augustine's view of these aspects of marriage as *bona*—good things— that mark its dignity and endow it with a noble attractiveness.[58] There is a basic pessimism in any assumption that human nature is more afraid of, than attracted by, the commitment aspect of the marital covenant. Since the permanence of the marriage bond is particularly devalued today, an anthropological analysis of how indissolubility corresponds to the "forever" aspiration of human love is especially called for. But a deep reappraisal of the human attractiveness of the fruitful one-spouse aspects (procreativity and exclusiveness) of the marital covenant also needs to be undertaken. We will attempt such an analysis in subsequent chapters.

These views would seem to be based on some confused notion that natural marriage involves people in a lesser commitment than Christian marriage, that it is less demanding, or that its demands are more easily ignored or dispensed with. But natural marriage, we repeat, is in fact as much of a commitment as Christian marriage. The difference is that it is not as enriched. It does not confer

58. See chapter 6.

the same strength or receive the same help from above to achieve in practice the fulfillment it promises. Sacramentality is an expression of God's largesse, not of his exigency. It is something that strengthens, remedies, and enriches. In this respect, it imposes no peculiar obligation over and above natural marriage, other perhaps than one of particular gratitude—for the calling and the unique gifts which it confers.

Let us pass on to consider that calling, and the gifts and graces involved in Christian marriage.

2

Marriage
Sacrament and Sanctity

A strong case can be made for holding that the fifth chapter of *Lumen Gentium* presents the most important, innovative, and even the most revolutionary doctrine of the Second Vatican Council. Under the title of "The Universal Call to Holiness," an utterly personalized message is presented to every member of the church, each of whom, whatever his or her position in life, is called to sanctity, to the fullness of friendship and intimacy with God. To help each one become truly aware of what this implies and to help each person to see and use the ways and means of responding effectively to this personal call from God remains a top priority in the ongoing work of ecclesial renewal. The call to holiness can appear discouraging, and an effective response to it impossible, if people measure the enterprise in terms of their own strength alone. There must certainly be a personal response and effort on the part of each one, but it is God who gives the strength—the grace—to answer effectively and to achieve the goal. All of us need constant reminders of the generosity and power with which God meets our efforts not only to avoid sin but to persevere and grow in prayer and in all the virtues characteristic of Christian life. In particular we need to be reminded of the special power to be found in the sacraments, those "masterworks of God,"[1] where he communicates his grace with singular power and efficacy.

It seems particularly important to relate this latter point to those sacraments which have a special "constitutional" value, that is, which confer a character that configures the person to Christ in a unique and unrepeatable way and thus give a permanent title to continuing graces necessary to live according to one's Christ-like configuration. The life of each person in accordance with his or her state (lay person, married or single, religious or priest) should be marked by constant reference to these sacraments and reliance on the specific sacramental graces that they offer. In practice one sees a major pastoral problem in the fact that many Christians live their lives with little or no awareness of or reference to the graces accruing to them from the "constitutional" sacraments.[2] Regarding baptism, for instance, insofar as many Christians think about their own baptism at all, they often see it as something which burdens them with obligations rather than as a source of strength and of filial rights, inasmuch as the main gift of baptism is to make us children of God. I think it is true that they seldom note or recall the day they were baptized, and this is probably true even of the sacrament of confirmation. Perhaps these remain as important moments of grace received in the past, but they are seldom recalled as occasions when a source of grace for the present was opened in one's life.

With regard to the sacrament of ordination, it is no doubt easier for a priest to avoid this pitfall and to recall that his *whole* activity is specified by a priestly mission and identity. Paul's words

---

1. CCC, no. 1116.
2. We regard matrimony as a "constitutional" sacrament; not of course in the sense of conferring sacramental character, but in that of constituting a person in a special state of life: a human state that by divine will is also a sacramental state.

to Timothy, "stir up the grace that is within you,"[3] are more likely to keep striking his consciousness and be a source of strength. Should one not expect something similar in the case of the sacrament of matrimony? How often does one find it? How is it that many married Christians, who perhaps celebrate their wedding anniversary in joy and gratitude, seldom seem to be motivated by a consciousness of sacramental graces once received and constantly operative? If there appears to be something inadequate in the way they understand this sacrament, could it be because it has often been presented to them in a way that is not totally adequate?[4] These questions have led to the considerations that follow.

Matrimony: A "Transient" or "Permanent" Sacrament?

All the sacraments apply the merits of the passion of Jesus and communicate or restore Christ's life to the soul, or increase this life in it. One notes the difference between the three sacraments of baptism, confirmation, and ordination, which impress a permanent *character*—a special configuration to Christ's priesthood— and the other four which do not. A difference not be confused with that between sacraments which can be called "transient" (because the sacramental power of the "matter" used does not extend beyond the moment of its use; it is there only *in usu*) and those that have an aspect of "permanence" about them because, after the sacrament is made or confected (and not only *in usu*), a sacramen-

---

3. 2 Tim 1:6.

4. "In the minds of both clergy and laity alike, the canonical, or legal, aspect of the sacrament of matrimony is strongly accentuated. This is understandable, proper, and necessary and is also genuinely pastoral in its effects. Marriage as the union of a man and a woman must be fully legitimized in the eyes of society, including the Church; it must be socially justified. But this is not its only or even its most essential aspect. The most fundamental aspect of marriage in the Church is its sacramentality" ("Pastoral Reflections on the Family," in Karol Wojtyla, *Person and Community: Selected Essays* [New York: Peter Lang, 1993], 346).

tal reality remains. In the first case, the natural realities utilized are endowed with efficacy only in actual "use," while in the latter they are substantially affected or changed, and the sacramental reality remains after the sacrament itself has been confected or conferred.

Baptism, in this sense, is a "transient" sacrament for in its conferral a particular use of natural realities—ablution by water—has the immediate effect of washing away original sin and the permanent ontological effect of making a person into a child of God. But once the sacrament is conferred, the natural reality used—the water—retains no supernatural virtue. The eucharist is the most significant example of a "permanent" sacrament. In its confection, natural realities—bread and wine—are used. They are however not merely endowed with a supernatural efficacy just in the moment of use, but are substantially changed. After the sacrament has been effected, the reality that remains is wholly supernatural, although it continues to be accompanied by the appearances—no more—of the natural realities that were used. The natural realities are in fact no longer there.

There has been a great deal of theological discussion regarding whether matrimony constitutes a "transient" or a "permanent" sacrament. A line of thought going back to Scotus views sacramentality as properly applying only to the moment of the actual celebration of marriage (matrimony *in fieri*); in consequence, only the moment of consent and perhaps that of consummation would confer grace *ex opere operato*. According to St. Thomas, not just matrimonial consent but also the bond established by it is the sacrament of matrimony, which thence becomes a continuing source of grace—he says that the bond is "dispositively ordained to grace."[5] Bellarmine expresses the same opinion: "The sacrament

---

5. "Actus exteriores et verba exprimentia consensum directe faciunt nexum quendam, qui est sacramentum matrimonii; et huiusmodi nexus ex virtute divinae institutionis dispositive operatur ad gratiam" (*Suppl.*, q. 42, a. 3, ad 2).

of matrimony can be regarded in two ways: first, in the making, and then in its permanent state. For it is a sacrament like that of the Eucharist, which not only when it is being conferred, but also while it remains, is a sacrament; for as long as the married parties are alive, so long is their union a sacrament of Christ and the Church."[6] Pope Pius XI, in *Casti Connubii*, quotes this passage from Bellarmine.[7] Pope John Paul II, in *Familiaris Consortio*, says:

The gift of Jesus Christ is not exhausted in the actual celebration of the sacrament of marriage, but rather accompanies the married couple throughout their lives. This fact is explicitly recalled by the Second Vatican Council when it says that Jesus Christ 'abides with them so that, just as he loved the Church and handed himself over on her behalf, the spouses may love each other with perpetual fidelity through mutual self-bestowal' (*Gaudium et spes*, no. 48).[8]

Therefore, according to this opinion,[9] it is not consent alone, not only the act of marrying, but also the conjugal bond—the married state—that is a sacrament, a sign and cause of grace.

It may be objected that the term "permanent sacrament" is improperly applied to matrimony[10]—rather, one should refer to it as one of the consecratory sacraments. This thesis, already suggested by theologians such as Scheeben, Karl Adam, and Dietrich von Hildebrand, was clearly, though qualifiedly, proposed in *Casti Connubii* where Pope Pius XI, having stated that spouses are "strengthened, sanctified and in a manner *consecrated*" by the sacrament of matrimony, went on to say:

---

6. Bellarmine, *De Sacramento*, cap. 6. Thomas Sánchez holds the same; see his *De sancto matrimonii sacramento* (Lugduni: 1739), lib. II, disp. V, 121, n. 7.

7. AAS 22 (1930): 583.

8. FC, no. 56.

9. Barberi holds it to be the common opinion today; see *La celebrazione*, 26.

10. The same can no doubt be said of baptism, confirmation, or ordination; see E. Boissard, *Questions théologiques sur le mariage* (Paris: Cerf, 1948), 66.

As St. Augustine teaches, just as by Baptism and Holy Orders a man is set aside and assisted either for the duties of Christian life or for the priestly office and is never deprived of their sacramental aid, almost in the same way (although not by a sacramental character), the faithful once joined by marriage ties can never be deprived of the help and the binding force of the sacrament.[11]

Recent statements by the magisterium strengthen this view. The Second Vatican Council states:

Christian spouses have a special sacrament by which they are fortified and receive a kind of consecration in the duties and dignity of their state. By virtue of this sacrament, as spouses fulfill their conjugal and family obligations, they are penetrated with the Spirit of Christ, who fills their whole lives with faith, hope and charity. Thus they increasingly advance towards their own perfection, as well as towards their mutual sanctification, and hence contribute jointly to the glory of God.[12]

The 1992 *Catechism of the Catholic Church* quotes this passage in putting matrimony alongside ordination as involving a "particular consecration."[13] Canon 1134 of the 1983 Code of Canon Law states: "In Christian marriage the spouses are by a special sacrament strengthened and, as it were, consecrated for the duties and the dignity of their state."

A "continuing" right to sacramental graces derives from certain sacraments whose effect is to constitute a person in a state of life: the state of a Christian, of a priest, or of a married person. Matrimony is like ordination in that by it a person enters into a new state, yet it is also singularly different, in that while there is not a natural non-sacramental priesthood to which the sacramental priesthood corresponds or upon which it is based, there is a natural

11. AAS 22 (1930): 555; see G. Baldanza, "La grazia matrimoniale nell'Enciclica *Casti connubii*," *Ephemerides Liturgicae* 99 (1985): 43–46.
12. GS, no. 48.
13. CCC, no. 1535.

matrimonial covenant, and it is precisely this which is sacramentalized. Matrimony is unique among the sacraments in that it is a
natural reality raised to the permanent dignity of a sacrament.[14]

The "transient" concept, which would reduce the sacrament
to the exchange of consent, seems less than satisfactory. A comparison with the eucharist can help: in the eucharist, the words of
consecration can be called "sacramental words" in the sense that
they give rise to the sacrament, but these words are not *the* sacrament. The sacrament remains after the words by which it is effected have passed. The words of matrimonial consent can similarly
be described as sacramental words by which the sacrament itself,
which remains, is constituted.[15] This sacrament also remains even
after the moment of consent has passed (and even if consent were
subsequently withdrawn).

Signification and Efficacy

There are good reasons to maintain that a refocus and development of ideas about the working of sacramental grace in marriage
are in order. It is natural that liturgical reflection, while respecting
the essential substance of each sacrament as instituted by Christ,
should pay special attention to modes of perfecting the symbolic
rites so that they express and intensify faith-filled celebration by
Christians. Theological and ascetical reflection, however, center
more on the ultimate purpose and sanctifying effect of each sacrament.[16] For sacramental theology, what is most important is that
a sacrament is an effective symbol more than a symbolic action; it

14. "Marriage is the only one of the sacraments which transforms a human institution into an instrument of divine action" (Jean Leclercq, *Le mariage Chrétien* [Paris:
Cerf, 1950], 32).

15. Both examples naturally presume that the words are accompanied by the necessary intention.

16. See St. Thomas's dictum that a sacrament "is a sign of a sacred thing inasmuch
as it sanctifies man" (*Summa Theologiae* III, q. 60, a. 2).

effects what it signifies. Dogmatic treatises on the eucharist reflect on its value—for the individual and the community—in bringing about a real participation in Christ's life and sacrifice, in effecting conformation to Christ. This is generally true of theological reflection on the other sacraments, which has dwelled more on what each does and effects than on what each signifies. Peculiarly, this has not been the case with the sacrament of matrimony. Theological reflection on the sacramentality of marriage has centered almost exclusively on its sign-function—Christian matrimony as signifying a great supernatural reality (the union of Christ and the church)—and has largely neglected investigation of its effect on the recipients.

If it is true that theological reflection on the sacrament of matrimony has lagged behind consideration of its moral, canonical, and pastoral aspects, a development of this theme would seem to be called for.[17] To my mind, reflection on this topic should seek above all to correct the imbalance just noted: the much greater attention given to the signifying role of the sacrament than to its sanctifying effect, and the limited analysis in practice which has been made of the relation between the two.

In the case of the other sacraments, the sign aspect is related very directly, though in clear subordination, to the sanctifying effect. The *res sacra* of which the sacrament is a sign is not only contained in the sacrament but is applied by it to the recipient, with sanctifying effect. It is this effect above all which matters; the sign simply illustrates or clarifies the particular nature of the effect. The sign of cleansing in baptism, or that of nourishing or a common meal in the reception of the eucharist, serve to illustrate to the human understanding the mode of sanctification that takes place in the individual and among the community.

17. See Barberi, *La celebrazione*, 6.

With marriage, as we have said, the sign aspect—the union of husband and wife representing the union of Christ and his church—has tended to occupy theological reflection, while the sanctifying effect has been given rather scant attention. The mainstream of Catholic thought has always resisted theses (such as expounded by Durandus), holding that matrimony is different than the other sacraments, being a sign without sanctifying efficacy.[18] Nevertheless that same mainstream theology has made only very tentative approaches in suggesting in what way the *res sacra* sanctifies the spouses. Bellarmine, who severely criticizes Durandus's view, focuses on the grace specifically contained in this sacrament. However, he too relates these graces to the objective (or perhaps "static") holiness of what is signified by married union rather than to the subjective holiness that is progressively and dynamically achieved by the living out of married life itself. With reference to the fifth chapter of Ephesians, he dwells on the demonstrative meaning:

Marriage could not signify that [the union of Christ and the church], unless between husband and wife, over and beyond the civil contract, there were also a spiritual union of souls. . . . If God joins man and woman for this purpose, that by their spiritual union they should signify the spiritual union of Christ and the Church, he then doubtlessly gives them the grace without which they could not achieve that spiritual union.[19]

It may well be that theologians, unaccustomed—at least until the present time—to regarding marriage as involving a specific call to holiness, have passed too lightly over matrimony as a sacrament of

18. "Nevertheless it is otherwise with this sacrament compared with the others; for in the others the sacred reality of which each is a sign is not only signified but also contained; in marriage however the sacred reality of which it is a sign, is signified only, and not contained" (Durandus of Saint Pourçain, *Super quattuor Sententiarum*, lib. IV, q. III, art. 1).

19. Bellarmine, *De Sacramento*, cap. II, 500.

sanctification.[20] It does seem that there is an imbalance here calling for a correction, above all in the light of the universal call to holiness, which includes the holiness of married people no less than that of other Christians.[21]

If we turn to scripture, I think we can find support for this view in Ephesians 5:21–33. Exegesis of this passage has tended to dwell on the Pauline presentation of the sign aspect of matrimony, that is, the image of the loving relationship and union between Christ and his church. However, perhaps exegetical efforts have not paid sufficient attention to the fact that this truth is presented by Paul in a preeminently practical context, where his main concern is pastoral exhortation and catechesis. Paul's teaching that marriage signifies the union of Christ and his church appears as a *consequence* of his reflections on the conjugal call to mutual love, sacrifice, and fidelity. "Husbands, love your wives, as Christ loved the church. . . . Even so husbands should love their wives. . . . For this reason a man shall leave his father and mother and be joined to his wife, and the two shall become one. This is a great mystery, and I mean in reference to Christ and the church; however, let each one of you love his wife as himself, and let the wife see that she respects her husband" (5:25, 31–33).

In this passage, Paul clearly views the husband as figuring Christ, while the wife corresponds to the church. Perhaps the subordination which this might be taken to imply has been overstressed, while insufficient attention has been given to the Pauline

20. St. Thomas, in affirming that matrimony "has a minimum of spirituality" (*Summa Theologiae* III, q. 65, a. 2, ad 1), is not denying its sanctifying effect (on the contrary), but simply giving a reason why it is generally listed last among the sacraments.

21. See LG, nos. 39–42; and GS, no. 48. St. Josemaría Escrivá, a precursor of Vatican II in many other ways, was particularly so in this point. See his "Marriage, a Christian Vocation," in *Christ Is Passing By* (New York: Scepter Press, 1995), 43–53. See further references to his teaching on this matter in Cormac Burke, "Love and the Family in Today's World," *Homiletic and Pastoral Review* (March 1995): 26–28.

comment about "no one hating his own flesh" (Eph 5:28–29), which indicates the underlying idea that marital love is intended to be in some way a purified form of self-love. Christ is really the model for *both* spouses. In quoting Ephesians 5:21, "Be subject to one another out of reverence for Christ," the *Catechism* applies it to the married relationship without any distinction.[22]

Paul is drawing attention not only to the significance of the sacrament of marriage but also to its sanctifying power, to its efficacy. It seems not only legitimate but obligatory to read into Paul's exhortations to married love and union a promise that the conjugal covenant confers special graces, sacramental graces, for this end. The balance of Paul's thought would seem to be: (1) the *signifying* aspect of matrimony as a sacrament is that conjugal union images Christ's love for his church, while (2) the *sanctifying* aspect is that, in loving one another with the help of sacramental grace, spouses become conformed to Christ in the generous dedication of his love. Thus both aspects are stressed.[23] St. Thomas, it will be remembered, rejected the opinion of those who saw *only* the sign aspect of matrimony and denied its efficacy in causing grace.[24]

The particular suitability of marriage having been raised to the dignity of a sacrament is not so evident if one makes its *raison d'être* that of imaging Christ's sacrificial love for his church; one could argue that this imaging is better done in the eucharist. It is more from the angle of its efficacy than of its signification that the unique importance of the sacramentality of marriage appears. The special fittingness of marriage being a sacrament is seen in how it is directed to sanctifying the highest form of human community;

22. CCC, no. 1642.

23. It is not a question of ignoring the sign-value, nor of denying that it is the origin and key to the sanctifying effect, but of analysing the graces which this sign (and Paul's comments) indicate.

24. "Some have said that matrimony is in no way a cause of grace, but only a sign. But this cannot be maintained" (Aquinas, *Suppl.*, q. 42, a. 3).

conferring grace so that the fruitful union of the sexes, made in the trinitarian image of God, can infuse supernatural love into the conjugal and family relationship between Christians.

Along the same lines we can note that while all the sacraments are sacraments of union, eucharist and matrimony are especially so. The eucharist makes each individual one with Christ, while matrimony makes two individuals one with one another, identifying them at same time with Christ. The love and union of persons is the whole scope and purpose of existence; its paragon is in the Trinity. Christ comes to incorporate all of us into this loving union, but such a union can only be achieved for us through self-giving that entails generosity—that is, through sacrifice, just as Christ unites himself to his church in this way. While the priesthood also mirrors Christ's sacrificed love for his church, Paul does not dwell on that but rather on matrimony, the common way of Christians. He knows that love and union between married persons is difficult but salvific. Surely his point is that, in the present state of mankind and in the plan of salvation, the love and union of persons must be sacrificial.

A further consideration of a very practical nature can be noted here. Though the sign aspect of matrimony provides a broad horizon for theological reflection, it might seem to offer little by way of motivating the majority of Christian couples in the actual living of marriage. In these times when the renewal of married life is being so urgently sought, theology could render notable service if it dwelt more on that particular aspect of the sacrament of marriage that can easily inspire properly instructed spouses, that is, its effect in communicating graces which enable the couple to live unitedly in faithful, fruitful, and growing conjugal love, so as to beget Christ in each other and to beget children in Christ.[25]

25. St. Bonaventure makes the point that while Christians, through the eucharist, are each first united more to Christ, and in consequence to one another, in matrimony,

St. Thomas, as we have seen, clearly places the sacrament not in consent, but in the *bond* deriving from it; in other words, he places sacramentality mainly in the *in facto esse* aspect of matrimony. After *Casti Connubii*, most theologians came to regard this as the common opinion.[26] It seems to me that the Second Vatican Council's presentation of marriage reinforces this view of the *whole* of the married covenant—marriage *in facto esse* as well as marriage *in fieri*—being sacramental. It is not just a momentary meeting of wills which matrimony as a sacrament is designed to sanctify, but a relationship, a state. The natural relationship acquires a continuing supernatural power.

Nature and Grace

The sacrament of matrimony is an outstanding example of "grace perfecting nature": ordinary realities are supernaturally transformed from within. Christian marriage does not create new obligations substantially distinct from those characterizing non-Christian marriage,[27] but simply provides the spouses with help and strength to fulfill their natural conjugal obligations and achieve their Christian goal. As Pius XI teaches in *Casti Connubii*, spouses are "not fettered but adorned, not hampered but assisted by the bond of the sacrament."[28] If pastors were to dwell more on this truth, they might be better able to dispel the prejudices which some Christians have against "sacramental" marriage. When marriage is considered as a means and source of grace, its demands are seen as positive, exhibiting such greatness of purpose as to appear worthwhile on a totally new level and in a totally new light.

---

the spouses are first united more to one another, and hence to Christ: *Sent. Lib. IV*, d. 26, art. 2, q. 2 (Ed. Quaracchi, vol. IV, 668).

26. Palazzini, "Il Sacramento," 755–56; see Michael Schmaus, *Katholische Dogmatik* (Münich: M. Hueber, 1957), 289.

27. The obligation of sanctity, common to all Christians (Mt 5:48), derives from baptism rather than marriage.

28. AAS 22 (1930): 555.

If grace builds on nature, then we should not only stress the privilege and richness of the sacramental graces of Christian marriage, but should do so on the basis of a renewed appreciation of the natural goodness and attraction of marriage itself. Only then can the demands of marriage—sacramental or non-sacramental— be met with optimism and determination. The current emphasis on a peculiarly Christian personalist philosophy is particularly helpful for our analysis. The basic Gospel rule of "losing oneself so as to find oneself" is equivalently found in that axiom of the Second Vatican Council which expresses the essence of Christian personalism: "man can fully discover his true self only in a sincere giving of himself."[29] Marriage contains a strong natural force drawing the human person out of self-centeredness and self-isolation due to what can rightly be called the conjugal instinct.[30]

Conjugal love, as well as being natural to man and woman, is the most intimate form of human relationship, with a variety of urges, satisfactions, and difficulties. Conjugal self-donation is therefore a great act of love—independently of the presence of feelings and sentiment, or of their absence. But it demands self-giving, involving a commitment that draws the person out of solitude and isolation, setting his or her life on a course of concern for another and for others, wishing them well, desiring what is "good" for them, which, according to St. Thomas, is the very essence of love.[31]

It is natural for husband and wife to wish to deepen the love which first drew them to each other. While perseverance and growth in that love demands constant effort, it would be unnatural for couples to conclude that the first onset of difficulties marks

29. GS, no. 24.
30. One could say that this is an instinct super-added on the human level to the mere sexual instinct. Animals seek a mate. Man and woman, if they understand their own nature, seek a spouse.
31. "To love is to wish someone what is good" (Aquinas, *Summa Theologiae* I–II, q. 26, a. 4).

the end of love, or that the effort to maintain and strengthen it is not worthwhile. The more human sense of marriage has always involved a commitment "for better or for worse." In difficult times, there is therefore a natural basis on which one can evoke a call to be faithful. It is pastoral wisdom to remind people that such reactions of the "conjugal instinct" are no less natural and noble than the similar dispositions to be found in parental love or instinct. There is something deeply unnatural, and even denaturalized, in the reaction of a father or mother who calmly stops loving his or her children, or does not care if he or she is no longer loved by them. It is equally unnatural, from the conjugal point of view, not to want to protect and maintain love for one's partner.

Christians, like non-Christians, marry because they are attracted by the good things that marriage offers: love, companionship, support, a stable home, and children. However, such good things are always threatened by individual selfishness, and today in particular couples receive no support—rather, the opposite—from the prevailing atmosphere in society. Such a life-long intimate relationship is not possible without developing an open and generous heart, which is a condition of human and supernatural charity. This, in our present state, can only be achieved with the help of God. The divine logic of matrimony being raised to the level of a sacrament can be perceived here. In marrying, Christians, perhaps without realizing it, receive graces or gifts to strengthen them for maintaining a marriage in the fullness of the conjugal commitment and thus to achieve its true ends.[32]

The Specific Graces of Marriage

Conjugal and family self-giving are revealed in the sacrament of matrimony as a way to achieve union with God. In loving each

---

32. "Sacraments are first and foremost Christ's free offer of grace. As such, they are gifts before they are choices" (Wood, "Marriage," 292).

other and their children, married couples learn to love God. Any genuine love leads a person to God, as the *Catechism* states: "Charity upholds and purifies our human ability to love, and raises it to the supernatural perfection of divine love."[33] In what follows, I suggest some possible specifications of the graces that this sacrament offers, without wishing to set forth their content in any depth.

The first grace is, naturally enough, designed to reinforce the couple's love so that it does not give way under the inevitable difficulties of a lifelong commitment but is strengthened and grows with the passage of the years. As the *Catechism* states: "This grace proper to the sacrament of Matrimony is intended to perfect the couple's love and to strengthen their indissoluble unity. By this grace they help one another to attain holiness in their married life."[34]

Love means loving the other as he or she is, that is, as a real person with defects. The hardest tests of married life come when romance wanes and couples begin to discover the extent of each other's defects. The sacrament must offer special and particularly strong graces for living through such moments, learning to forgive, to ask for forgiveness, and to develop the aptitude for dwelling on one's partner's positive characteristics and avoiding obsessions with those that appear negative—in a word, to keep loving one another in a truly self-sacrificial, Christ-like, way.[35]

One might legitimately suggest that matrimonial grace is further specified in the way it strengthens each spouse in sexual identity and donation: helping the man develop his distinctive spousal self-gift in a masculine mode and dedication, and the woman

33. CCC, no. 1827.
34. CCC, no. 1641.
35. "Learning to love each other with each one's defects" was one of St. Josemaria Escrivá's most constantly repeated points of advice to married couples; see further Burke, "Love and the Family," 23–24.

equally in a feminine mode and dedication. The unity of marriage after all is not just indissoluble, nor simply interpersonal; it is intersexual. It calls for a growth in sexual identity which is threatened today by those who seem to belittle God's gift of sexual differences, character, and function.[36]

A particular task of married love—for which the sacrament provides grace—is to purify the sexual relationship between husband and wife of the elements of selfishness and of possible exploitation which, in the present state of human nature, can affect it. The *Catechism* is quite explicit about the dangers here:[37]

This experience [of evil] makes itself felt in the relationships between man and woman. Their union has always been threatened by discord, a spirit of domination, infidelity, jealousy and conflicts that can escalate into hatred and separation. . . . According to faith the disorder we notice so painfully does not stem from the *nature* of man and woman, nor from the nature of their relations, but from *sin*. As a break with God, the first sin had for its first consequence the rupture of the original communion between man and woman. Their relations were distorted by mutual recriminations; their mutual attraction, the Creator's own gift, changed into a relationship of domination and lust.

Original sin caused man and woman to become too immediately absorbed with the exterior physical aspects and attraction of sex, preventing them from reaching, "seeing," and understanding the inner meaning and real substance and value of sexual differences and complementarity, and especially to share in the full meaning of conjugal-sexual self-giving.

The sacrament of matrimony therefore provides special graces for living conjugal chastity. This chastity calls for a certain strength and restraint between husband and wife, born of their vigilance

36. See Cormac Burke, "Sexual Identity in Marriage and Family Life," *The Linacre Quarterly* 61, no. 3 (1994): 75–86.
37. CCC, no. 1606–7.

as regards the tendency not to honor the mystery of their reciprocal sexuality, and not to act according to the laws which their
mind discovers in this mystery: a tendency which is a temptation
to use, and not to respect, the other. It is natural to each person to
be aware of the presence of a selfish element in the realm of sexuality, just as it is natural for a married couple to want to free and
purify their mutual love from the self-seeking which can be present in their intimate relations. Little is said today of conjugal chastity, and yet its absence leads to the undermining of that mutual
respect which should characterize the love of the spouses as well
as the true freedom in which their reciprocal spousal donation
should be made.[38] Marital chastity is an essential safeguard for the
strength and permanence of conjugal love, but it is not likely to be
attained without the help of special graces. "To heal the wounds
of sin, man and woman need the help of the grace that God in
his infinite mercy never refuses them. Without his help, man and
woman cannot achieve the union of their lives for which God created them 'in the beginning.'"[39] In the eighth chapter of this volume we will give further consideration to the topic of marital chastity within the context of the history and implications of the term
"remedy of concupiscence" which was for so long presented as a
'secondary' end of marriage.

The abundance of pleasure in marital intercourse is surely
meant to correspond to the joyous sense of mutual spousal surrender and possession. But if spouses allow pleasure to matter too
much to them, if they act as if nothing in their mutual physical

---

38. "That interior freedom of the gift, which of its nature is explicitly spiritual
and depends on a person's interior maturity. This freedom presupposes such a capacity
of directing one's sensual and emotive reactions as to make self-donation to the other
possible, on the basis of mature self-possession" (Pope John Paul II, *General Audience*,
November 7, 1984; see *The Theology of the Body: Human Love in the Divine Plan* [Bos-
ton: Pauline Press, 1997], 414 [hereafter "TB"]).

39. CCC, no. 1608.

relationship calls for restraint, or as if their mutual love is in no way endangered by the element of selfishness which habitually threatens sexuality, then they are in danger of taking rather than of giving, and of so losing the sense and reality of mutual donation. Conjugal chastity will help them to keep the truly personalist values of physical sexuality paramount in their minds, that is, the reaffirmation of their conjugal gift and acceptance of one another by means of sexual intercourse which, in its sharing of open-to-life procreativity, expresses the uniqueness, totality, and exclusiveness of their self-giving.

The married couple usually and naturally become a family. Spousal love is normally meant to become parental love, and the sacrament of marriage undoubtedly offers particular graces for the unfolding of personalities, redirection of affections, and acquisition of new abilities involved in this gradual and vital process, so powerfully geared to the maturing of persons. It is a particular mission of parents to mediate God's paternal and maternal love. The sacrament of matrimony should therefore grant spouses special graces to grow in parental identity and love, so that each learns to be a true father or mother, as the case may be. A sanctified marriage means a marriage where the partners have learned to be holy spouses and holy parents. From the purely natural viewpoint, the family, with its unique functions of humanizing and socializing, is rightly called the first vital cell of society. From the Christian point of view, married couples with their children are called also to be a Gospel "leaven" in the world. The sacramental graces peculiar to the married state must be considered as providing powerful apostolic stimulus and strength. If a couple is not aware of these graces—if they are not often reminded of them, in pre- and post-marriage preaching and catechesis—they may fail to activate them or rely on them, thereby neglecting a large part of the Christian evangelizing mission which is so peculiarly theirs. Nothing can so contribute to bringing the world to God as the example of married couples who, in keen awareness of the graces coming to them from the specific sacrament they have received, are living their conjugal and family life in active reliance on these graces.

These are some of the graces that the sacrament of marriage offers. It is urgent that preaching and pastoral attention help couples to realize that they, as much as any priest or religious, have a true *vocation* to holiness precisely in and through their married state. This is the calling implied in the sacrament the spouses administer to each other. If they correspond to the distinctive graces of this sacrament, God will work powerfully in their lives, helping them to fulfill the natural and generous aspirations of their conjugal love. This leads to the ultimate supernatural purpose of sanctity; through their faithful dedication to each other and to their children, they are led to the fullness of personal growth in Christ as well as to the realization of the particular evangelizing potential of their calling.

For every Christian, then, matrimony is a vocation, a call from God, with interpersonal and supernatural ends which affect both the conjugal-family society and the whole of the surrounding social atmosphere. So considered, the ends of sacramental marriage could be tentatively expressed as (1) the sanctification of the spouses themselves through their faithful grace-sustained love for one another, (2) the sanctification of the home in which the children born of this spousal love grow up, and (3) the evangelizing effect of this growing marital and familial holiness. However, this is not the way in which the ends of marriage have been presented by traditional theological and canonical teaching. This is a complex and perhaps confusing tale that we will examine in the next chapter.

3

The Ends of Marriage
A Personalist or an Institutional Understanding?

We concluded the previous chapter with a tentative suggestion regarding the logical ends of marriage when considered as a genuine calling from God, a true vocation to holiness. However, our suggestion, as we noted, does not align with the traditional formulation of the ends of marriage. For many centuries these ends were expressed in very different terms, ranged in a hierarchical order of primary and secondary ends. After the Second Vatican Council, dating concretely from the 1983 Code of Canon Law, the hierarchical ordering seemed to disappear, while a new term, the "good of the spouses" (*bonum coniugum*), made its appearance as one of simply two ends. These changes certainly seem momentous, and have provoked widely differing reactions and interpretations. The analysis of the changes can be facilitated by recalling the prolonged debate over the ends of marriage, and indeed at times about its very nature, which theologians, canonists, and Christian anthropologists engaged in over a large part of the last century.

In this debate, there was on the one hand the traditional (often termed the "procreative" or "institutional") understanding, which presented the ends of matrimony in a clear hierarchical manner: a "primary" end (procreation) and two "secondary" ends (mutual help and the remedy for concupiscence). On the other hand, there emerged a new view which, without necessarily denying the importance of procreation, urged that at least equal standing to be given to other personalist values linking husband and wife: mutual love, the physical conjugal union as an expression of this love, etc. In the traditional view, the practical consideration of marriage remained almost exclusively in the hands of moral theologians and canonists, the former principally centered on the ethical aspects of physical sexuality, the latter on the validity of matrimonial consent. Marriage was studied in light of its primary end, and its essential properties of unity and indissolubility were understood and explained mainly as a function of this end.

The secondary ends of marriage were given very summary treatment. The aspect of mutual help was seen as extending simply to the sustenance and comfort that the spouses could give one another in the hardships of life, especially in old age. St. Thomas mentions a view (without making it his own) which would seem to reduce it even further: "Woman is said to have been made as a help for man. But it can only have been to help him in procreation through intercourse, since for any other work a man could be more effectively helped by a man than by a woman."[1] The "remedy for concupiscence" was generally considered as another secondary end of matrimony added, after the fall of man, in a sort of "second institution" to compensate for a powerful tendency to sin which had now entered man's state.[2] (Chapter 8 will be devoted to a critical-historical study of the concept and usage of the term "remedy for concupiscence.")

---

1. "Dicitur mulier esse facta in adiutorium viri. Sed non ad aliud nisi ad generationem quae fit per coitum: quia ad quodlibet aliud opus, convenientius adiuvari posset vir per virum quam per feminam" (Aquinas, *Summa Theologiae* I, q. 98, a. 2).

2. Bonaventure, for instance, takes up the thesis from Hugo de St. Victor: "There was a two-fold institution: one before the Fall as a mission, and the other after the Fall as a remedy" (*Sent. Lib. IV* d. 26, a. 1, q. 1 [662]); see Hugo de St. Victor, *De sac. coniugii* (PL 176:481).

A strong counter-opinion held that these views of the aims of marriage were too exclusively centered on its procreative function, relegating to the periphery aspects which most people (including the married couples themselves) would hold as being at the heart of the marital relationship: love between man and woman as the main motive of marriage, the promise of personal happiness or fulfillment that marriage seems to offer, and the human values felt to underlie physical sexuality. No doubt modern romantic literature (as well as the developing science of psychology) influenced the evolution of these ideas. In the first decades of the twentieth century, a growing number of ecclesial thinkers began to highlight these more personal values present in marriage.

Especially well-known among the early "personalist" writers are Dietrich von Hildebrand and Herbert Doms.[3] Von Hildebrand emphasized the love-relation implied in marriage, while Doms saw the essence of marriage in physical union and its end as the fulfillment and realization of the spouses as persons. Though von Hildebrand insisted that the conjugal act must remain open to life, he does affirm that the act "already has full meaning in itself" and is to be understood as the "full attraction of conjugal love."[4] Doms went further, maintaining that "the conjugal act is full of meaning and carries its own justification in itself, independently of its orientation towards offspring."[5] B. Krempel, another personalist writer of the early twentieth century, ignored offspring as an end of marriage; its end is the "life-union" of man and woman, the child being simply the expression of this union.[6]

---

3. D. von Hildebrand, *Die Ehe* (Münich, 1929) and *Il Matrimonio* (Brescia, 1931). Herbert Doms, *Vom Sinn und Zweck der Ehe* (Breslau: Ostdeutsche Verlagsanstalt, 1935).

4. Hildebrand, *Il Matrimonio*, 49–50.

5. Herbert Doms, "Conception personnaliste du mariage d'après S. Thomas," *Revue Thomiste* 45 (1939): 763.

6. See A. Perego, "Fine ed essenza della società coniugale," *Divus Thomas* 56 (1953): 357.

Many of these writers have tended to be hostile to, or at least critical of, the notion of a hierarchy of ends on the grounds that it presented an excessively *institutional* view of marriage, which emphasized its procreative aspect or finality to the detriment if not the exclusion of the personal fulfillment which man and woman naturally look for in marrying. It was this point of the hierarchy of the ends, or more accurately of the relationship between them, that provoked the strong though carefully nuanced official opposition which this incipient view of married "personalism" encountered during the pontificate of Pope Pius XII.

The Magisterium and Development of Views on the Ends of Marriage

In a 1941 address to the Roman Rota, Pope Pius XII insisted that the tendency must be avoided "which considers the secondary end as equally principal, freeing it from its essential subordination to the primary end," and he criticized "any undue dividing or separating of the conjugal act from the primary end."[7] This was followed by a Holy Office decree regarding the ends of marriage, of April 1, 1944, which rejected the thesis that the "secondary" ends can be considered independently of the primary end and not as subordinate to it.[8] In a 1951 address, Pope Pius XII clearly reemphasized the hierarchical notion of the ends of marriage, and made a point of recalling how the Holy See, in the 1944 decree, had considered unacceptable the opinion of those who "taught that the secondary ends are not essentially subordinate to the primary end, but are of equal importance and independent of it."[9]

It is very arguable (especially in hindsight) that this rejection of the "independence" or *non*-connection between the ends was the most significant aspect of the magisterium of Pope Pius XII on

7. AAS 33 (1941): 423.   8. AAS 36 (1944): 103.
9. AAS 43 (1951): 849.

the matter, the peculiar vigor of his stance being explained by the fact that in the 1930s some presentations of the personalist thesis, such as those we have mentioned, appeared to completely undercut the procreative finality of marriage, suggesting that the act of conjugal love between the spouses can be fully significant in itself even if one annuls its procreative orientation. One thus sees how the thinking of Pope Pius XII links in with that of Pope Paul VI in *Humanae Vitae*, where he argues for the natural and essential inseparability of the unitive and procreative aspects of the conjugal act. The link with the thought of *Gaudium et Spes* should also be noted.[10] The magisterium was firm in rejecting presentations of married personalism which could lend support to a contraceptive philosophy.[11]

In any case, despite the opposition which these particular approaches encountered during the pontificate of Pope Pius XII, the main thrust of the theories did not lose strength. The Second Vatican Council witnessed their reemergence in full force on the conciliar floors, carrying off what appeared to many to have been a definitive victory. Without question, the vision of marriage presented by the Pastoral Constitution on the Church in the Modern World is strongly personalist. *Gaudium et Spes* describes marriage as an "intimate partnership of life and love," presents married consent "as the mutual giving of two persons," and insists on how husband and wife, in helping and serving each other, "become conscious of their unity, and experience it more deeply from day to day" (no. 48).

Much emphasis is placed on the role and dignity of conjugal love (not presented, however, as an *end*). The Constitution extols its importance, describing it as "an eminently human love because it is an affection between two persons rooted in the will and it embraces the good of the whole person; it can enrich the sentiments

10. GS, no. 51, para. 2.
11. See chapter 7.

of the spirit and their physical expression with a unique dignity and ennoble them as the special elements and signs of the friendship proper to marriage." The text continues: "[It] leads the spouses to a free and mutual giving of self, experienced in tenderness and action, and permeates their whole lives." The Constitution also stresses "the equal personal dignity of husband and wife," and says that this is "acknowledged by mutual and total love" (no. 49).

While marriage is stated to have been endowed by God "with various ends," what these ends are—besides procreation—is not specified, and no hierarchy between them is indicated (no. 48). More strikingly, while the natural and intrinsic ordination of matrimony and married love to procreation is twice expressed (nos. 48, 50), there is only a passing reference to the *mutuum adiutorium* (not clearly indicated as an end), while the *remedium concupiscentiae* is not mentioned at all. This would seem to lend support to the impression we have mentioned, which is fairly common: that it was only after half a century that personalism, with the Second Vatican Council, prevailed over the institutional view of marriage and at last received official, though perhaps reluctant, recognition from the magisterium.

This impression, though common, is not quite right. It is incorrect to suggest that married personalism encountered nothing but opposition from magisterial teaching until the Second Vatican Council. If one goes back to the era before Pope Pius XII, one finds the first charter for the development of this personalist understanding granted in 1930 by the papal magisterium itself, in Pope Pius XI's *Casti Connubii*. The statement that conjugal consent and union involve the "generous surrender of one's own person" is in fact already to be found in this encyclical and thus antedates the council by more than thirty years.[12] The encyclical extols

12. One enters on marriage "through the generous giving of one's own person made to another for the whole of one's life" (AAS 22 [1930]: 553).

the love between husband and wife "which holds pride of place in Christian marriage," and in a momentous passage emphasizes how it should lead to their personal and spiritual growth: married love "must have as its primary purpose that man and wife help each other day by day in forming and perfecting themselves in the interior life. . . . This mutual interior formation of husband and wife, this persevering endeavor to bring each other to the state of perfection, may in a true sense be called . . . the primary cause and reason of matrimony."[13] We will have occasion to return to this passage.

The married personalism delineated by the Second Vatican Council had its precedent, therefore, in the magisterium at the time of Pope Pius XI. After the Council it was of course a dominant note of the teaching on marriage of Pope John Paul II. Sexuality and marriage, interpreted in a strongly personalist light, were in fact the themes chosen for a lengthy papal catechesis covering the first years of his pontificate and frequently echoed thereafter.[14] By the turn of the millennium a personalist view of marriage had become firmly established in magisterial teaching.

Married Personalism and the Code of Canon Law

With this in mind, let us turn not only to the conciliar texts on marriage, but particularly to the post-conciliar magisterium which seeks to channel the Council's desire for renewal (expressed at times in terms that are as suggestive as they are vague) into concrete notions and practical dispositions. Surprising as it might seem, the first and most important document in this regard is the 1983 revised Code of Canon Law. Indeed, in promulgating it, Pope

13. Ibid., 547–48. So strong is the encouragement which this passage appears to give to a personalist understanding of marriage that some vernacular editions (for example, the U.S. text published by The Daughters of St. Paul, Boston), more papist than the Pope himself, actually omitted it from their version of the encyclical, apparently in the conviction that it could only be explained as a curial lapsus.

14. *Catechesis on Human Love*, written in 1979–84 and commonly referred to in English as "theology of the body" and collected in TB.

John Paul II described it as "the last document of Vatican II."[15] The
fruit of fifteen years of post-conciliar study, the Code sought to
give juridic precision to the spirit of the Council. The personalist
note of this spirit is particularly present in the revised expression
of the church's teaching on marriage. One outstanding example is
the new definition of the object of matrimonial consent (c. 1057),
which will occupy us in the next chapter. Moreover, the effect of
personalist ideas can be seen in several canons related to matrimonial consent: deceit (c. 1098), for instance, or fear (c. 1103), and also
c. 1095. For the moment let us center our attention on the very first
canon in the title on marriage, which defines the nature and purpose of matrimony itself: "The matrimonial covenant, by which a
man and a woman establish between themselves a partnership of
the whole of life, is by its nature ordered toward the good of the
spouses and the procreation and education of offspring" (c. 1055).

Here we are offered a brief formula of the greatest importance
which marks not only a magisterial application but a clear *development* of the married personalism of *Gaudium et Spes*. Particularly
to be noted is the progress from the rather vague statement about
matrimony being endowed with "various" or "other" ends besides
procreation to the specific enunciation of two ends to marriage.[16]
Of special interest in this definition or description of marriage is
the highly personalist concept of the "good of the spouses," the *bonum coniugum*, presented now, along with procreation and education of offspring, as one of the ends of matrimony.

It is important to bear in mind that we are dealing with a
new term which is scarcely to be found in ecclesial writing before
it was accepted in 1977 into the *schemata* for the new Code. Its

15. AAS 76 (1984): 644.
16. GS, nos. 48 and 50. In *Casti Connubii*, Pius XI in some way also anticipated
this expression of a double end: "Its purpose which is the begetting and educating of
children for God, and the binding of man and wife to God through Christian love and
mutual support" (AAS 22 [1930]: 570).

acceptance came at the end of a thorough debate within the Pontifical Commission for drafting the Code regarding ways of juridically expressing the "personal[ist]" end or ends of matrimony.[17] It should be noted that the Commission at first spoke of the *bonum coniugum* as a way of expressing the *"finis personalis."* Some commentators took this to suggest that by the *bonum coniugum* the Commission wished to express the subjective ends of the spouses. In this interpretation the *bonum coniugum* comes to signify the *"finis"* or *"fines operantis"*: love, security, happiness, personal satisfaction, etc. The Commission itself, some time later (precisely in defending the expression *bonum coniugum* against criticism), found it wise to explicitly reject such an interpretation. It made it quite clear that *finis personalis* is intended in an objective, not a subjective sense: "The ordination of matrimony to the *bonum coniugum* is truly an essential element of the matrimonial covenant, and not a subjective end of the person marrying."[18] It is important to bear this in mind: the expression *bonum coniugum* refers to the *"finis operis"* rather than to the *"finis operantis."* That is, it relates to the intrinsic design of marriage, to the institutional ends which it has of itself and not to the ends of the concrete person(s) marrying.

This rather sudden introduction of a new term, the *bonum coniugum*, to take its place alongside the procreation and education of children as an end of marriage, is all the more striking in that the particular term itself, in this precise usage, is nowhere to be found in the documents of the Second Vatican Council, to which one might reasonably expect to trace its genesis.[19] *Gaudium et Spes*, in

17. *Communicationes* (Reports of the Pontifical Commission for the Revision of the Code of Canon Law) (Rome: Libreria Editrice Vaticana, 1969–83), 123.

18. *Communicationes* (1983), 221.

19. In fact, the term *bonum coniugum* as expressive of an end of marriage has practically no precedent in theological or canonical writings. Its insertion in 1977 (by unanimous vote of the Pontifical Commission) into the draft of what was to become

line with the whole tradition of the church, twice states that marriage and married love are naturally ordered to procreation, as to their end: "By their very nature, the institution of matrimony itself and conjugal love are ordained for the procreation and education of children" (no. 48, and repeated in the opening line of no. 50). What is surprising is that, despite the personalist note dominant in nos. 48–49 of the Constitution, it contains no phrase or formula which could be said to express the personalist end with the clarity with which the procreative end is stated. There is a brief phrase which recalls, and is no doubt meant in some way to express, the former "secondary end" of the *mutuum adiutorium*: "Man and woman . . . help and serve each other by their married partnership" (no. 48). However, we are not told what is the content or final purpose of this mutual help. Vague references are made to the "various" or "other" ends of marriage besides procreation, but these are not specified. All in all, we have to face up to the fact that the concise formula of c. 1055—that marriage is ordered to the good of the spouses—is nowhere to be found in the conciliar documents, nor is it easy to draw from them a clear notion of the precise meaning of the phrase, which remains nevertheless as a notion of exceptional theological interest.

This lack of clarity perhaps makes it understandable that some (arguing also that there can be only one main end) maintain that the Council did not in fact introduce any real modification in the previous doctrine about the distinction and hierarchy of primary and secondary ends. This seems a difficult thesis to sustain, for it fails to give any explanation for the deliberate avoidance by the

---

the present c. 1055 meant that the 1983 Code became in fact the first magisterial document to use the term to express one of the ends of marriage. Of course, its subsequent introduction into the 1992 CCC (nos. 1601, 1660, and 2249) and the later *Compendium* of 2005 (no. 338) (*Compendium of the Catechism of the Catholic Church* [Rome: Libreria Editrice Vaticana]) signifies that it cannot be treated as a merely canonical formulation, but has passed into general magisterial teaching.

Council of the terminology formerly used. The more common view is that the doctrine of a hierarchy of ends has been replaced by one in which we have two ends of equal standing: the procreative-institutional and the personalist. Others, no doubt feeling that the prolonged debate of the past decades has created an unjustified and regrettable tension or opposition between the various ends or aspects of marriage, see the mind of the Council as wishing to overcome such sense of opposition and to show the essential unity between these aspects. We are told, for instance: "Vatican II sought to remake the unity between the two aspects—the personal and the institutional—so that conjugal love would not be separated from procreation."[20]

Two Interconnected Institutional Ends

My own opinion is that the debate about the hierarchy of the ends of marriage is a potential dead end, and that it is rather the interrelation and inseparability between these ends that matters and needs emphasizing. We will go into this in a moment, but first there is an important point that calls for clarification, a major misunderstanding which seems to have constantly accompanied the debate on this subject, and which will continue to create confusion unless it is highlighted and corrected. Both those who insist on the equal dignity of the ends of marriage and those who continue to defend the idea of a hierarchical subordination (as well as those who would like to underline the unity between the ends, as in the quotation just given) tend to contrast or simply distinguish the ends involved, as if one (the procreative) was the *institutional* end, and the other (the "good of the spouses"), the *personalist*. To my mind, such a contrast is to be firmly rejected. *Both*

20. A. Favale, "Fini e Valori del Sacramento del Matrimonio" (Rome, 1978), 203. Barberi describes the text of GS, no. 48 as a "synthesis of the two views: juridico-institutional and human-personalist" (*La celebrazione*, 119).

ends—procreative and personalist—*are institutional*! Both, that is (and it is vital to see this),[21] derive from the very institution of marriage. Marriage, in other words, has two institutional ends. By the institutional ends of marriage is obviously meant those ends established in its very institution, that is, those with which marriage was endowed by its "institutor" or creator—by God himself. God's plan as originally revealed to us has to ground our analysis of the ends for which marriage was instituted.

It seems to me that little importance has been attached in this debate to something that, to say the least, is intriguing for those who seek a key in Scripture to God's design—the two distinct accounts that the book of Genesis, in its first and second chapters, offers of the creation of man, male and female, and of the institution of marriage. One account expresses a clearly procreative finality, while the other can fairly be described as personalist. The first, the so-called elohist text, reads: "God created man in his own image, in the image of God he created him; male and female he created them. And God blessed them, and God said to them, "Be fruitful and multiply" (Gen 1:27–28). The other, the "jahwist" text (considered the earlier in date of composition), says: "The Lord God said, "It is not good that the man should be alone; I will make him a helper fit for him," that is, woman: "Therefore a man leaves his father and his mother and cleaves to his wife, and they become one flesh" (Gen 2:18–24).

The Two Scriptural Accounts of the Institution

We do not have to be scholars of Scripture to suggest that this dual narration is no "accident" or a slip of the pen on the part of the Holy Spirit. The presence of the two accounts is scarcely to be dismissed as casual, or the connection between them as simply extrinsic. Surely we have to deal rather with something deliberate, with two complementary narratives, connected in a way that

---

21. Just as it is vital to see that both are, in the proper sense, personalist.

corresponds to the logic of God's plans, a logic within which the institutional purpose of marriage appears as *both procreative and personalist*.

In the elohist text, man's relative *perfection* is underlined. He is made in the image of God and is the highest visible expression of the goodness of creation. The distinction of sexes ("male and female he created them") appears as a key to man's mission to carry on the work of creation by procreation. The idea of the goodness of this assigned mission characterizes the passage. In the jahwist version, it is rather man's *incompleteness* which is stressed. Man (male *or* female) is incomplete if he remains on his own, and this is not a good thing: "*non est bonum.*" The normal plan of God is that man will find the goodness he lacks in union with a member of the other sex, and this union should lead to the good of each and of both, to the *bonum coniugum*.

As appears from Scripture, then, God's purpose in instituting marriage is also personalist. Marriage is institutionally directed not only to the increase of the human race through ordered procreation in a family setting, but also to the "increase" of the persons who marry, to their development or perfecting in their ability to love. It is by going back to marriage as it was "in the beginning" that we find the biblical roots and the true content of the *bonum coniugum*. The "good of the spouses" regards not primarily their passing happiness but their maturing in the love that brings one to eternal happiness. The theme is so important, and so often misunderstood, that we will devote the next chapter to it.

The Demands of Married Personalism

I have written elsewhere[22] on the modern tendency to see the Augustinian *bona* not principally as "values" or "benefits" of the married state, but rather as burdensome obligations that it impos-

---

22. See *Covenanted Happiness* (New York: Scepter Press, 1999), ch. 8.

es on the couple. This applies particularly to the *bonum sacramenti* (indissolubility) and the *bonum prolis* (offspring). It is true that the wholehearted acceptance of these "goods" takes a sustained effort; but it also true that this effort, besides being a source of happiness, has a deep maturing effect on the persons who face up to it.

Gaudium et Spes (following *Casti Connubii*) teaches that it is "for the good of the spouses, of the children, and of society" that the marriage bond has been made unbreakable.[23] Indissolubility therefore positively favors the *bonum coniugum*. The point is surely that all the effort and sacrifice involved in fidelity to the unbreakable character of the bond—in good times and in bad, etc.—serves to develop and perfect the personalities of the spouses. A similar reading is no doubt to be made of that passage in no. 50 of *Gaudium et Spes* which states that "children greatly contribute to the welfare of their parents." Children enrich their parents' lives in many human ways, and not least in virtue of the generous dedication they tend to evoke in them.

The fact is that it is not easy for two people to live together for life in a faithful and fruitful union. It is "easier" for each to live apart, or to unite casually or for a short time, or to avoid having children. It is easier but it is not happier, nor does it contribute to their growth as persons. "*Non est bonum homini esse solus*": it is not good for man—male or female—to live alone or in successive temporary associations that tend to leave him or her increasingly trapped in selfish isolation. Married commitment is not an easy endeavor, but, apart from typically being a happy one, it is one that matures. There is no true married personalism which ignores or fails to understand and stress the goodness, for the spouses, of the conjugal commitment.

---

23. GS, no. 48; see CC (AAS 22 [1930]: 553). This is the only mention of the phrase *bonum coniugum* in the conciliar documents; it is proposed here not as an end of marriage but as a simple effect of indissolubility.

The Personalism of the Human Procreative
Power and Relationship

It is bad not to see the institutional character of the personalist end of marriage. It is worse not to recognize the personalist
character of conjugal procreativity. To speak disparagingly about
"biologism," whenever stress is laid on the procreative aspect of
marriage, betrays a fundamental lack of understanding of married
personalism. Nothing can so uniquely express the marital relationship and the desire for marital union as conjugal intercourse
when it is open to its procreative potential. Why after all should
sexual intercourse between husband and wife be called "*the* conjugal act"? What makes it, among all the possible expressions of love
between the spouses, so singular, so uniquely capable of expressing
their desire for union? Nothing else, in last analysis, than the fact
that it is the gift and acceptance of the seed of life. A married couple uniquely express their love for one another and are uniquely
united in intercourse, because each in effect says to the other: "By
this act I am prepared to share with you, and with you alone, this
most singular power God has given us: the power to fuse together
a part of the life of each of us so that, in uniting, they become a
new life: our child, the living expression and fruit of our union and
love."[24] The union of the spouses' two selves "in one flesh" tends to
become incarnated in a new self which is a mirror and expression
of their married community and love. True union between free
persons always involves donation. In the case of the conjugal act,
intercourse is unitive because of the absolutely unique nature of

24. See Aquinas: "Parents love their children because they are in some way part
of themselves, because the children are procreated from the seed of the parents. Hence
the child is in some way a part of the parent, separated from him [Parentes diligunt
filios eo quod sunt aliquid ipsorum. Ex semine enim parentum filii procreantur. Unde
filius est quodammodo pars patris ab eo separata]" (*In VIII Ethic.*, lect. 12).

the donation involved: the gift of procreativity. Hence derives the *intrinsic inseparability* of the unitive and the procreative aspects of the marital act.[25] We will expand on this in chapter 7.

Another personalist aspect of open-to-life conjugal inter-course is that it tends in a legitimate way to self-realization and self-perpetuation (both personalist values), but raises them, by the very donative and generous nature of the act, to a higher level.[26] When open to life, the act tends not to assertion or perpetuation of each spousal self in egoistic isolation, but precisely to the per-petuation of something common to both and most intimate to them: the love binding them together. It is precisely this aware-ness of the deep personalist meaning of procreativity that renders marital intercourse so uniquely capable of contributing to the *bo-num* of each spouse, maturing and "realizing" each one and linking them together. Further, each child that they have becomes a visible incarnated link strengthening the conjugal bond, the maintenance of which is so essential to their own personal realization and au-thentic good.[27]

Conjugality and procreativity are thus seen to have a natu-ral complementarity. Conjugality means that both the man and woman are destined to become *spouses*: to unite themselves to each other in an act that is unitive precisely because it is oriented to procreativity. And procreativity means that he or she is destined to

25. *Humanae Vitae*, no. 12 [hereafter "HV"].

26. What is more singular as a form of self-realization than the begetting of one's own child—another person, in all its irrepeatability—as the fruit of the gift of self that each of the spouses gives to the other? Here we see the radical defectiveness of the personalism of Doms, who reduced the child to a simply physical complement to the conjugal community.

27. "The stable and firm cause of the union [between a man and his wife] would seem to be the children. So it is that sterile couples, who lack offspring, are more prone to separate. . . . And the reason is that children are a common good of both, that is, of husband and wife. . . . That which is common maintains and holds friendship to-gether" (Aquinas, *In VIII Ethic.*, lect. 12).

become a *parent*: the union of the spouses tends to fruitfulness by its very nature. Conjugality and procreativity taken together draw man out of his original solitude, which limits him as a person and is an enemy of his "self-realization," of his *bonum*.[28]

A 'Right' to the Ends?

Bonum prolis and procreation need to be accurately distinguished. The *bonum prolis* (or "openness to procreation") is an essential feature of the marital relationship, and no true marriage can be constituted if it is absent. Procreation is an end of marriage: a marriage can be valid even if that end is not achieved. The reason is clear. It lies within a person's power to share his or her procreative potential with another, and to be prepared to do so is necessary for valid marital consent. There is therefore a *ius ad bonum prolis*, a right that the other accepts the "procreativity" of the conjugal relationship; to exclude the *bonum prolis* from one's marital consent invalidates it. However, there is no *ius ad prolem*, no right to actual procreation, for that does not lie totally under a person's will but depends ultimately on God.

It is true that some canonists have used the term *bonum prolis* as simply equivalent to procreation. This is incorrect (the confusion of a property with an end), and it has become especially important today to avoid such error. There is just one step from saying, correctly, that there is a *ius ad bonum prolis*—a right to openness to offspring—to incorrectly positing a *ius ad prolem*, a right to actually having a child. Questions related to *in vitro* fertilization, etc. are seen by many people in terms of such a "right." The *Catechism* (no. 2378) addresses this point very firmly: "A child is not something owed to one, but is a gift. The 'supreme gift of mar-

28. Pope John Paul II reflects on how sexuality holds out the promise of overcoming this original solitude; see TB, 35.

riage' is a human person. A child may not be considered a piece of property, an idea to which an alleged 'right to a child' would lead." There is a right that one's partner in the married covenant does not exclude what God may give, but each child is in the end a gift of God.

Synthesis and Inseparability

Modern personalism, therefore, encouraged especially by the Second Vatican Council and subsequent magisterium, offers a renewed vision of marriage and its institutional ends. The major points of this vision, as I understand them, could be presented synthetically as follows: (1) the natural ordering of marriage to given ends is emphasized, (2) the hierarchy between the ends is not emphasized,[29] (3) *both* the good of the spouses *and* the procreation/education of children are *institutional* ends, (4) *both* the good of the spouses *and* the procreation/education of children have *personalist* value, (5) the ends are naturally (institutionally) inseparable, (6) their inseparability is more important than any hierarchy between them, and (7) inseparability means an *inter*-ordering, rather than a sub-ordination, between the ends.

Let us dwell briefly on the last three points: the inseparability of the two ends of marriage as they are presented to us in c. 1055. Is it possible to separate these two ends? Conceptually, yes. In reality, no, at least not without undermining the vital structure of matrimony. Marriage was instituted for the maturing of the spouses, particularly through having a family and dedicating themselves to the task of raising children, and it was instituted for the procreation/education of children, to be achieved through the passing

---

29. Pope John Paul II made a passing reference to the hierarchy of ends in an address of October 10, 1984 (TB, 407). This one reference does not seem to me to detract from the fact that the matter is now expressed otherwise by all major magisterial documents.

physical union and through the abiding and growing existential and organic unity between husband and wife. The institution was one, although it is described in Genesis in two distinct accounts. It is God who has put these ends together in one institution, and man should resist the tendency to separate them.

A procreative marriage with many children in which neither of the spouses has a sense of family life, or of how dedication to it contributes to their own maturing or happiness as persons, has lost its distinctive human dimension, and will with difficulty contribute to the good of the spouses or of the children. A marriage *à deux*, from which children (or more than one or two children) are excluded—because they are regarded as potential enemies to the couple's happiness—is not likely to make the couple happy for long and is too undemanding to contribute to their authentic good.

That is why there seems little point in centering attention on the possible hierarchy between these two institutional ends of marriage. The procreative aspect is not better defended because it is said to stand higher in importance than the good of the spouses.[30] It is better defended when married couples see that their own mutual love, their happiness together, and the personal growth of each, are furthered by the enterprise of building a family according to God's plans. The good of the spouses is only understood in all its personalist potential when it is seen to depend on the unique human enrichment that comes with each child. Only then is it saved from reductive tendencies which, while perhaps speaking of the good "of the spouses" (conjointly), actually mean the "good" of each one individually, thus leading to those common existential

30. To defend this may only serve to exacerbate a sense of opposition between the ends and incidentally to buttress the pseudo-argument of those who say that the church is interested only in numerical offspring, and not in the spouses' legitimate aspirations of happiness.

THE ENDS OF MARRIAGE 69

situations where the "good" of one comes in the end to be seen as rival and enemy to that of the other, and the stage is set for the collapse and dissolution of a common venture of happiness.

Inseparability gives a better idea of the mutual relation between these ends. It passes over the question of hierarchy and looks rather to the essential *inter*-ordering of the ends. Each relates vitally and existentially to the other. Each depends on the other; they stand or fall together. It seems in fact idle to debate whether the ends are of equal dignity or whether there is a subordination between them, just as it is pointless to debate the same points regarding the relationship between man and woman. It is the complementarity, the inseparability, which needs to be underlined.

In chapter 7 we will attempt a fuller anthropological-personalist analysis of the main teaching of *Humanae Vitae* regarding the inseparability of the unitive and procreative aspects of the conjugal act. It is suggestive that Scripture-based study of the institution of marriage leads us to a parallel conclusion regarding its ends: two ends inseparably connected in one divine purpose. There is a natural and intrinsic connection between the two ends of the good of the spouses and the procreation and education of children. They are intimately linked, and the pursuit of each end should help the other while being at the same time conditioned and helped by it.

Further Perspectives

The new presentation of the ends of marriage given in the 1983 Code of Canon Law, in the 1992 *Catechism*, and in the current magisterium opens up broad and important perspectives for investigation, not only in the juridic field, but also in Scripture, theology, morals and anthropology, as well as in the pastoral area. In substantial continuity with the past, we need a reappraisal (1) of the concept of marriage, based on a more comprehensive understanding of its original institutional purpose and dignity, overcoming in particular the suggested opposition between the procreative and the personalist aspects; (2) of conjugal sexuality, which is in danger of being cut down to a meaningless exercise of self-seeking, where any vestige of donation of self is submerged in a growing instrumentalization of the other spouse, reduced to the level of a sex-object; (3) of the three Augustinian "goods" or *bona*, in particular of the *bonum prolis*, rehabilitated and integrated into true Christian married personalism; (4) of the family, particularly by preventing the true concepts of fatherhood and motherhood in all their human reality, content, and dignity, from being lost; and (5) of the pastoral pre- and post-wedding ministry, to help people strengthen their understanding of marriage as a way of Christian dedication and sanctification.

In the short and in the long run, the last point is of predominant importance. Couples need help to deepen their awareness of the sacramental riches of matrimony. More particularly still, they need to realize that marriage is a genuine *vocation*, a personal call from God to a way of life aimed at achieving sanctity. Pre-marital instruction must seek above all to awaken in the future spouses this awareness of a divine calling, designed to help them so live their human love that it becomes for each one a means of growth in love for God, and to help them to build a family together.

4

A Further Look at the "Good of the Spouses" as an End of Marriage

In the previous chapter, we noted the church's contemporary presentation of the "good of the spouses" as one of the ends of marriage. The term is as important as it is new, and it invites, indeed calls for, interpretation as to its precise meaning. We have given a summary exposition of one possible interpretation, backing up this view with Scriptural and magisterial references, and have also noted the misleading tendency to present procreation as the institutional end of marriage and, as if in contrast, to *bonum coniugum* as the personalist end. Both ends, we have sought to show, are institutional, and both are personalist. It is important to develop our consideration of the latter point.

The harder task may well be to illustrate the personalist content of the procreative aspect of marriage. We will attempt to do so in chapter 7. The purpose of the present chapter is to analyze the personalist nature of the *bonum coniugum*. Many might consider this an easy and indeed almost a superfluous endeavor, so much does it seem to them that the personalism of the "good of the spouses" is self-evident. I cannot agree. To my mind, many so-called personalist interpretations of the *bonum coniugum* have been extremely superficial, and at times quite wrong, both in the personalism they invoke and in the nature and purpose they assign to the *bonum coniugum* itself.[1] Moreover one must note the recurring (and surprising) tendency among certain theological and canonical writers to treat the *bonum coniugum* as if it were the central and almost only expression of the personalism characterizing contemporary church teaching on marriage. This passes over the new way in which matrimonial consent is now expressed, which is even more unquestionably and evidently personalist, and arguably provides the key to the deeper understanding of the nature of the *bonum coniugum*. However, before we look into this, it may be useful to recall what is distinctive to a personalist philosophy of life, and then try to draw well-grounded conclusions from the ways in which the modern church magisterium has chosen to use personalist notions in describing both the nature and the ends of marriage.

Personalism

Christian personalism can be rightly regarded as the philosophical or anthropological view underlying the teaching of the Second Vatican Council on individual and social life, and particu-

---

1. Among popular canonical writers, Lawrence Wrenn is probably emblematic in this sense. In his 1986 essay, "Refining the Essence of Marriage," he concludes that "six of the more obvious qualities that might constitute the essence of the *bonum coniugum* [are] partnership, benevolence, companionship, friendship, caring, and finally love" (*The Jurist* 46, no. 2 [1986]: 537). E. G. Pfnausch follows much the same line in his article, "The Good of the Spouses in Rotal Jurisprudence: New Horizons" (*The Jurist* 56 [1996]: 548). In the field of theological analysis, William May has commented on the inadequate treatment often given to the *bonum coniugum*: "Some theologians, e.g., Antonio Miralles, identify the "good of the spouses" with the old good of "mutual assistance" and discuss it only very briefly. See his *El Matrimonio* (Pamplona: EUNSA, 1993), 102. This view, however, is hardly correct, [although] also championed by many canonists." ("The 'Good of the Spouses' and Marriage as a Vocation to Holiness," October 3, 2004; http://www.christendom-awake.org/pages/may/marriage-2.htm). I have sought to bring out the inadequacy of these and similar analyses in a lengthy article, "Progressive Jurisprudential Thinking" (*The Jurist* 58, no. 2 [1998]: 437–78).

larly on marriage. What does this personalism mean in practice? The key personalistic text is from *Gaudium et Spes* (no. 24): "Man can fully discover his true self only in a sincere giving of himself." The same document (no. 48) applies this notion directly to marriage, speaking of it "as a mutual giving of two persons," or a union in which the spouses "mutually give and accept one another."

This is not abstract philosophizing on the part of the Council. Christian personalism is being proposed as an alternative, as a remedy, to the destructive secular individualism that so strongly characterizes modern life. But, it may be objected, is there any great difference between the two? Do not both, after all, center on the person or the individual? No; they represent totally different approaches both to personal growth and to social life. Pope John Paul II dwells on "the antithesis between individualism and personalism":

Love, the civilization of love, is bound up with personalism. Why with personalism? And why does individualism threaten the civilization of love? We find a key to answering this in the Council's expression, a "sincere gift." Individualism presupposes a use of freedom in which the subject does what he wants. . . . He does not want to "give" to another on the basis of truth; he does not want to become a "sincere gift." Individualism thus remains egocentric and selfish. The "ethos" of personalism is altruistic: it moves the person to become a gift for others and to discover joy in giving himself.[2]

This Christian view of fulfillment is radically opposed to the idea of self-centered fulfillment which not only dominates almost all of modern psychology and psychological training, but also colors the outlook of many Catholics.

Christian personalism, then, is not individualism; just the opposite. It is concerned not mainly with the rights of the individual,

2. *Letter to Families* (1994), no. 14.

but with his or her growth. Its focus is not self-concern and self-protection, but self-giving, calling the individual out of himself. It is by sincere giving in response to worthwhile values that the individual realizes or fulfills himself or herself.[3] The Gospel roots are clear: seek your life, selfishly, and you will lose it; give your life, generously, and you will find it (cf. Mt 10:39).

The Heart of Married Personalism Lies in the New Definition of Consent

We have already considered the personalist overtones of the *bonum coniugum* as one of the institutional ends of marriage. The almost total newness of the term perhaps explains why, as I see it, so much theological and canonical writing zeroed in on the expression as if it contained the essence and almost the whole of the personalism now present in the magisterial teaching on marriage. Insofar as this has occurred, it involved a serious narrowing of perspective, for it passed over or relegated to a secondary position any consideration of the new and much more directly personalist description of matrimonial consent which the 1983 Code gives to us. One must make this point vigorously, not only because the two notions—the *bonum coniugum* of c. 1055 and the *sese mutuo tradunt et accipiunt* (the "mutual giving and accepting of each other" by the spouses) of c. 1057—are closely interrelated, but particularly because the clear terms in which marital consent is formulated arguably contain essential clues to understanding the somewhat obscure content of the "good of the spouses."

Canon 1057 describes what is involved in the act of marital consent, thereby offering one of the most vital reformulations of the church's teaching on marriage.[4] We read: "Matrimonial con-

---

3. See the author's *Man and Values: A Personalist Anthropology* (Nairobi, Kenya: Scepter Press, 2007).

4. The 1917 Code (c. 1081) gave an unappealing (and what was generally con-

sent is an act of will by which a man and a woman by an irrevocable covenant mutually give and accept one another for the purpose of establishing a marriage."[5] The new and eminently personalist expression in this canon of what the spouses consent to in marrying holds the key to the correct interpretation of the ends of the marriage to which they consent and thus helps to clarify the imprecise concept of the *bonum coniugum* of c. 1055.

Our standpoint is that the *sese tradere-accipere* (c. 1057) and the *bonum coniugum* (c. 1055) together highlight the personalist spirit characterizing the new ecclesial way of thinking about matrimony. We also hold that any deeper analysis of this married personalism must begin with the implications of marital consent as involving the gift of self. Our reason for holding this is that the notion of the *bonum coniugum* as an end of marriage is, as we have already remarked, a totally new term in ecclesial parlance, while that of marital consent as self-gift is not. This latter notion was already expressed in 1930 in *Casti Connubii*, which says that people "enter on marriage through the generous gift of their own person for the whole of their lifetime."[6] *Gaudium et Spes* enriches this notion in a very significant way, speaking of the "act by which the partners mutually give *and accept* one another."[7] That spouses mutually "give and accept each other" is pure personalism, Christian personalism in its essence, applied to marriage. In marriage too, it is only in the decision to make such a reciprocal and committed self-gift that man and woman can

---

sidered an over-physicalist) description of matrimonial consent: an act of the will "by which each party gives and accepts a perpetual and exclusive right over the body, for acts which are of themselves suitable for the generation of children." This stressed the potential role of the parties marrying as parents, but failed to take account also of their present desire to unite as spouses.

5. "Consensus matrimonialis est actus voluntatis, quo vir et mulier foedere irrevocabili sese mutuo tradunt et accipiunt ad constituendum matrimonium."

6. "Per generosam quidem propriae personae pro toto vitae tempore factam alteri traditionem" (AAS 22 [1930], 543).

7. "Actu humano, quo coniuges sese mutuo tradunt atque accipiunt" (GS, no. 48).

fully discover their destiny and fulfillment. But we should note well that, as applied to marriage, it is not just a meaning-filled decision to give oneself; it is equally a decision to accept another, which is even more meaningful. Personalism, especially in marriage, always carries a challenge with it. It is demanding: come out of yourself, open yourself, give yourself; be more generous, more receptive, more understanding, and more forgiving.

There is a deep contrast between the idea of "self-sufficiency" presented by much of modern psychology and the Christian ideal of realization through self-giving. "Only by transcending themselves and living a life of self-giving and openness to truth and love can individuals reach fulfillment."[8] Self-sufficiency has always been a radical temptation for man, one that he needs to overcome if he is to give himself and realize himself, and in the end attain eternal life. Marriage, being by essence a covenant of self-giving, presents itself in the plan of nature as a safeguard against the trap of self-sufficiency. As the Second Vatican Council states, "this [conjugal] partnership of man and woman constitutes the first form of communion between persons. For by his innermost nature man is a social being; and if he does not enter into relations with others he can neither live nor develop his gifts."[9] People are especially made for conjugal interdependence. It is natural therefore to understand marriage in terms of mutual sharing and support. To regard it simply as a means of personal satisfaction is individualistic, as well as a sign of defective anthropological thinking.

This is why I maintain that the "self-giving" and very particularly the "other-acceptance" of marital consent hold the key to the proper understanding of the *bonum coniugum*. It is not good for man or woman to be alone, to live without some committed re-

---

8. Pope John Paul II, "Address to Members of the American Psychiatric Association, Jan. 4, 1993," *Osservatore Romano* (English Edition) (Jan. 13, 1993), 4.
9. GS, no. 12.

lationship with others. To be alone is a great enemy to personal development and indeed to salvation. The "good" that God wants for the spouses through the married commitment is the final result of the generous and unconditional conjugal giving of self as one is and, perhaps even more so, of the generous and unconditional acceptance of one's partner as he or she is—both prolonged, with the help of grace, throughout a life time of exclusive fidelity and of openness to the fruit of mutual conjugal love.

While I regard this new personalist formulation of matrimonial consent as a very positive development, I naturally hold that the idea of mutual and total self-gift cannot be taken in any absolutely literal sense.[10] The *traditio suiipsius* must necessarily involve an element of metaphor. The right that each spouse acquires is not and cannot be a right over *every* aspect of the person or life of the other. Some of these are absolutely inalienable, such as personal dignity, freedom, responsibility, etc. Without questioning that the spouses should seek a high degree of mutual understanding and moral unity, it is evident that marital consent does not confer any juridic right over those aspects of the person which can be considered supra- or meta-conjugal. For instance, along with the obligations proper to the married state, each spouse retains the untransferable duty to work out his or her own salvation; a duty that can and ought to be powerfully helped by the married commitment but cannot be absorbed into it.

The Condition or Effect of Conjugal Self-Giving: Coming Out of Self

If we believe in the continuity as well as in the development of doctrine, we need to show how the apparently new personal-

10. See my book, *L'Oggetto del Consenso Matrimoniale: un'analisi personalistica* (Turin: Giappichelli, 1997); an English version was later published in *Forum* 9 (1998): 39–117. See also my study, "The Object of the Marital Self-Gift as presented in c. 1057, §2," *Studia canonica* 31 (1997): 403–21.

ist emphasis characterizing ecclesial reflection on marriage has roots traceable back to the beginning of Christianity, even if these roots have at times developed below the surface of theological or canonical thinking. Jesus, in answering a fundamental question regarding marriage (that of its indissolubility), referred back to the "personalist" narrative of Genesis 2:18–24 regarding how marriage was in the beginning (Mt 19:4–8). Along with Pope John Paul II in his "Theology of the Body," we also take this as our main reference point.

"*Non est bonum esse hominem solum faciamus ei adiutorium similem sui*": "It is not good that the man should be alone; I will make him a helper fit for him" (Gen 2:18). From this divine purpose of taking man or woman out of individual solitude by providing a helpmate and spouse in marriage, ecclesial reflection came to consider mutual help (*mutuum adiutorium*) as an end, a "secondary" end, of marriage.[11] And yet, though the concept of the spouses being a mutual help to each other is so clearly rooted in Scripture, it is striking that it has been the object of so little consideration on the part of theologians over the centuries, and that there has been very little developed analysis of what this mutual aid involves. Having said that, I think that in whatever analysis there has been, one can legitimately trace a certain "personalist" trend of thought.

In one of his later works, St. Augustine writes: "The good of marriage is always a good indeed. In the people of God it was at one time an act of obedience to the law; now it is a remedy for weakness, and for some a solace of human nature."[12] Most of the theologians of the twelfth century scarcely mention the concept of the *mutuum adiutorium*, and when they do, it is largely with un-

11. In chapter 8 we will consider the question of the *remedium concupiscentiae*, formerly classed as another secondary end.

12. *De bono vid.*, c. 8, n. 11 (PL 40:437).

expanded reference to Augustine's "*humanitatis solatium.*"[13] The position of Thomas Aquinas, however, merits mention. If we ask a peculiarly modern question—whether he saw in sexuality as such a role for the "realization" of the human person—no doubt the answer is that, in common with the rest of medieval theology, he did not.[14] Does it follow from this that he gives no thought whatever to the mutually enriching role, outside the purely procreative sphere, of the complementary relationship between husband and wife, in the development of human maturity?

Not at all; he teaches that man and woman are naturally inclined to marriage not only because of offspring but also because of the "the mutual help given to each other by the spouses in the home." He presents the difference between the sexes as a special expression of man's need of help from others: "Just as natural reason tells us that men should live together, because each one alone cannot be self-sufficient in all the aspects of life (and so man is said to be naturally social), so of those things that are necessary for human life, some fall naturally to the competence of men, others to that of women." And so, he concludes, "nature brings it about that there be a definite association of man and woman which consists in matrimony."[15]

Further, with specific reference to the text of Genesis, Thomas speaks of the special friendship that exists between husband and wife: "The friendship between man and woman is unique, for they are united not only in sexual intercourse which even among animals creates a closeness of companionship, but also in their life together which covers the whole of their domestic relations. As a

13. See P. M. Abellán, *El fin y la significación sacramental del matrimonio desde S. Anselmo hasta Guillermo de Auxerre* (Granada, 1939), 168.
14. See M.-J. Nicolas, "Remarques sur le sens et la fin du mariage," *Revue Thomiste* 45 (1939): 792.
15. Aquinas, *In IV Sent.*, d. 26, q. 1, a. 1; and *Suppl.*, q. 41, a. 1.

sign of this therefore, as we are told in Gen 2:24, a man will leave his father and mother for the sake of his wife."[16] He quotes and approves Aristotle: "According to the Philosopher, in VIII *Ethic.*, the friendship which exists between husband and wife is natural, and comprises what is virtuous, useful and enjoyable."[17] Aquinas adds: "The form of matrimony is an inseparable union of souls, by which husband and wife are pledged irrevocably to maintain faith toward one another,"[18] and elsewhere insists that "in marriage there is not just a corporal, but also a spiritual union."[19]

Aquinas makes it clear that, in his conception, woman's role as man's helper does not place her on an inferior level for she remains his equal partner: "As regards the second end, which is the running of the family and their mutual sharing together, the wife is joined to the husband as a partner."[20] He insists that marriage is not just for the sake of procreation, but has other, more personalist, ends: "Marriage exists among men, not only for the begetting and nurturing of offspring, but also for the partnership of common life through mutual sharing." Hence he considers the question whether this *operum communicatio* or mutual sharing between husband and wife should not be described as a *bonum matrimonii* on a par with the *bonum prolis*: "Therefore, as offspring [are] considered a good of matrimony, so [it seems] should mutual sharing."[21] He answers the question in the negative.

It is important neither to overlook nor to overvalue these texts. They offer a basis on which a deeper understanding of the "mutual help" could have been developed (although, in fact, it was not). It is not my intention to contest that the dominant understanding of marriage held through the centuries tended towards

---

16. Aquinas, *Summa contra Gentiles* III, c. 123.
17. Aquinas, *Suppl.*, q. 49, a. 1.
18. Aquinas, *Summa Theologiae* III, q. 29, a. 2.
19. Aquinas, *Suppl.*, q. 56, a. 1, ad 3.   20. Ibid., q. 65, a. 5.
21. Ibid., q. 49, a. 2.

a procreative interpretation, but simply to suggest that certain notes of married personalism are also to be found in the writings of major ecclesial thinkers of the past, and therefore that modern personalism can rightfully claim to have a tradition behind it of which it is indeed a development.[22]

Nevertheless I think we must acknowledge that St. Thomas's (and in general his successors') concept of the *mutuum adiutorium* moves on a basically natural and earthbound level, with little or no suggestion that the mutual help has a supernatural purpose as its ultimate goal. Thomas, along with others before him (including Augustine), and especially along with those who follow them down to the present day, seems to interpret the divine purpose in giving a helpmate to man or woman as simply that of assisting them in the hopes and vicissitudes *of earthly life alone*. It can well be contended that this view is inadequate. Such an earthbound consideration can only stem from a general and prolonged tendency to consider marriage almost exclusively as an *officium* in the sense of a social mission as well as a failure to see it also as a divine calling to growth in personal and Christian perfection.[23]

What is the relationship between the *mutuum adiutorium* and the *bonum coniugum*? One interpretation would be to identify them, or at least to suggest that the *mutuum adiutorium* should now be considered as absorbed into the *bonum coniugum*. This might be so, but if we once more look attentively at the second book of Genesis, I think we can formulate a deeper and more harmonious analysis.[24] As we have seen, however innovative the term *bonum coniugum* may appear to be, its Scriptural credentials are

22. Hugo of St. Victor is of course noted for ideas that may be considered personalist.

23. See Nicolas, "Remarques," 779.

24. Notably, GS does not anywhere refer to *mutuum adiutorium* as an end, simply stating that spouses "render each other mutual help [mutuum sibi adiutorium . . . praestant]" (no. 48).

as valid as those of *mutuum adiutorium*, being drawn from the very same passage in Genesis. It was precisely because it was not good for man or woman to be alone that a helpmate was given to them: *Non est bonum esse hominem solum; faciamus ei adiutorium.* The helpmate, therefore, was given for the sake of their *good*: their "*bonum*." God wished the woman, as wife, to be a help towards the good of the man, her husband; and the man, as husband, to be a help towards the good of the woman, his wife. The *mutuum adiutorium* appears clearly as ordered to the *bonum coniugum*. If theological tradition was hitherto content to stop at the *adiutorium* aspect of Genesis 2:18 with little analysis of what this "help" should consist in and, more importantly, no analysis of what it is aimed at, we are now in a new situation where the emphasis is transferred from the means (the "mutual help") God chose, to the end he intended (the "good" of man and woman).

It is not good to be alone. It is good to have a helpmate. Good for what? The purpose of the helper is to aid in achieving the good that God has in mind. What is that good? What does God have in mind when he bestows the good of life and other goods upon man? Merely human consolation and earthly happiness? No; that is not sufficient, it does not last. The true good for which we are made, the good that is our destiny, is God himself. The limited and passing goods God gives us here on earth are designed to fit us for the enjoyment of that good. The conjugal *adiutorium*, then, is the *means* to the *bonum*, which is the *end*. This, I suggest, provides the key to the ultimate analysis of the *bonum coniugum*.

Nature and Purpose of the *bonum coniugum*

The "help" that the spouses are meant to provide for one another is directed to the integral perfecting of each as a person called to eternal life; in this consists the genuine *bonum coniugum*. Strong magisterial support can be found for this view. The official volume annotating the "sources" of the new Code[25] gives *Casti Connubii* as a main source of canon 1055. In that important encyclical we find words which to my mind describe the essence of the *bonum coniugum*. Pope Pius XI there insists that married love "demands not only mutual aid [*mutuum auxilium*] but must go further; it must have as its primary purpose that man and wife help each other day by day in forming and perfecting themselves in the interior life, so that through their partnership in life they may advance ever more and more in virtue, and above all that they may grow in true love towards God and their neighbor."[26] Pius seems to say here that interpretations, however traditional, which make the *mutuum adiutorium* consist in mere physical or psychological support for earthly affairs are insufficient. It is for their ultimate *bonum*—growth in virtue and sanctity—that the spouses are meant to help each other.

Confirmation of this can, I think, be drawn from other indicated sources of c. 1055, including the 1951 address of Pius XII, where the Pope spoke of the "personal perfecting of the spouses" as a secondary end of marriage.[27] *Gaudium et Spes* (no. 48) is also indicated, as well as nos. 11 and 41 of *Lumen Gentium* and no. 11 of *Apostolicam Actuositatem* (the Decree on the Apostolate of Lay People). *Gaudium et Spes* speaks in terms of the human and supernatural growth of the spouses: "Husband and wife . . . help and serve each other by their married partnership; they become conscious of their unity and experience it more deeply from day to day. . . . Fulfilling their conjugal and family role . . . they increasingly further their own perfection and their mutual sanctification." The supernatural aspect of this is particularly drawn out in the per-

25. *Codex Iuris Canonici, fontium annotatione auctus* (Rome: Libreria Editrice Vaticana, 1989).
26. AAS 22 (1930): 548.
27. AAS 43 (1951): 848–49.

tinent paragraphs of *Lumen Gentium*, especially in no. 11: "Christian spouses help one another to attain holiness in their married life and in the accepting and rearing of their children." Similarly *Apostolicam Actuositatem* insists: "Christian spouses are for each other . . . cooperators of grace and witnesses of the faith."[28]

That marriage is essentially directed to the sanctification of the spouses is a conclusion that would seem to flow necessarily from the fact of its sacramentality. In this sense the personalism of *Casti Connubii* was simply developing the teaching of the Council of Trent, namely, that grace in marriage is directed to "perfecting love and sanctifying the spouses."[29] In other words, the sacramental grace of marriage leads spouses to sanctity by perfecting (in the truest sense) their conjugal love.[30] It is interesting here to recall a passage from St. Augustine. He writes that God, after creating man, "made the woman to be a helpmate for the man . . . that the man might at once have glory from the woman in so far as he went before her to God, and present in himself an example to her for imitation in holiness and piety."[31] Thus considered, the mutual help consists especially in being an inspiration for advancing toward God "in holiness and piety." This insight is not explicitly extended to the *reciprocal* aspect of the male-female relationship divinely instituted. But we do so extend it, affirming that as man is to woman, so is woman to man: a help and an inspiration in the joint effort to advance toward God in that fundamental *bonum* (that ultimate "self-realization") which is represented by personal holiness.

28. AA, no. 11.

29. "Amorem perficere . . . coniugesque sanctificare" (Denz., 969). See also Bellarmine, who states that matrimony "is a union that consecrates and sanctifies souls [*unio sacrans, et sanctificans animas*]" (*De Sacramento*, cap. 5).

30. "The sacramental grace of Christian marriage . . . by which the natural love between the spouses is brought to its perfection for the sanctification of husband and wife" (Paul Anciaux, *Le Sacrement du Mariage* [Louvain: Nauwelaerts, 1961], 249).

31. *De catechizandis rudibus*, c. 18, n. 29 (PL 40:332).

The Conjugal Commitment: The Scope and Consequences of Spousal Self-Giving

Marriage is a form of sexual commitment to which a man and a woman in love are normally drawn as a means of fulfilling their desire for union and life-communion. Lovers who love with a conjugal love would like to give themselves totally to each other, to be fused into one. Of course, such a total union cannot be literally achieved. All that lovers can do (and it is very much) is to establish between themselves a relationship so close and unique that it places each in the privileged position of spouse and so singles him or her out from all others. Marriage is a covenant where a man and a woman have consented to make each other the object of a personalized relationship (the most unique relationship possible between two human persons), exclusive of all others in respect of its distinctive mutual rights/obligations, meant to last for life, and open to sexual union and to the most personalized fruit—the child—of sexual intercourse, which itself is the most distinctive bodily expression of the conjugal love-union between the spouses.

Here we have the major personalist connotations of the conjugal self-gift of c. 1057. Any analysis of this marital self-gift naturally centers in the first place on these three unique expressions of the conjugal commitment between a man and a woman: that the choice be exclusive of others, at least in a similar relationship; that it be permanent (a gift for a time is a loan, not a gift); and that it be open to the life-giving power of sexuality (a couple can express the uniqueness of their relationship in no more striking a way than having a child together).

Each human person, in the awareness of his or her contingency, wishes to be loved, to be in some way unique for someone. Each one, if he or she does not find anyone to love him or her, is haunted by the temptation to feel worthless. Further, it is not enough to be loved; it is necessary to love. A person who is loved can be unhappy if he or she is unable to love. Everyone is loved (at least by God), but not everyone learns to love. To learn to love is as great a human need as to know oneself loved; only thus can a person be saved from self-pity or self-isolation (or both). To learn to love demands coming out of self through firm dedication, in good times and bad, to another and to others. What a person has to learn is not passing love, but committed love. We all stand in need of a commitment to love. Such is the priesthood, or a life dedicated directly to God; and such is marriage, the dedication to which God calls the majority. To bind people to the process of learning to love was God's original design for marriage, confirmed by the Lord (Mt 19:8). The married commitment is by nature something demanding. This is brought out by the words with which the spouses express their mutual acceptance of one another: "For better or for worse, for richer or for poorer, in sickness and in health . . . all the days of my life."

Giving as One Is: Defects and All

A point needs to be made here which might seem trivial but is extremely important in practice. Self-giving in matrimonial consent means giving oneself as one is. Hence it always means giving a *defective* self. Similarly, it means accepting the other party as he or she is, also with his or her defects. Since we all have defects, marriage is always a union of two defective persons. And a large part of the *bonum*, the good effect, of marriage comes from the effort involved in the giving and accepting of imperfect selfhood. Marriage is—is meant to be—a state in which two persons who are imperfectly lovable learn to love each other with their imperfections. No other realistic way of learning to love is possible. This is the demanding reciprocity of marriage. The gift of a defective self has its noble marital complement and correspondence in the acceptance of a defective other. Human love, made faithful with God's help, can turn the meeting and union of two imperfect selves to a great good for both.

Thus one can and should find a natural and vital connection between the two ideas: "good of the spouses" and marital "giving/ accepting." Marital consent means not just to "give" oneself, but also to accept one's partner with his or her limitations. This is not easy, least of all for a lifetime. But if tackled with the help of grace, it can be achieved. Such a mutual and demanding commitment powerfully matures the spouses, from which develops the good implied in the *bonum coniugum*.

Superficial Analyses

There are some interpretations of married personalism and concretely of the *bonum coniugum* which, while at times using personalist language, tend to be fundamentally individualist in character.[32] Yet married personalism goes far beyond a simple acknowledgment of "the dignity of conjugal love," as some would express it. This sort of analysis tends to remain at the surface of the matter, especially if it dwells on the "rights" or expectations of love and not, at least in equal measure, on its "duties" and demands. Such superficial marital personalism was common in the 1970s and 1980s, and still inspires some writers. One result, for instance, is to take the *bonum coniugum* as consisting in the psychic, affective, physical, or sexual "integration" of the spouses. The suggested criterion seems inadequate from a Christian standpoint, not only because it fails to look at the spouses' "good" supernaturally but also because it tends to resolve the *bonum coniugum* into a question of natural "compatibility." One can then be easily led into holding that seeming incompatibility is an enemy of the "good of the

32. See my "Progressive Jurisprudential Thinking," 472–75.

spouses," whereas pastoral experience shows that many highly "integrated" marriages are of couples whose characters are extremely diverse and even apparently opposed, and who could well have ended up "incompatible" unless they had resolved (in an evidently maturing effort) to avoid this result.[33]

Similarly, to take the *bonum coniugum* simply in the sense of the "well-being"[34] of the spouses or their "mutual welfare," or to make it consist in the achieving of a comfortable or untroubled life, is scarcely in harmony with a Christian understanding of the real good of the human person. The Christian sense of life suggests that "the bad times" as well as "the good" are meant to serve the achievement of the ultimate divine purpose of marriage. Such views are inadequate because in the last analysis they reduce the notion of married personalism to the promise that marriage should turn out to be an easy, harmonious love affair. This is pure romance; it is not realism, and it is certainly not personalism.

The character of Aunt Betsey in Dickens's *David Copperfield* is a bossy but wise woman. When David began to experience the difficulties that came from having married Dora, a very immature and childish girl (only a "child-wife," as Dora herself pleaded to David), Aunt Betsey declined to intervene so as to try to correct or even train Dora, and she told David:

You have chosen freely for yourself, and you have chosen a very pretty and a very affectionate creature. It will be your duty, and it will be your pleasure too, to estimate her (as you chose her) by the qualities she has, and not by the qualities she may not have. The latter you must develop

---

33. See "Sentence *coram* Burke," *Rotae Romanae Decisiones* 90 (March 26, 1998): 259.

34. This is the translation which the Canon Law Society of Great Britain and Ireland gives to "*bonum*" in the *bonum coniugum* of c. 1055. The word is too important to be so loosely translated. The latest English translation, prepared under the auspices of the Canon Law Society of America, properly renders it as "the *good* of the spouses" (Rome: Libreria Editrice Vaticana, 2003).

in her, if you can. And if you cannot, you must just accustom yourself to do without them. . . . This is marriage.[35]

To accustom oneself to the fact that one's spouse is not exactly as one would like is a very basic condition of married love, and perhaps has good claim to be considered an essential obligation of marriage.

A happy married life together is no doubt the aim or hope of almost all who marry. Yet to identify the *bonum coniugum* as a divinely given end of marriage with "shared happiness" is anything but adequate. If one is to make any sense of what seems to be the practical working of God's providence, the achievement of the "good of the spouses" also involves many things that, to human eyes at least, cannot be termed "happy": ill health in spouse or children, loss of employment, financial hardships, etc. "Shared hardships" can contribute enormously to the "good," the growth as a person, of each of the spouses. Even what might be considered unilateral hardships such as the burden of a disabled husband falling totally on the wife, or the more extreme case of infidelity of one partner, where the other remains faithful to the bond, can serve the deeper good of at least one of the parties in a way that perhaps would not have been brought about by some easier lot.

End, Not Essential Element: An Important Distinction

Any analysis of the *bonum coniugum* needs to set out from this evident fact: that it is an end of marriage. This paves the way for a further clarification. If it is an end, it cannot be an essential property or element of marriage. While this too should appear as logically evident, I realize it may cause some initial surprise. Therefore we could take a moment to recall some elementary notions regarding essence ("essential" means what necessarily pertains to the essence), properties, and ends.

35. Charles Dickens, *David Copperfield* (New York: Penguin, 2004), ch. 44.

The essence of any reality is its irreduceable nucleus (stripped of all accidental aspects) without which the reality cannot be. What is essential to any thing must be present, at least in its constitutional moment; otherwise the thing cannot itself come into existence. This helps us to see the relationship between essence and end. As one of the best-known modern canonical theorists writes in relation to marriage:

> The essence is something different from the end, and so they may never be confused, nor can one fall into the error of understanding the end as essential, in the sense of being part of the essence. It is necessary therefore to carefully avoid any confusion between the essence of marriage and its ends; this is an elementary precaution which some authors have nevertheless not always kept in mind. By dint of speaking without due precision of essential ends (the expression is correct if one means by it that the ordination to them is essential, but absolutely inappropriate if it is used to suggest that the end is constituent of the essence), it is not infrequent that, at least in certain contexts, one falls into confusion between end and essence, with all the inaccuracies and errors that this leads to.[36]

The essential properties or elements of a being qualify its essence in a fundamental or constitutional way. If an essential element is missing, the being itself cannot come into existence. An essential quality or property of friendship is the readiness to help each other mutually. Friendship is naturally ordered to mutual help, and actual help given is one of its natural consequences or ends. Even if two friends are separated and totally lose touch, their friendship remains intact for as long as their mutual disposition continues, even though actual mutual help is no longer possible. If the readiness to help is missing on one or other side, then (whatever the appearances) there is no true friendship.

---

36. J. Hervada, *Vetera et Nova* (Pamplona, 1991), 1.357.

It follows that while each reality is ordered to an end, it does not depend for its existence on the end. Therefore, the end is said to be extrinsic to the essence, while the essential properties are intrinsic. At the same time, the very fact that a reality is ordered to its ends means that although the ends as such do not enter the essence, the essence cannot be without an "ordination to" its ends. This is why an end cannot be an essential property or essential element. Each being or reality must have its essential properties within it. Without its essential elements or properties it cannot exist. Each reality also has an essential ordering to an end. The properties necessarily enter the essence; so too does the ordination to the end. However, it bears repeating that the actual end itself remains extrinsic to the essence, for the end may fail ever to be achieved without the essence failing in its existence.

The "*bonum coniugum*" and the Augustinian "*bona*"

Technical as the point may be, it is nevertheless an elementary error (and inexcusable if one wants to write seriously on this subject) to treat the "good of the spouses" as if it were in the line of the traditional three *bona* of marriage formulated by St. Augustine. In 1985, Francesco Bersini, one of the first authoritative Italian canonists to comment the matrimonial norms of the new Code, unhesitatingly affirmed that the *bonum coniugum* "has nothing to do" with the three Augustinian *bona*.[37] Urbano Navarrete similarly insists on the radical difference between the *bonum coniugum* and the Augustinian *bona*: "The term 'bonum' of c. 1055 has a completely generic sense and in no way the specific meaning which the word has in the Augustinian trilogy."[38]

It is to remain on the surface of the matter to let a linguistic

37. F. Bersini, *Il Nuovo Diritto Canonico Matrimoniale* (3rd ed.) (Turin, 1985), 10.
38. U. Navarrete, "I beni del matrimonio: elementi e proprietà essenziale," in *La nuova legislazione matrimoniale canonica* (Rome, 1986), 97.

similarity confuse fundamental differences of category and meaning. In the Augustinian view, as we shall consider in greater detail in chapter 6, the three *bona* refer to "goods" or values of the married state: they are positive features of matrimony that show its worth and dignity. Marriage is good because it is characterized by faithfulness, permanence, and fruitfulness. Each *bonum* is predicated of or attributed to marriage. The readiness to have children is a *bonum matrimonii*, and so is exclusiveness or permanence. It is evident that Augustine is speaking of the values or essential properties of marriage, not of its ends or finalities.

It helps to present this analysis schematically. The three *bona* or attributes of matrimony are as follows: *bonum fidei,* exclusive fidelity, is a *bonum* or attribute of matrimony; *bonum prolis,* procreativity or openness to having children, is a *bonum* or attribute of matrimony; and *bonum sacramenti,* indissolubility, is a *bonum* or attribute of matrimony.

As is immediately evident, we cannot proceed to add the *bonum coniugum* to this list. It would make no sense to say that the *coniuges*—the spouses—are a *bonum* or a value of matrimony. The term *bonum coniugum* does not express a value, property, or attribute of marriage in any sense parallel to that of the Augustinian "goods." The *bonum* of this new term is referred not to marriage (as if it were a value that makes marriage good), but to the spouses (as involving something that is good for them). It denotes not a property of marriage (a *bonum matrimonii*), but something—the "good" or growth as persons of the spouses—which should result from marriage. The Augustinian *bona* are fundamental qualities or properties that describe and identify aspects of the essence of marriage, while the *bonum coniugum* is an end of marriage, an effect that marriage should produce on the persons of the spouses themselves. It is predicated not of marriage (a "*bonum coniugii*"), but of the spouses (a "*bonum coniugum*"), as something that marriage ought to cause or lead to. Careless thinking creates confusion here, rendering adequate analysis of the meaning and force of the new term unnecessarily difficult and even impossible.

None of this means that there is not an interrelation between the Augustinian *bona* and the *bonum coniugum*. On the contrary, it is only logical that the different aspects of marriage—properties, elements, ends—should stand in close connection. I consider the *bonum coniugum*, as an institutional end of marriage, to be intimately linked to the three Augustinian *bona*. They are clearly different—end as distinct from properties—yet are closely interrelated. I do not think any adequate analysis of the *bonum coniugum* can be made which does not see it as an end of marriage achieved in the first place through the force and effect of the three *bona*.

Though the point will recur later on, we should here note the modern tendency to see the Augustinian *bona* not in their natural attractiveness as values or "benefits" of the married state, but simply in the aspect of the obligation which accompanies each. This betrays a grave lack of human perspective, an anthropological defect. This negative viewpoint applies particularly to the *bonum prolis* (offspring) and the *bonum sacramenti* (indissolubility). It is true that the wholehearted acceptance of these "goods" takes a sustained effort; but it also true that this effort is a source of happiness and also has a deep maturing effect on the persons who face up to it and hence contributes to their spousal good.

Children and the Good of the Spouses

Spousal self-giving has its most unique physical expression in the union of the genital-procreative organs. Many people today do not understand (and rather rebel against) this "accident" of nature which so intimately connects conjugal union with procreation. In chapter 7 we will consider why the procreative aspect of the conjugal act is inseparable from its personalist-unitive aspect. For now, our purpose is to show how having and rearing children is an intrinsic part of the purpose of marriage and serves to mature the spouses and make them better persons; in other words, to show the interdependence (already mentioned at the end of chapter 3) and the necessary connection between procreation and the good of the spouses.

Earlier we presented the mutual "self-giving" of the spouses expressed in their marital consent (c. 1057) as the key to a true understanding of the *bonum coniugum*. Now we should note that the later magisterium, while repeating this personalist formulation of marital consent, broadens its scope and purpose. The 1983 Code simply states: "Matrimonial consent is an act of will by which a man and a woman by an irrevocable covenant mutually give and accept one another for the purpose of establishing a marriage." The *Catechism* says much the same (in a slightly less juridical form), but specifies further the purpose of this self-giving, and amplifies it. The purpose is not just to give each to the other faithfully, but also to give together fruitfully: "Marriage is based on the consent of the contracting parties, that is, on their will to give themselves, each to the other, mutually and definitively, in order to live a covenant of faithful and fruitful love" (no. 1662). The *Compendium* of the *Catechism* states the same: "Matrimonial consent is given when a man and a woman manifest the will to give themselves to each other irrevocably in order to live a covenant of faithful and fruitful love" (no. 344).[39] The self-giving is now said to be one not only of mutual, definitive, and faithful love, but also to be one of "fruitful love." This simply underlines the teaching of the Second Vatican Council: "Children are the supreme gift of marriage and contribute to the greatest extent to the good of the parents themselves."[40]

In light of this, the point made earlier about marriage being a

39. *Compendium* of the CCC.
40. GS, no. 50.

"safeguard against the trap of self-sufficiency" needs to be refined. Peculiarly, two selves can want to be sufficient to and with each other. They can plan their union around themselves alone, reluctant to open that union to others. Then they remain caught in a trap of *égoisme à deux*, of shared and calculating selfishness. It is their openness to a family, to the children that their union—if the love inspiring it is genuine—will normally give rise to, that saves them from this trap. Our modern world has forgotten that love does not want just satisfaction and comfort, but also growth and challenge. Two persons in love want to do things together: to design or make or buy or furnish together something that will be peculiarly *theirs*, because it is the fruit of their united decision and action. Nothing is more proper to a couple than their child. The sculptor hews his vision of beauty into lasting stone. Only parents can create *living* works of art, with each child a unique monument to the creative love that inspires and unites them.

A society, through the monuments it builds, evokes the memory of the great things of its past in order to keep its values alive in the present and for the future. Spousal love needs such monuments. When romance is fading, when perhaps it has died and the spouses are tempted to think that love between them has died with it, then each child remains as a living testimony to the depth and uniqueness and totality of the conjugal gift of self which they made to each other in the past—when it was easy—and as an urgent call to keep giving now, even when it is difficult.

Children strengthen the goodness of the bond of marriage, so that it does not give way under the strains that follow from the inevitable waning or disappearance of effortless romantic love. The bond of marriage, which God wants no one to break, is then constituted not simply by the variables of personal love and sentiment between husband and wife, but more and more by their children, each child being one further strand giving strength to that bond. It is through devotion, effort and sacrifice, especially when made for the sake of others, that people grow and mature most; only in this way can each come out of himself or herself and rise above solitary selfhood. We remarked above that man and woman are "especially made for conjugal dependence"; we could add that they are by the same token made for familial dependence and dedication. No one can achieve fulfillment and goodness—his or her authentic *bonum*—without a dedicated reaching out to others.

The "good of the spouses," we insist, is the good of learning to love, of preparing for heaven, of seeking holiness. Holiness consists in loving God's will, and God's particular will for those called to marriage is that, in him, they love each other and love the children he blesses them with. This ultimate content of the *bonum coniugum* is summed up in a passage from *Lumen Gentium* (no. 11): "Christian spouses help one another to attain holiness in their married life and in the accepting and rearing of their children."

The Maturing "Good" of Living Up to One's Word

Having devoted some lines to showing how a couple's children, generously accepted and cared for, tend powerfully to make better and more mature persons of the parents, let us now offer a parallel, though brief, consideration of the related effect of the unbreakable nature of the bond uniting the spouses. Loyalty to the commitment of married life contributes more than anything else to the true good of the spouses, a fact that is powerfully brought out when one reflects that this freely accepted commitment also becomes a duty owed in justice. In his 1987 address to the Roman Rota, Pope John Paul II described this duty as involving "a conscious effort on the part of the spouses to overcome, even at the cost of sacrifices and renunciations, the obstacles that hinder the success of their marriage."[41] In *Familiaris Consortio*, he speaks

41. AAS 79 (1987): 1456.

of indissolubility in an emphatically positive way, presenting it as something *joyful* that Christians should announce to the world: "It is necessary," he says, "to reconfirm the *good news* of the definitive nature of conjugal love."[42] If this comes as a surprising statement to many people today, it is a sign of how far contemporary society is from understanding the divine plan for man's authentic good. One of the special missions facing Christians in the work of reevangelizing the modern world is to spread the news that the bonds of married and family love are too sacred and too important—also for human happiness—to be broken. This is clear when one considers the "good of the children." What child prefers his or her parents to separate, even if they do not enjoy each other's company? What children want is that the parents *learn* to carry on with the shared task of marriage. It is a matter of justice that the parents so learn, and in the end it leads to their own personal maturity and fulfillment.

Extreme Cases

Undeniably there are many marital situations where a purely human judgment can conclude that the "good of the spouses" has not been or cannot be achieved: the cases, for instance, where one of the spouses, reneging on his or her conjugal commitment, walks out on the other. Does it make any sense to talk of the *bonum coniugum* as applying to such situations? As regards the reneging spouse, certainly the marriage would scarcely seem capable of working any longer toward his or her "good." Yet it can still work powerfully for the good of the other if he or she remains true to the marriage bond. If that fidelity is maintained, moreover, it may in God's providence act as a call to repentance and as a force of salvation for the unfaithful spouse, perhaps in his or her very last moment on earth—when one's definitive *bonum* is about to be de-

42. FC, no. 20 (AAS 74 [1982]: 103).

cided. That the positive potential of such situations can be grasped only in the light of the Christian challenge of the cross does not in any way weaken the analysis. If it is true that the positive potential may never be actually realized, that simply reflects the risk and mystery of human freedom. As the *Catechism* states (no. 1615):

Jesus has not weighed down the spouses with a burden that is impossible to bear, heavier than that of the Law of Moses. Having come to reestablish the initial order of creation upset by sin, he himself gives the strength and grace to live marriage in the new dimension of the Kingdom of God. Following Christ, denying themselves, taking upon themselves their own cross, the spouses can "understand" the original sense of matrimony and live it with the help of Christ. This grace of Christian Matrimony is a fruit of the Cross of Christ, the source of all Christian life.

Some Canonical Observations

If we interpret the *bonum coniugum* to mean something along the lines of a life together in which each spouse feels himself or herself "realized" or "fulfilled," or if we take the notion of marital consent presented in c. 1057 not in a personalist sense ("I give myself, I accept you") but in a contractualist *quid pro quo* sense ("I give as much as you give, not a whit more; I will put up with as much from you as I calculate you are accepting or putting up with from me"), then indeed one can construct arguments that in a concrete case the personalist purpose of marriage was not fulfilled. In this case, something was missing from the start, and therefore the couple can enter a plea for a declaration of nullity due to failure to minimally understand what marriage is about, or to incapacity to assume its essential obligations, or to the exclusion of the *bonum coniugum*, or to deceit, etc. I do not say that there may never be a nullity underlying such a situation; but I do hold that the attitudes as I have described them (somewhat caricatured, no doubt), and perhaps the juridic grounds invoked to justify the plea, have everything to do with individualism and nothing to do with personalism.

As we have seen above, true married commitment—for better or for worse, till death do us part—is always the pledge of two defective people trying to love each other as they are, flaws and all, and to stick to the task of marriage. And that, we repeat, contributes powerfully to their maturing, their growth and fulfillment as persons, and their genuine personalist good—their *bonum*. Thus defects give little grounds to suppose incapacity, though their growth may indeed imply poor effort or even bad will. One's response to the defects of one's partner may also be defective, or it can be generous, helped by the experience of how hard it is to battle against one's own defects.

Exclusion of (and Capacity for) the *bonum coniugum*

Valid consent requires the acceptance of marriage in its essence; that is, as the union of a woman and a man characterized by the properties of exclusive fidelity, openness to having children, and indissolubility of the bond. If a contracting party excludes one of these essential properties or elements at the moment of consent, then the marriage is null (c. 1101). Cases of unilateral or even bilateral exclusion do occur; one (or both) of the contracting parties positively excludes, say, offspring or indissolubility from their union, and the consent is consequently invalid. Such cases, however unwise and unfortunate, probably occur with greater frequency today in our consumerist and calculating society.

If we turn from the exclusion of the properties to that of the ends of marriage, the new formulation of the ends as enunciated in c. 1055 has given rise to some debate (perhaps not all of it necessary). The debate has not concerned the possible exclusion of procreation, since what is involved in such exclusion is clear in canonical jurisprudence.[43] But with regard to the hypothetical exclusion of the *bonum coniugum*, the matter is different. Certainly, if this end—the ordering of marriage to the "good of the spouses"—is positively excluded at the moment of consent, then consent is invalid. What is not at all clear however is how such an exclusion could take place. In fact the case in which the hypothesis might occur at consent is hard even to imagine. That one or other, or both, should want to exclude offspring is conceivable, however lamentable. That one or other, or both, should want to exclude their own good (or the good of the other), however they understand this good, is almost impossible to envision. It seems as far-fetched as the "Jemolo case" which canonists given to fantasy debated under the pre-1983 codicial regime (a man marries a woman, consenting to all the properties of marriage, but with the deliberate purpose of making her suffer). The introduction into the 1983 Code of c. 1098, on *dolus* (the invalidating effect of *deceit* deliberately used to obtain consent) renders the old debate moot and suffices to cover these unlikely cases if they were ever to occur.

Incapacity

Valid consent requires certain dispositions toward or acceptance of the ends of marriage. If these are positively excluded, consent itself is invalid. Here however one must not confuse a positive exclusion of the ends with an incapacity to achieve them. While church law has always required an openness to the ends of marriage, it has never made a capacity to achieve the ends essential to a valid marriage, and so an incapacity to achieve an end is neither an

---

43. Besides, the exclusion of the end (the ordering to procreation) coincides for all practical purposes with the exclusion of the property (openness to having children). For the difference between *bonum prolis* (procreativity) as a "good" (i.e., as an essential property of marriage) and actual procreation as an end, see Cormac Burke, "The *Bonum Coniugum* and the *Bonum Prolis*: Ends or Properties of Marriage?" *The Jurist* 49 (1989): 704–13.

impediment nor a ground for the invalidity of consent. This has always been clear in relation to the end of procreation. Canon 1084 states explicitly: "Sterility neither prohibits nor invalidates marriage." The same must logically apply to an incapacity to achieve the *bonum coniugum*, prescinding from the real difficulty, or perhaps impossibility, of determining what might constitute such an incapacity.

Among the new dispositions of matrimonial law contained in the 1983 Code, there is no doubt that c. 1095 has been the most used (and to some, the most abused) in tribunal work. The canon lays down that "those who suffer from a grave lack of discretionary judgment concerning the essential matrimonial rights and obligations to be mutually given and accepted" and "those who, because of causes of a psychological nature, are unable to assume the essential obligations of marriage" are incapable of contracting marriage.

The attempt to fit a hypothetical incapacity for the *bonum coniugum* within the terms of this canon will simply not work. As pointed out above, an incapacity for the end has no invalidating effect on consent. More to the point, the object of consensual incapacity under c. 1095 are the essential rights/obligations of matrimony. There is clearly no right to the *bonum coniugum* (just as, we repeat, there is none to the other end of procreation). While one can allow that there is a moral obligation on the each of the spouses to work towards their "good," canon law (excepting of course the cases of deliberate deceit or positive exclusion) has refused to give juridical status to this moral obligation.

One has the right to what must be given by the other, not to what marriage itself may or may not give. The gift of offspring depends not just on the spouses but ultimately on God. And the gift of the "good" of the spouses, however one chooses to understand it, depends indeed on God (who certainly wants it), but also on the free response of the spouses to God's grace as it comes to them through the peculiar plans of his providence. Sometimes God's plan for the good of the spouses involves a childless marriage, and it not infrequently seems to involve a union where personality differences create tensions between the spouses that can pull the marriage apart unless they have recourse to prayer and generous sacrifice so as to learn to get on together. Incapacity and lack of effort or of generosity are not to be confused. What then of a claim that one person was not consensually capable under c. 1095 because he or she was unable to assume the obligation of making the other person happy? I doubt that it could be juridically upheld. I am sure that such a claim does not accord with any true understanding of the married commitment.

5

Church Law and the Rights
of Persons

The theological studies and reflections that make up this book have been prompted in part by my research and experience as a canon lawyer and rotal judge. This experience deepened my awareness of the extent to which a lot of post-conciliar theological (and indeed canonical) writing has worked from the premise that the main obstacle to true pastoral renewal is found in the institutional-juridical structures and related mentality still prevalent in church life. This, as a principle, I cannot share. Institutions, even divine institutions, have their limitations when their governance is (as it must be) in the hands of men. And the same, *a fortiori*, is true of canon law and its administration. However, as the reader has no doubt already sensed, I do not go along with any broad presumption that the institutional aspects of the church or its juridical structures are an impediment to pastoral renewal or a reinvigorated pastoral life. I particularly regard the 1983 Code of Canon Law, with its stress on ecclesial rights and duties in general, and with its presentation of matrimonial law in particular, as a major instrument for renewal; and I believe that its proper understanding and proper application are essential for this renewal.

Hence, I think it opportune here to analyze briefly the "law *versus* pastorate" or "institution *versus* renewal" mindset that is still common in many circles. This excursus will be philosophical-juridical rather than theological, centering on the nature and function of law precisely in the context of Christian personalism, and also on how church institutions are at the service of individual Christians in their call to come to Christ, as well as (in our specific context) how this is particularly true of the indissolubility which God, in instituting matrimony, gave to it as an essential property.

The Pastoral Function of Law

The renewal envisaged by the Second Vatican Council was to be pastoral; in other words, it was to be a renewal of the church's role in caring for souls as it carries on the work of Christ, the eternal pastor.[1] A pastorally renewed church, according to the mind of the Council, should therefore be a church where souls are cared for and where the care they receive is given according to the fullness of Christ's design. Though the Council speaks rather rarely of charisms or that which is charismatic (eleven times in all), "charismatic" became the watchword or test of numerous post-conciliar attempts at renewal. One major result was to regard the institutional and juridical aspects of church life as inimical to the charismatic spirit considered necessary to pastoral renewal. Charism implied freedom whereas institution and law implied restriction. For many, the traditional inflexibility of the law came to be considered an anti-pastoral force. Instead of caring for people, the thesis went, it harms them. It seeks to keep Christian life in set molds, thus stifling initiative, spontaneity, experimentation, and the use of personal charisms.

In this way, a "law-versus-pastorate" mentality came to characterize many post-conciliar approaches. For some, it seemed axiom-

---

1. See *Christus Dominus*, no. 1 [hereafter "CD"].

atic that whoever thinks in juridical categories is no longer think-ing pastorally. For them, "pastoral" and "juridical" became opposed and even incompatible terms. It follows within this logic that inso-far as the Second Vatican Council emphasized the pastoral aspects of the church's life, it initiated—and its spirit countenances—a de-emphasis on law and on all the canonical aspects of ecclesial life. All of this suggests several questions. Which, if any, justifica-tion does the approach just outlined have in conciliar thinking? What is the relationship between law and pastoral care? Must we see opposition or can we find harmony between them? If we are to answer these questions properly, I think we have to highlight and to harmonize two important features of Vatican II: the personalist note that characterized its thinking, and the new understanding of law and authority that it offered.

Vatican II was Personalist

We have already noted the personalism of Vatican II. Here we need to carry our considerations somewhat further. The Council is of course personalist, in a primary sense, in that it is centered on the person of Jesus Christ. But it is also personalist in the very im-portant sense that it stresses the dignity and inviolability of each human person. Now, in stating that Vatican II is personalist in this latter sense, we need to keep some points clear.

First, personalist is not the same as individualist. Vatican II is not individualist; in other words, it does not accentuate the indi-vidual above the community. It is community centered and accen-tuates the community and the person simultaneously. *Communio* is its main theme and is the main basis that it proposes for a renewed church.[2] To be gathered together as sons and daughters, brothers and sisters, within the great family communion of the blessed Trin-ity, of God's own life, is the vision and inspiration it offers.

2. LG, no. 1.

Second, Vatican II is therefore both personalist and community-centered. There is no contradiction. Personalism stresses the dignity and rights of each person seen in his value as God's creation and in his calling to divine sonship in Jesus Christ. However, in stressing rights, personalism also stresses duties (any genuine philosophy of rights is also a philosophy of duties). It stresses duties towards other persons—towards the community—and sees the fulfillment of these duties as a means of personal growth and self-fulfillment in the fulfillment of the community. Individualism, in contrast, stresses the interests and advantage of the individual regarded as an end in himself, unrelated to any community. The individualist may at times pay lip service to duties but has no real concern for them. Self-interest is his rule. Where individual interests and common interests seem to clash, the individualist will always put what he considers his own interests first. One can be personalist and community centered. One cannot be individualist and community centered. The failure to keep this basic truth in mind has largely bedeviled renewal in the post-conciliar years.

Third, to be personalist is not to be anti-law. The individualist spirit can be (and generally is) anti-law. The personalist spirit cannot be anti-law, since a main function of law is precisely to defend the personal rights of each individual and to harmonize the relative rights of different persons, so that all can grow within the community. If one does not keep the difference clear between individualism and personalism, one may fail to perceive that the use of personalistic language (invoking freedom, rights, conscience, etc.) can at times be simply a cover for individualist anti-community attitudes.

Another feature of Vatican II that is of interest here is its understanding of authority and of law. There is no doubt that Vatican II called for a rethinking of the nature of law and authority in the church as well as a new approach regarding the way in which authority is exercised. Authoritarianism and arbitrariness clearly violate the spirit of the council, but to call for a new understanding of law is not to reject law. To call for new modes in the exercise of authority is not to say that there should be no authority or that authority should not be heeded.

The Second Vatican Council Never De-emphasized Law

Vatican II nowhere countenances a de-emphasis on law, and less still does it put an *"Ecclesia Spiritus"* of charismatic gifts and pastoral spontaneity above an *"Ecclesia iuris"* of laws and discipline. On the contrary, when Vatican II seeks to reduce the theologically pregnant (but broad and somewhat vague) theme of *communio* to a more concrete image, it chooses "people of God," a term which necessarily carries with it a juridical emphasis in a way that other traditional descriptions of the church, such as "body of Christ" or "bride of Christ," do not. It should be obvious that while an ecclesiology of the body of Christ can be developed without any special emphasis on the reality or necessity of law, an ecclesiology of the people of God cannot, since the very notion of a "people" necessarily stresses interpersonal relationships, rights and duties, and therefore questions of justice and law.

This point is surely elementary and offers an all-important key to renewal. Nevertheless, certain attempts at renewal over the past decades have not only totally ignored it, but have contradicted it and sought to generate a renewal movement based on an anti-law mentality. This must be stated emphatically: an individualist anti-law mentality cannot lead to renewal. It can only lead to the dissolution of community, to a lawless situation where rights are not respected, duties are not fulfilled, and the many—the people—are exploited by the few.[3]

3. I have tried to develop this point at greater length elsewhere; see *Authority and Freedom in the Church* (San Francisco: Ignatius Press, 1988), published in a revised version in 2009 as *The Lawless People of God?* (Nairobi, Kenya: Scepter Press, 2009).

Pastoral Concern and Juridical Function

I will now try to pinpoint the connection between pastoral concern as Vatican II understands it and juridical system and function. Communion with Christ, and with others in Christ: this is the great pastoral theme and aim of Vatican II. This pastoral concern evidently presupposes not only a possibility of communion, but a *right* to communion, a right of access to Christ. Here we see how quickly the pastoral and the juridical interlink, because once we speak of rights we are of course speaking in juridical terms. Rights, after all, need to be defined so that people know their own rights and the rights of others, in order that they know what is owed to each one and what each one owes to others. Rights also need to be defended so that each person is in fact given what is due to him. And this is where law and authority necessarily enter the picture, because without law and authority there can be no proper definition, and especially no proper defense, of rights.

This can be indicated by taking a deeper look at the content of the right to *communio*. The right to *communio* is the right to find the grace, truth, and will of Christ in and through his church, using the means that Christ himself has instituted and left us. Canon 213, one of the most basic canons in the 1983 Code, says tersely: "Christ's Faithful have the right to be assisted by their Pastors from the spiritual riches of the Church, especially by the Word of God and the Sacraments." Canon 762 further stresses one aspect of this, also put in terms of a right: "The People of God are first united through the word of the living God and are fully entitled"—they have the full right—"to seek this word from their priests."

There are some important points to be noted regarding these canons, which are taken word for word from the conciliar documents *Lumen Gentium* (no. 37) and *Presbyterorum Ordinis* (no. 4). In the first place, the canons, in underlining the rights of certain persons, necessarily underline the obligations of others (one person's right always implies another person's obligation). Secondly, while the terms "Christ's Faithful" and "people of God" in themselves include clerics as well as laity, nevertheless in these passages—which emphasize what the people are entitled to seek from their pastors—the Council is evidently speaking in particular of the rights of the laity.

Duties Come with Rights

In fact, renewal as presented by the Council depends largely on the laity's becoming aware of their ecclesial rights (and, of course, duties) and exercising them. This special stress on the rights of the laity is undoubtedly something new. It is also something with an immediate consequence, for it evidently puts special stress on the obligations of those who are called to be ministers to the people—that is, the clergy. That is why it is not a healthy sign for renewal when some clerics today who talk emphatically about ecclesial rights do not speak with equal emphasis about ecclesial duties; when they do not seem to be aware that, within the people of God, it is the laity who have more rights than duties and the clergy who have more duties than rights; and when they are vague about clerical duties, whereas the Council is specific (as is the Code), or when they are negative about them—about obedience or celibacy, for instance—whereas the Council is totally positive.[4]

After *communio*, another major theme of Vatican II is that of *diakonia*, of service, with particular reference to clerical service. To serve is the great task, privilege, and duty of clerics. A large part of church law is in fact aimed at safeguarding and enforcing the proper service offered by the clergy to the whole people of God. If we then ask what is the pastoral role or function of law, the answer

---

4. LG, nos. 24, 36, 41, and 42; *Presbyterorum Ordinis*, nos. 15 and 16 [hereafter "PO"]; and cc. 273, 277, and 284.

is clear: it is the defense of ecclesial and personal rights. Without law, these rights are not defined, clear, or safe. Without law, violations of rights go unchecked. Without law, abuses creep in, pastoral abuses included.

A further point should be mentioned here. Some contemporary pastoral theorists seem not only to accept the view that law is meant to defend persons, but to have also taken on themselves to vindicate this view in the face of those who, they allege, see the function of law as the defense not of persons but of institutions. It is scarcely an exaggeration to say that whole areas of canon law have become for them a battlefield between what they would call a conservative legalistic-canonical school, which defends institutions as against persons, and a progressive pastoral-canonical school (their school) which defends persons as against institutions.

Law, Persons, and Institutions

The presuppositions underlying this approach seem to raise two questions: (1) is it a function of law to defend institutions? And (2) if so, does the law, in defending institutions, show a lack of concern for persons and for their rights? The surprising thing about the first question is that it should be raised at all within a Catholic context. Surely it is elementary to Catholic ecclesiology that Christ did not set up a purely spiritual church but a church that, as *Lumen Gentium* (no. 8) puts it, is a "hierarchically ordered society" and a "spiritual community" at one and the same time. In this society there are realities that pertain to the constitutional essence of the church: the sacraments, the deposit of faith, the hierarchy, the magisterium, etc. These institutions were instituted by Christ himself; they are entitled to the defense of the law, and, insofar as the law defends them, it is defending the constitutional will of Christ for his church and his people.

If the suggestion that canon law has no mission to defend

church institutions is out of step with the ecclesiology of Vatican II, the suggestion that, in defending institutions, canon law shows a lack of concern for persons and their rights betrays a radical failure to understand the true personalism of the Council. Persons, in God's plan of redemption, need institutions and access to institutions for their personal growth in Christ. For instance, this growth would be severely limited without the proper use of the sacraments. It also enters into God's plan that persons, if their growth in Christ is to be complete, need the concrete demands that institutions at times make on them. Law, therefore, in defending institutions, is defending persons. It is defending institutions *for* persons so that, also through them, each member of the people of God can reach and be reached by the fullness both of Christ's personal grace and help, and of Christ's ambition and particular demands for him or her.

So, if we have to make choices in the whole matter, the choice is not between defending institutions *or* defending persons; it is between *defending persons* by defending the institutions designed for their help and enrichment or *failing to defend persons* by allowing them to be deprived of the full power and efficacy of Christ's institutionalized gifts to his church and, through his church, to his followers.

Law, Truth, Justice

A truly Christian and personalist analysis reveals the positive and essential function of law in the life and renewal of the church. Law, truth, and justice are pillars of every society that proposes to offer its members the incentives, channels, and guarantees necessary so that interpersonal life and relations develop in harmonious solidarity. Law is at the service of the truth and even more concretely of justice: of what, according to the most attainable measure of truth, regulates the relations between persons, whether physical or juridical. That is why Saint Thomas Aquinas says that "justice is at times called truth,"[5] because it implies acting according to right reason or truth. In 1942 Pope Pius XII told the Roman Rota that "the world has need of the truth which is justice, and of that justice which is truth."[6] And in a 1961 address, also to the Rota, Pope John XXIII referred to the ministry of the ecclesiastical judge as a "*ministerium veritatis*," a ministry or service of the truth.[7]

More than ever before, we need practitioners of the law who are in love with justice and truth, who are deeply conscious of the "*Splendor Veritatis*" and—a subject to which Pope John Paul II devoted his 1994 address to the Rota—of the "*Splendor Legis*" or the "*Splendor Iustitiae*," the splendor of law and of justice. Only such jurists can help the great body of the faithful to understand the service given by the law to the life and vigor of the people of God. Turning more specifically to the field of our present interest, one could add that only such jurists will be capable of comprehending and reflecting the deep attractiveness of the church's teaching on marriage, while also understanding the challenges it undoubtedly offers.

Our thesis so far, therefore, is that the institutions with which Christ endowed his church are defended in the church *not against* persons but *for* persons. Let us now consider how this principle applies to marriage, and very particularly to indissolubility which the church holds to be an essential property of marriage as instituted by God.

Indissolubility and the Rights of Persons

The opinion has not infrequently been voiced that the preconciliar church, in its defense of the institution of marriage—and

---

5. Aquinas, *Summa Theologiae* II–II, q. 58, a. 4, ad 1.
6. AAS 34: 342.
7. AAS 53: 819.

especially in its insistence that indissolubility is one of its essential properties—was unmindful of the personalistic aspects of marriage and particularly of each individual spouse's right to fulfillment and happiness. According to this opinion, Vatican II offered a new understanding of marriage, seeing it less as an institution and more as a person-to-person relationship, and so opened the way for a more flexible and more truly pastoral approach to marital situations and problems.

The main pastoral problem is of course posed by broken marriages, and—so we are told—the obstacle to the pastoral solution of these problems remains the institutionalized concept of indissolubility. An inflexible approach on indissolubility is seen to be not only pastorally sterile but also unjust and cruel, as condemning many individuals whose marriages have irremediably broken down to a choice between two forms of bitter frustration: sacrificing their hopes for happiness in a new marriage if they wish to remain within the communion of the sacraments, or sacrificing their sacramental communion within the church if they remarry.

That all null marriages be declared null must always be a pastoral (and, I would hope, a juridical) concern of the church. But the truer pastoral concern is surely to see that such marriages are *avoided*; in other words, a true pastorate must be concerned that people enter *real* marriages, which means, among other things, marriages that are indissoluble. If some priests and pastoral workers find difficulty with this last statement, it is, I think, because they have let themselves be persuaded that indissolubility, from any pastoral viewpoint, is not a positive factor; it is negative. It is something that does not contribute to Christian life but rather impedes it. To my mind an effective and renewed pastorate concerning marriage depends largely on whether we can correct this conviction and see indissolubility in a positive rather than a negative light; and on whether we can clarify our understanding of indissolubility and see that its defense signifies the defense not just of an institutional aspect, but also of a personalist aspect of marriage. Clarification of this point is of the utmost importance.

Let us consider the matter in relation precisely to marriages where true conjugal harmony between husband and wife seems to have collapsed and where both want, or one of them wants, freedom to look for happiness elsewhere. Why does the church defend such completely failed marriages? In defending them, is the church not defending the institution—devoid, in these concrete instances, of life and meaning—at the expense of the persons involved? No. In defending the indissolubility of such marriages, the church is also defending three categories of persons.

First of all, the children; there should be little difficulty in seeing this point. Children do not prefer to see their parents fighting or to have them separate. They prefer them to be united. Further, they have a *right* to that parental unity which the church defends[8] and which, after all, it is within the parents' power—if they wish—to create. Even if one of the parents refuses to live up to his or her obligations to create and maintain married and family unity, the children still have the right to the fidelity of the other.

In defending indissolubility, the church is also defending the rights and expectations of other persons who are outside the immediate family circle: other married couples, people preparing for marriage, and young people in general. Here it is important to state that, however much we emphasize the personalist aspects of marriage, no Christian or truly human view can ignore its social aspects. Marriage is never a purely personal affair; it is also social. Married couples have rights and duties towards the rest of society,

8. "When the conjugal covenant is broken, those who suffer most are the children who are the living sign of its indissolubility" (Pope Benedict XVI, *Address*, April 5, 2008) (http://www.vatican.va/holy_father/benedict_xvi/speeches/2008/april/documents/hf_ben-xvi_spe_20080405_istituto-gpii_en.html).

and the rest of society has duties and rights towards each married couple. Concretely, it is good for the other members of a society to see an example of fidelity in the commitment lived by married people. It is good to have the witness of couples around them whose lives say, "Yes, it is possible to be chaste and faithful; it is possible to get along with someone else despite his or her defects; it is possible to overcome one's own pride, limitations, and selfishness." A society where no one bears witness to this fidelity is a society where no one takes marriage seriously, and that is a society heading for collapse. Couples preparing for marriage or who are already married need to be reminded that to marry means to enter a state of life with important obligations and responsibilities toward the community. No true pastoral understanding or presentation of marriage can ignore this social aspect.

The third category of persons that indissolubility is meant to defend is the *spouses themselves*. This is indeed the pastoral *quid* of the matter. This is the point that might seem hardest to see, and yet should, on reflection, be clearly seen, at least by pastors. It is true that an individual or a couple, in a self-centered mood, may not see it for as long as that mood lasts. Even then, however, the pastor who sees it can help them. To clarify, let us examine more closely the ever recurring objection; why should not people whose marriage has irremediably failed be free to seek happiness in a second marriage? The simple answer, the *pastoral* answer, is that it is not the Lord's will (their ultimate pastor's will) that they should do so.

The Lord Wants Us to Be Happy

Does God not want such a couple to be happy? On the contrary, it is precisely because he *does* want them to be happy with the limited happiness that is possible here on earth and with unlimited happiness hereafter. But he knows that happiness depends on love: on the ability to love and on *developing* this ability, and his design for marriage is that it should be a constant contributor to this development of the capacity to love. This, from the personalist point of view, is in fact what marriage is about. It is on this that the true *bonum coniugum*—the genuine "good" of the spouses—depends. Marriage in God's plan is not a haven of love but a school of love. Married people are apprentices of love, as indeed we all are in this life. The main difficulty in learning to love is the fact and force of personal selfishness. The happiness that love offers depends on the gradual overcoming of selfishness; that is why it is the sort of happiness that takes effort. And that too is why the "bad" moments of marriage—the hard moments—can also be good moments, providing that a person is prepared to rise to the challenge that they pose.

It is precisely the unbreakable character of the marriage bond that makes it contribute so powerfully to the *bonum coniugum*. It tells the spouses that God wants them to remain committed to one another even when commitment seems pointless or impossible; that he wants them to keep loving one another even when all feelings of love seem to have died. *Gaudium et Spes* (no. 49) says that what makes married love an "eminently human love" is that it is "an affection between two persons rooted *in the will*." Love tends to begin on the level of feelings, but it can never mature and deepen if it remains on that level, which, after all, is the surface level of human relations. In order to grow, love must not remain a purely emotional matter; it needs to become a matter of deliberate and voluntary choice. Its firmness and maturity must come from the will; it is in the will, as the Council says, that it must be rooted.

Love Is Rooted in the Will

If emotional love is not yet a true or deep love, conditioned love is a very questionable love, and calculating love is not love at all. What sort of love does a person have whose approach is, "I'll love you provided this does not require an effort or demand a sacrifice of me," "I'll love you provided you do not have any defects," or "I love you because I calculate you will make me happy"? This is self-centeredness, not love. And yet, at the start of all love affairs and all marriages, along with some elements of genuine love ("I love you for what you are"), certain elements of calculation are no doubt also present. A sound pastoral program for marriage guidance aims at helping people to realize this, and to gradually purify their understanding and living of love. No pastoral approach wants to make happiness harder than it is. But it would be a false pastorate which let people have the impression that happiness is easy or can be had easily. We are not being pastoral towards people if we tell them that they are entitled to effortless happiness.

The law of indissolubility says to a married person, "You have no right to give up the effort to love even if marriage proves difficult or runs into unforeseen obstacles. You have no right to let your spouse down, or your children down, or other people down. Finally, you have no right to let yourself down or to think you can find a better happiness than the one God has planned for you. You will not be happy that way. It simply will not work."

The warm-heartedness of so many dedicated pastoral workers is a great gift, provided it does not detract from their clear-mindedness. Counseling suffers if one or other quality is lacking. Good pastoral workers seek to feel and encourage with the heart of Christ but also to think and counsel with the mind of Christ. The more their sympathies are stirred by the difficulties in which someone is placed, the more they try to remember that both they, the counselors, as well as the person seeking counsel, need the guidance of the moral law that Christ has given us. A pastoral worker may, for instance, empathize with all the emotional factors urging a girl to have an abortion, yet should be clear-minded enough to know and to tell her that abortion is not only homicide before God, it is "suicide" for her conscience and for her chance of happiness.

Everyone has a chance of happiness in life, but many people throw their chance away because they do not or will not face up to the challenge involved in that chance. Any true pastoral work needs to take into account this element of challenge that enters into God's plan for human happiness. People in difficulties need consolation; they need to be helped out of these difficulties insofar as this is possible. But sometimes the only truly pastoral possibility is to help them face these difficulties and the challenge they imply.

A law forbidding abortion or divorce does not create problems; rather, it is seeking to avoid false "solutions" to problems. This is the clear-sightedness required of our pastoral workers: to see that it is not the law which creates the problems or the difficulties—the difficulties are already there—but rather it is the "solution" which would make them worse. It is a superficial and mistaken pastoral vision, therefore, that sees law as an obstacle blocking the way to happiness. Law is a challenge indicating the way to happiness. These reflections need to be meditated upon by those priests and counselors who feel that if they give a pastoral "no" to a person in trouble, they have nothing further to offer. They have a challenge to offer!

Reluctant to Challenge?

Why do we seem reluctant to put challenges to people today—the challenge of chastity, of generosity, of fidelity? Perhaps we do not have the same confidence in people that Christ had; he challenged his followers constantly. Perhaps we need to examine ourselves and see how positively and forcefully we in turn accept and live these same challenges in our own lives. The challenge of marriage holds even for what one may be tempted to classify as utterly hopeless cases. For instance, marriages where one of the spouses has become totally alcoholic or has been given a life sentence in jail. It is easy to argue that when a spouse promised to accept the other "in sickness or in health," "for better or for worse," he or she did nor foresee eventualities like these. Nevertheless, the anticipation of even such eventualities is what is literally and directly implied in the promise. Otherwise this promise expresses nothing more than that conditioned and worthless "love" of which we spoke earlier: "I promise to love you provided loving you involves me in no great sacrifice."

Besides, it makes no pastoral sense to describe such situations as "hopeless." Pastoral terms of reference can never be exclusively human. Otherwise, if we take the case of something like a terminal cancer, the medical judgment that the case is hopeless would signify that, pastorally speaking, there is nothing more to be said. This is not true. The doctor may have no hope to offer, but this is not the case for the pastor or indeed for any Christian. Similarly, in these extreme marriage cases, if indissolubility is to stand, human wisdom may have no hope to offer. Yet the wisdom of the church offers hope, the hope of the immense reward reserved for the person who keeps fidelity—not only with his or her spouse, but also with Christ—in carrying the cross.

The pastoral consolation offered in reminding people of such hope is immense. Yet it is not only on that purely supernatural or other-worldly level that pastoral consolation can be offered. As a matter of pastoral justice, there are human considerations which should be put to people in this situation, in which they can also find consolation and encouragement. They should be reminded that the spouse who is faithful to his or her matrimonial commitment in conditions of particular difficulty is, as we mentioned earlier, an example and a source of immense strength to other people. There is another consideration that one needs to mention as well: faithfulness in such difficult circumstances has something deeply *natural* to it, in the challenge that it offers to the better and more generous side of human nature. Just as it is not natural for a mother to reject or abandon her son, no matter how dissolute his life may become, it is neither truly natural nor in any way Christian for a husband or wife to abandon the other just because he or she is imprisoned or an alcoholic. Any effective pastoral program needs to build on this conviction. If the pastor senses that some married people tend to think or react differently—with too little natural loyalty and courage and with too much natural self-concern and cowardice—then this should be seen as a pastoral problem to be worked through, so as to help people acquire a more Christian understanding of all the demanding strength and beauty of the married relationship.

Declarations of Nullity

Some have said that the response to a petition for nullity should be "at least as pastoral as it is judicial." Behind this seems to lie the implication that it is the affirmative response to the petition (that is, the declaration of nullity) *and it alone* which is pastoral, whereas the negative response (which actually means the upholding of the validity of the marriage) must necessarily be branded with the *non*-pastoral or *anti*-pastoral stigma of "juridical." Perhaps here we can more easily bring to light the fundamental unsoundness of the "pastoral *versus* juridical" mentality.

Any matter where the interlinking interests of several persons are involved is a matter of justice, and justice is a pastoral as well as a judicial concern. No doubt one can distinguish between, on the one hand, the delicate and often difficult process of discerning and declaring what is just (a process that is rightly termed judicial), and on the other hand, the equally delicate and not infrequently equally difficult task of getting people to see that what has been declared to be just *is* in fact just, and to accept it as such (a task that is rightly termed pastoral). But these distinctions are *comple-*

mentary rather than in opposition. If a judicial decision is just—if it respects and vindicates rights—then it is pastoral. Conversely, nothing can be pastoral if it is not also just. After all, if it is not just, this means that someone's rights are being violated. Surely no one is going to suggest that being pastoral means allowing a person to ignore justice, to get away with injustice, or to trample on the rights of others.

No genuine pastoral work is being done if a pastor fails to convey the full personal challenge that Christian living represents. This, it should be understood, is to *encourage* them, not to discourage them. Chastity, despite its difficulties, has an appeal; indeed, an immense appeal. And so has justice. Not only social justice, but also (and very particularly) commutative or interpersonal justice, with its call and challenge to each one to respect others, to face up to what he or she owes to others, and to give what is owed.

The Healing Power of Justice

Justice is a powerful stimulus to people. It appeals to their inner honesty, to their deepest values, calling on them to put the proper rights of others above their own personal convenience or advantage. That is why one is left perplexed at suggestions that a judgment has no power to "heal" persons. This is not at all the case. A just judgment—a declaration of justice—has great power to heal, or at least to point out the path to health. It is true that the judgment alone (the declaration) may not be sufficient to restore health; it needs to be accepted personally and put into effect. That is why even though justice always possesses healing power, in the end it is not just the declaration but the acceptance of justice that heals. To bring about that acceptance is properly the role of pastoral work.

When we say that good medicine heals, we mean that the healing process demands not only making a proper diagnosis but also getting the patient to accept the necessary treatment or medicine, even if it is painful or bitter. The diagnosis or prescription—the judgment—is useless if there is no one capable of helping the sick person to accept and apply the remedy. Both judges and pastors have a capacity to heal, but their healing capacity is not exercised if they let people think that a violation of rights or a failure to fulfil obligations is a healthy and not a pathological situation.

One does occasionally come across cases where a judgment seems to leave a person "wounded," and he or she lapses into a bitter and resentful attitude. But if the judgment is just, the person should not be resentful, or at least should not remain in that state for long. The pastoral concern in such cases must be to help the person out of the attitude through seeing that the judgment, despite the personal hardships it may seem to cause him or her, defends other people's rights. Only if the person accepts this will the "wound" gradually disappear and the healing process be brought to completion. The pastor who does not share this aspect of pastoral concern may tell people they are well, but he is in fact allowing them to remain sick.

Some commentators seem to look on the current multiplication of matrimonial annulments as a triumph of canonical procedure. My own view is that it rather indicates a failure of pastoral practice. In matrimonial matters as in life in general, there will always be hard cases, and some of them can never be solved, humanly speaking. Even then, their burden and hardship can become lighter if they are understood in terms of a share in the cross of Christ. To help those concerned to achieve this Christian understanding is the truly pastoral contribution in such cases.

Hard Cases

Many of the "hard cases" that keep materializing today were never meant to become so hardened, and their hardening can in fact be avoided if they are made the object of more thoughtful pastoral care based on the major convictions that I have sought to outline and which can be summarized as follows. (1) Christian marriage is a way of sanctity and therefore, like any other calling to holiness, must be built on a life of prayer and frequent reception of the sacraments (see c. 1603) and on effort, that is, the acceptance of the cross. (2) God knows what he is doing in making the bond of marriage indissoluble. He knows that love means giving and being faithful to one's gift, and therefore he wants husband and wife to be *bound* to the liberating task and saving effort of learning to give and learning to love. (3) Earth is not heaven; but human love on earth is meant to be a preparation for love in heaven. (4) Therefore, and finally, if God wishes to bind husband and wife to one another for life, it is also so that, in the end, he can bind each one of them to himself for eternity.

Pastors who are diffident about the human value of indissolubility would do well to follow the subsequent personal history—over the next decade, for example—of those who have followed the way of divorce or who have managed to get an "easy" annulment. For every one case that seemed to have worked out happily, I think they will find ten (or a hundred) who, having failed to measure up to the challenges of love, have continued down the slope of isolating selfishness, and who, apart from any possible sense of having failed God, are dogged by a deep and intimate self-disillusionment, for having failed their partner, their children, their relations, other people, or themselves. If we, in effect, subscribe to a "no-confidence" vote in God's law, and so do not maintain the pastoral thrust of helping people stick to the task of learning to love, we will see a worsening of the basic pastoral problem of more and more isolated and loveless people. The ultimate horizon may or may not be distant; but it is clear. If we let people think that happiness is easily found, or found through self-seeking, or found without self-giving, and if our pastoral advice endorses letting Christians be governed by feelings instead of helping them govern themselves through the exercise of mind and will, then—in the long or short run—we risk seeing ecclesial society turn into a non-community, a "non-people," where the bonds of mutual respect, support and loyalty have been dissolved, and each one, in wishing to be a law to himself, ends up by being a world to himself: a diminished and deprived world of isolation, self-centeredness, and fundamental unhappiness.

6

The "Good" and the "Bad" in Marriage according to St. Augustine

A Battle on Two Fronts

In the previous chapter we sought to place the doctrinal issue of indissolubility within a positive pastoral perspective. Now we return to a more dominantly theological note, examining some aspects of the thought of St. Augustine, who might well be considered the first theologian of marriage. How would St. Augustine react if he returned to the world at the start of the third millennium and had to evaluate the modern attitude toward marriage and toward human sexuality? I believe that (with surprise, or perhaps without it) he would identify two phenomena that he experienced in his own time (even if somewhat differently modulated), two attitudes that he combated; two evaluations, seemingly located at opposite poles but nevertheless intimately related to each other.

Disesteem for Marriage: Exaltation of Sex

On the one hand, there is the disesteem in which marriage is held in our time. Modern public opinion accords it little standing and less trust, has increasing doubts about its value and is skeptical as to its possibilities of working out in the long run. Surrogates abound (free unions, trial marriages) to the point that the very notion of marriage is losing all objective content (for example, same-sex "marriages"). No doubt most of our contemporaries would not yet say that marriage is bad, but they might have some difficulty in specifying why it is good. On the other hand, this disesteem of marriage goes hand in hand with a certain omnipresence of sexuality in almost all aspects of life. While this might at first sight indicate an apparent reevaluation of sex, a more attentive analysis suggests in fact its absolute trivialization.

There is no longer any norm for sex: no understanding within which it attains full and proper meaning, and outside of which it must be considered *abnormal*. Indeed, what today seems to be considered normal—as if it should apply to everyone—is an "active" sexual life, in whatever form that activity takes. Sexual intercourse is no longer regarded as something sacred, filled with meaning, which characterizes one unique human relationship, that of marriage, and is reserved for those who are spouses. Sexual activity doesn't imply a deep dedication of persons; it can be casual, temporary, promiscuous. Anyone—even a person of the same sex—can be a good and legitimate sexual "partner." St. Augustine had already seen quite a bit of this in his own lifetime. Thus he probably would not be greatly surprised to see how errors and aberrations of the past keep turning up again in modern times. But I think he would help us to deepen our analysis of these errors and, with his positive presentation, help us to combat the current pessimism about marriage and about sexuality in general.

Augustine as a source to overcome pessimism about sexuality—one might ask, can this question be seriously proposed? Surely a basic accusation against St. Augustine is that his mind was marked by a deep pessimistic streak, especially with regard to sexuality, and that his subsequent influence—proportionate to the quality of that mind—has left the church's thought burdened down to the present day with a negative and defective ethic of sexuality and marriage. Modern critics have added another accusation: that his view of marriage was fundamentally defective inasmuch as he attributed importance and value to its procreative function alone and totally ignored its personalistic aspects.

I do not share these critical views. I consider them to be based on an inadequate reading of St. Augustine, as well as on a faulty understanding of conjugal sexuality itself. But the criticisms have been repeated so often than it seems wise to let them in some way condition our study. Certainly, Augustine's outlook, like that of every man, was marked by the experiences of his life. But the Manicheism of his early days remained for him a darkness from which he had emerged,[1] and not a source of recurrent pessimism.[2] Once he began to walk in the light of the Christian faith, his vision of sexuality and marriage became sharpened and refined by his efforts to keep a Catholic balance between the extremes of Manicheism on the one hand and Pelagianism on the other.[3]

Augustine: Pessimist? Anti-Personalist?

Two questions arise here. Firstly, was St. Augustine's view of marriage exclusively procreative, or does his thought also present aspects that can properly be called personalist? Secondly, was his

1. A certain parallel could plausibly be traced with Chesterton's emergence from the "poisonous period" of his agnostic days to "astonished theism." See William Oddie's perceptive study, *Chesterton and the Romance of Orthodoxy* (Oxford: Oxford University Press, 2008), 328–29.

2. See E. Schmitt, "Le mariage chrétien dans l'oeuvre de Saint Augustin," *Études Augustiniennes* (Paris, 1983), 107.

3. For the purpose of our study, it is enough to recall that the dualistic Manicheans saw matter as evil, only the spirit being good. Hence, the body, marriage, procreation were all evil. Pelagianism was naturalistic in spirit, professing an over-optimism about salvation as something that could be attained by human effort alone, without the help of divine grace. It denied that concupiscence is a disorder that can affect marriage.

view of sexual activity pessimistic, or can we find in it elements of real utility for our own correct emphasis regarding sexuality, especially as an expression of married love? The balance of Augustine's mind on sexuality and marriage can only be established by weighing the two great and very different controversies on these matters that he engaged in: first, with the Manicheans early in his Catholic life, and later on, with the Pelagians. The Manichean doctrines represented a frontal attack on marriage, while the Pelagian views involved a more subtle attack on the Christian norm for sexuality. The former were openly anti-marriage; the latter were apparently pro-sexuality, but in fact tended to undermine man's ability to respect and uphold the dignity of sex. St. Augustine's polemical exchanges with the Manicheans reflect his defense of marriage in general and of procreativity in particular, while those with the Pelagians reveal his reserve regarding views which present human sexuality as basically unproblematic.

In the dualist view of the Manicheans, the body is the work of the devil, and so its propagation is evil; marriage, considered as the institutional means of procreation, is also evil.[4] Given this peculiar Manichean tenet, it is natural that St. Augustine, in his reply, expounds the opposite thesis: conjugal sexual intercourse is good precisely because procreation is good.[5] This explains in large part his insistence on the generative purpose of sex.[6] But it is not true that the only value Augustine sees in marriage is procreation. His first major work on marriage, written in his early anti-Manichean days, has the very significant title of *De bono coniugali*, or "The Good of Marriage." In it his thought can at times legitimately be

4. "Is it not you who hold that begetting children, and so imprisoning souls in the flesh, is a greater sin than cohabitation?": *De moribus Manichaeorum* 18, 65.

5. *De moribus Manichaeorum* 18, 65; cf. *Contra Faustum Manichaeum*, lib. 30, 6.

6. See D. Covi, "El fin de la actividad sexual según San Agustín," *Augustinus* 17 (1972): 58; L. E. Samek, "Sessualità, matrimonio e concupiscenza in sant'Agostino," *Studia Patristica Mediolanensia* 5 (Milan: Università Cattolica del Sacro Cuore, 1976), 232.

termed "personalist." Observing that "it is proper to inquire for what reason marriage be good," he explains, "this seems to me not merely to be on account of the begetting of children, but also on account of the natural association between the two sexes,"[7] whose mutual faith he describes as "the first fellowship of humankind in this mortal state."[8] He insists on the value of love between husband and wife, and how the *ordo caritatis* unites those whom age or misfortune may have deprived of children: "Now in good although aged marriage, even if the vigor of youth between man and woman has faded, the order of charity between husband and wife remains in its fullness."[9] He presents fidelity as an exchange of mutual respect and service,[10] and insists that "the bodies of the married too are holy, when they keep faith to one another and to God."[11] In his later work on widowhood, he writes: "The good of marriage is always a good indeed. In the people of God it was at one time an act of obedience to the law; now it is a remedy for weakness, and for some a solace of human nature."[12]

Augustine goes further. In defending the goodness of matrimony, he offers an unsurpassed analysis of the essential values—profoundly human values and divine blessings at one and the same time—which characterize and show the beauty, nobility, and attractiveness of marriage. This is the Augustinian doctrine of the *bona matrimonialia*, which he presents repeatedly in the form of

7. *De bono coniugali*, 3, 3 (PL 40:375).

8. Ibid., 6, 6 (PL 40:377).

9. "Nunc vero in bono licet annoso coniugio, etsi emarcuit ardor aetatis inter masculum et feminam, viget tamen ordo caritatis inter maritum et uxorem" (ibid., 3, 3 [PL 40:375]).

10. "Fides honoris et obsequiorum invicem debitorum" (ibid.).

11. "Sancta sunt ergo etiam corpora coniugatorum, fidem sibi et Domino servantium" (ibid., 11 and 13 [PL 40:382]).

12. "Nuptiarum igitur bonum semper est quidem bonum; sed in populo Dei fuit aliquando legis obsequium; nunc est infirmitatis remedium, in quibusdam vero humanitatis solatium" (*De bono viduitatis*, 8, 11 [PL 40:437]).

canticles of praise of the three fundamental values or properties which evidence the goodness of marriage: its exclusiveness, its pro-creativity, and the unbreakable nature of the conjugal bond. For Augustine, each of these essential properties of the conjugal society is a *bonum*, a good quality, that gives dignity to matrimony and shows its deep correspondence to the innate aspirations of human nature which can therefore take glory in this goodness: "This is the goodness of marriage, from which it takes its glory: offspring, chaste fidelity, unbreakable bond."[13]

The three *bona*: *bonum fidei*, *bonum prolis*, and *bonum sacramenti*. We have here a formula that is typically Augustinian in its brevity and incisiveness. Writers down the centuries have tended to echo its brevity, perhaps without making sufficient effort to penetrate its depth and to discover its anthropological richness. St. Augustine is not to be blamed if later ecclesial reflection, dwelling on the procreative finality of marriage which he so well defended, has neglected to maintain and develop his positive view of the other deeply human values by which marriage is essentially characterized.[14] In this context it is arguably true that theology and especially canon law have fostered a restrictive and at times apparently negative view of the properties of marriage, laying special emphasis on the aspect of *obligation* involved in each *bonum* and concerning itself mainly with the juridical consequences of their *exclusion*. It seems to me beyond question that this insistence on the obligatoriness of the *bona* has tended to obscure their actual goodness. Augustine did not present the *bona* mainly as obligations, but as

13. "Illud esse nuptiarum bonum unde gloriantur nuptiae, id est, proles, pudicitia, sacramentum" *De peccato originali*, 37 and 42 [PL 44:406]).

14. While strongly defending the purpose of procreation, "St. Augustine focuses rather on the constitutive factors of marriage from the viewpoint of its moral goodness or value, and not of its end—the latter being the aspect under which the three "goods" we are considering will be taken up in later theology" (René Simon, "Sexualité et mariage chez saint Augustin," *Le Supplément* 109 [1974]: 158).

blessings. "Let these nuptial blessings be the objects of our love: offspring, fidelity, the unbreakable bond. . . . Let these nuptial blessings be praised in marriage by him who wishes to extol the nuptial institution."[15] There is nothing defective or negative in this forceful analysis. On the contrary, St. Augustine's thesis—that the marital relationship is good because of three exceptional *values*[16] which characterize it—appears as powerfully attractive to those whose natural sense of life has not been warped.

One is inclined to think that modern men and women, or at least those who have retained some true sense of marriage, will have little difficulty in accepting that there is a value in the *fides* of matrimony. It is a good thing that spouses pledge mutual and exclusive fidelity, thus showing the unique appreciation each has of the other. The good or value of fidelity is surely clear. "You are *unique* to me," is the first truly personalized affirmation of conjugal love and echoes the words God addresses to each one of us in Isaiah: *Meus es tu*, "you are mine."[17]

Today a greater effort may be required to understand and admit that this mutual fidelity is all the more a value because it is meant to be permanent; enshrined, that is, in an unbreakable bond. We moderns have developed a notion of our own freedom which makes us suspicious of any definitive commitment. We always want to be in a position to go back on our choices, even on a choice as natural as marriage. And that is why indissolubility, which is an essential *bonum* for St. Augustine, has become a "*malum*" for so many people today. A temporary or breakable bond is better than

15. *De nuptiis et concupiscentia*, 1, 17, 19; see 21, 23 [hereafter "*De nupt. et conc.*"].

16. I have a great regard for the term "values," properly understood and used (see my *Man and Values*). Yes, the term can be regarded as "loaded" inasmuch as some would substitute it for the traditional notion of "virtues." Such confusion of thought should be resisted. A "value" is something one appreciates or admires; or perhaps, at a lower scale, something one simply finds useful. A "virtue" is a positive habit or ability one acquires by effort. The terms have totally different meanings.

17. Is 43:1.

an unbreakable one. Only soluble marriage is good and acceptable; an indissoluble bond is bad and unacceptable. Yet it is Augustine who is right, and we moderns who are mistaken in our paralyzing diffidence and who need to correct a false perspective regarding the positive needs and fulfilling tendencies of our nature.

Truly, for whoever has not lost contact with his or her own humanity, the value of a bond of love that is permanent should be clear. To possess a stable home or haven, to know that one's "belonging" to another, and that other's belonging to one, is for ever: all of this is natural and highly attractive for the human person. While one knows it will require sacrifices, it is *natural* to sense that the sacrifices are worth it. Pope John Paul II insists on this point: "It is natural for the human heart to accept demands, even difficult ones, in the name of love for an ideal, and above all in the name of love for a person."[18] John Paul II, in full consonance with St. Augustine's vision, goes further in fact and speaks of indissolubility as good news: "To all those who, in our times, consider it too difficult, or indeed impossible, to be bound to one person for the whole of life, and to those caught up in a culture that rejects the indissolubility of marriage and openly mocks the commitment of spouses to fidelity, *it is necessary to reconfirm the good news* of the definitive nature of that conjugal love that has in Christ its foundation and strength."[19] Elsewhere he says: "The family achieves the good of being together. This is the good par excellence of marriage (hence its indissolubility) and of the family community."[20] Marriage is good: a deep and demanding good to be faithful to, not a superficial "experience" to be tried and discarded as soon as its first demands make their appearance.

---

18. *General Audience*, April 28, 1982 (TB, 281).
19. FC, no. 20.
20. *Letter to Families*, no. 15.

As already remarked, it is not true that Augustine saw marriage exclusively in a procreative light. At the same time it is clear that the *bonum prolis* or procreativity was a central marital value for him, and an essential one, along with the *bonum fidei* and the *bonum sacramenti*. Perhaps it is here where our modern men and women are furthest from understanding St. Augustine's thought, and where they could at the same time most benefit from it. Is procreativity a value for our contemporaries? Do they grasp the personalist dignity of procreation, seeing the fallaciousness of views which dismiss as mere "biologism" any defense of the intrinsic and inseparable connection between the procreative and the unitive aspects of marital intercourse?[21] Do they realize not only that marriage is naturally designed to be fruitful, but that this fruitfulness is a *good* thing, a "*quid bonum*," because, as the Second Vatican Council teaches, "children are the supreme gift of marriage and greatly contribute to the good of the parents themselves"?[22] Are people therefore convinced that the practice of contraception—or even of unneeded or misused natural family planning—impoverishes the personal and conjugal life of the spouses? If few would answer these questions with an unhesitant "yes," and many with a qualified or unqualified "no," then modern thought is certainly not aligned with that of St. Augustine nor, it would seem, with the judgment of the Second Vatican Council regarding how procreation enriches married life.[23]

The Augustinian "*bona*" and Christian Personalism

It will be helpful here to recall briefly what we considered in chapters 3 and 4: that some theological and canonical writers of

21. This connection will be studied in detail in the next chapter.

22. GS, no. 50.

23. See Janet E. Smith, "Conscious Parenthood," *Nova et Vetera* (English Edition) 6, no. 4 (2008): 927–50.

the past century held that church thinking had been long dominated by an institutional understanding of marriage, and that (also
in the spirit of the Second Vatican Council) this must be replaced
by a more person-centered understanding. In this view, the institutional understanding emphasized the social aspect of marriage
and, concretely, its role as an institution for propagating the human race. In contrast, according to this way of thinking (especially
in its post-conciliar phase), we are now called to a renewed understanding of marriage in a personalist way, with greater emphasis on
the relationship between husband and wife, on the role and aspirations of conjugal love, and on personal fulfillment; with greater
freedom, therefore, from institutional restraints. Part of this whole
process, it was suggested, must involve a shift of emphasis away
from the traditional Augustinian *bona* which were particularly regarded as institutional elements of matrimony unfavorable to the
development of personalism.

Both the presuppositions of this view as well as the contrasts it
makes strike me as unwarranted. For a Christian, after all, marriage
must surely be always seen as an institution not of positive human
law, but of divine law. In other words, it is not a mere historical
invention or a temporary arrangement devised by men—suited
perhaps to the human or social mores of some particular moment,
but which people of a later age could well modify or discard—but
a God-given reality which corresponds to man's nature and to the
divine plan for human development and destiny.

It is this institution, marriage itself, which can indeed be
viewed from a variety of standpoints. In considering it, one can
stress personalist values (self-fulfillment, conjugal love, etc.) on
the one hand, or legal realities (validity of consent, capacity, etc.)
on the other, and then one can certainly draw a contrast between
the two views. While one can quite legitimately draw a contrast
between a personalist and a legal (or even, if one wishes, a legalis-

tic) understanding of marriage, I find it quite misleading to draw a contrast between an "institutional" and "personalist" understanding. It was in defense of this viewpoint that I published a number of theological studies during my years at the Roman Rota which sought to show that the "institutional view" and the "personalist view" of marriage lend themselves to synthesis rather than to contrast, and (more to our present point) that the Augustinian *bona* are deeply personalist, both reflecting the aspirations of conjugal love and favoring the true human fulfillment of the spouses.[24]

In fact, to maintain that a procreative understanding of marriage is not personalist reveals a major defect in anthropological thinking. The contemporary loss of the sense of the goodness of human procreativity, of the uniqueness of the conception of each child, or of a spouse becoming a parent, suggests a devalued concept of life itself and of the privilege of being cooperators with God in its perpetuation. It was during his Manichean phase that Augustine had his only son—unplanned and unwanted. How significant it is that even then, despite the Manichean tenet that procreation is bad, he received this son as a gift from above, naming him *Adeodatus*, "Given-by-God."

St. Augustine's doctrine of the triple *bona* is fully entitled to be termed personalist. If we have largely lost that positive vision of these basic values of marriage, if we too easily tend to think of the burden and not of the goodness and attractiveness of an exclusive lifelong fruitful union between man and woman, then it

24. Chapter 3 covers my main views. Particular aspects are studied in the following: "La Indisolubilidad Matrimonial y la Defensa de las Personas," *Scripta Theologica* 22 (1990): 145–55; "Personnalisme et jurisprudence matrimoniale," *Revue de Droit Canonique* 45 (1995): 331–49; "Personalism and the *bona* of Marriage," *Studia canonica* 27 (1993): 401–12; "Personalism and the Traditional *Goods* of Marriage," *Apollinaris* 70 (1997): 305–14; "Personalism and the Essential Obligations of Marriage," *Angelicum* 74 (1997): 81–94; "La Indisolubilidad como expresión del verdadero amor conyugal," *Revista Española de Teología* 55 (1995): 237–50; and "Marriage: A Personalist Focus on Indissolubility," *Linacre Quarterly* 61 (1994): 48–56.

is perhaps we, and not St. Augustine, who could be charged with pessimism, or at least with an impoverished outlook on reality.

After all, the idea on which all genuine Christian personalism is built is expressed in that key passage in *Gaudium et Spes* (no. 24): "Man cannot fully find himself [*plene seipsum invenire non posse*] except through a sincere gift of himself."[25] Whoever does not really give himself to another remains alone, and "it is not good that man should be alone" (Gen 2:24), for in that way he cannot fulfill himself. That dedication to another can be directly to God,[26] or (more

25. It is plausible that the insertion of this phrase into GS was mainly due to Bishop Karol Wojtyla. The phrase appears repeatedly in the magisterium of Pope John Paul II. For our present purpose a passage commenting on the antithesis between individualism and personalism is particularly relevant: "Love, the civilization of love, is bound up with personalism. Why with personalism? And why does individualism threaten the civilization of love? We find a key to answering this in the council's expression, a "sincere gift." Individualism presupposes a use of freedom in which the subject does what he wants, in which he himself is the one to "establish the truth" of whatever he finds pleasing or useful. He does not tolerate the fact that someone else "wants" or demands something from him in the name of an objective truth. He does not want to "give" to another on the basis of truth; he does not want to become a "sincere gift." Individualism thus remains egocentric and selfish. The real antithesis between individualism and personalism emerges not only on the level of theory, but even more on that of ethos. The ethos of personalism is altruistic: It moves the person to become a gift for others and to discover joy in giving himself" (*Letter to Families*, no. 14).

26. It would be tempting, but too time-consuming, to dwell here on the personalism represented (in an eminent way) by dedication to God in celibacy. To give oneself to another, coming out of self, is the key of personalism. In final analysis this is because it is the way of the salvation of mankind effected through the incarnation. If God gives himself to man it is in order that man can unite himself with God, so as to fulfill himself and ultimately to find salvation in eternal wedlock. Marriage, *sacramentum magnum* (Eph 5:32), is a figure of Christ's union with his church and with each Christian. God wants to "marry," to enter into an eternal covenant or *con-iugium* with each soul in particular. Augustine does not hesitate to say that "we are called to marriage-union with God [vocamur ad coniugium Dei]" (*Contra Adimantum Manichaei Discipulum*, 13, 3); "the greatest marriage is that of the soul with Christ [maius coniugium est animae cum Christo]" (*Sermones* 335/G, 1). God is faithful and each one is called to be faithful to him with the fidelity that characterizes the true spouse. We all are called to be faithful spouses; there one discovers in a particular way the deep connection between Christian marriage and celibacy out of love for God. The danger that threatens the married person (as well as the celibate) is to lapse back into selfishness, abandoning the loving and faithful dedication to which one has freely committed oneself. On this point

commonly) to marriage. But it has to be a real dedication—an authentic donation made totally and without reserve—and it is here where dedication as love, and marriage as an institution, meet and coincide. If an unreserved dedication toward the other party is today no longer regarded as an essential value of the matrimonial relationship, neither is a commitment which is open to children, the possible fruit of the conjugal union. Generally speaking, marriage is still expected to be faithful and exclusive, but it is accepted that it can be temporary and sterile.

The main value that many of our contemporaries seem to see in the man-woman relationship is that simply of some form of sexual companionship, whether or not it is formalized in marriage. Sexuality, and not conjugality, has become the reference point. As a result, the distinction between licit and illicit sexual relationships (in more traditional terms, between marriage and fornication) becomes more and more blurred, and ends up by losing any real meaning. Many maintain that, provided a sincere love exists, matrimonial and extra-matrimonial relationships are almost indistinguishable from the moral point of view. Given the presence of such love, both are "good" (though some may grant that from a certain point of view the former is preferable).[27] But the basis for

---

St. Augustine also shows a highly personalist spirit. When exalting matrimonial fidelity he adds that the celibate for God is also in a *conjugal* state: "While those who dedicate their virginity to God have a higher degree of honor and sanctity in the Church, they are not unmarried; for they are conjugally united with the whole Church, in which marriage the spouse is Christ" [Nec illae quae virginitatem Deo vovent, quamquam ampliorem gradum honoris et sanctitatis in Ecclesia teneant, sine nuptiis sunt: nam et ipsae pertinent ad nuptias cum tota Ecclesia, in quibus nuptiis sponsus est Christus] (*In Evangelio Joannis tractatus*, 9, 2). The person who has chosen celibacy for God is not alone (that erroneous modern supposition); he or she is more immersed than anyone in the love of all loves. Nothing is more personalist (and "fulfilling") than the spousal dedication that the celibate person makes.

27. We have indeed come very far from that controversy with the Manicheans against whom St. Augustine maintained that marriage "is a good in itself and not only when compared, in contrast, with the evil of fornication. In other words, it is not that marriage and fornication are two evils, among which marriage is the lesser, but rather

this "goodness" no longer resides in the total mutual self-donation shown through the conjugal *bona*. It is placed instead in the fragile goodness of "love," devoid of any real aspect of self-dedication: a transitory love, without any promise of fidelity, and closed to its possible fruit in a new life. Such love does not really unite—more than for a moment and in passing—nor has it the capacity to take a person out of his or her existential solitude. The physical expression of love, no longer restricted to a truly married relationship, can easily fall under the sway of a force—that of uncontrolled sexuality—that isolates the individual and tends to dehumanize and devitalize love itself.

A proper reappraisal of St. Augustine's contribution to married personalism depends on our ability to interpret his doctrine of the *bona* in a personalist key and not only, as is so often done, in one that is juridical and that some would describe as merely "institutional." The doctrine of the *bona* is St. Augustine's great legacy in defense of the goodness of marriage. Contemporary Christian thought, in response to current pessimism about matrimony, should feel challenged to explore and expound in fuller measure the human content and appeal of these values.

St. Augustine and Conjugal Love

What place does conjugal love occupy in St. Augustine's thinking? He was no doubt too much a man of his times to give the same importance to the affective or sentimental aspects of love, as we tend to do today. For him the truth of conjugal love is to be found not in the area of feelings, but within the *ordo caritatis* where the emphasis is placed on faithful companionship independently of the variations or the possible waning of passionate or affective love. For him too the essence of the marital covenant lies in reciprocal self-

---

that marriage is a good" (P. Langa, "Equilibrio agustiniano entre matrimonio y virginidad," *Revista Agustiniana* 21 [1980]: 110).

giving.[28] But the quality of this mutual donation is put to the test by time, and there is no doubt that St. Augustine was more impressed with the goodness of the faithful marriage weighed down by years, the *bonum et annosum coniugium*—than with the romantic but untested conjugal encounter of youth. What a turn of Latin phrasing Augustine might have given to the saying that a young couple in love is a pleasing sight, but an old couple in love is a sight to marvel at.

Fidelity is the fruit of authentic marital affection. Love, like every virtue, is difficult and suffers moments of temptation. The faithful and chaste spouse is superior in her love to the one who lends herself to fleeting affairs. "And in what is the wife superior if not through her love for fidelity, her love for marriage, her more sincere and chaste love [towards her husband]"?[29] Her love is more genuine because it is more faithful.

In his great catechesis on human love, Pope John Paul II presented a personalist analysis of sexuality and marriage, seeing them as a divinely instituted means to help man overcome his "original solitude." In connection with this, it is interesting to note that in a work as early and important as *De bono coniugali*, Augustine begins his exposition by emphasizing the essential companionship of marriage. He too sees the goodness of the conjugal union evidenced in its being the first natural fulfillment of the human need for sociability. In the opening chapter, Augustine clearly sets forth the broad human foundation on which he grounds the goodness of marriage: man's sociable nature and the natural value that man finds in friendship. It is only after laying down that human sociability finds its first natural expression precisely in marital society

28. See Pope Gregory IX, *Decretales*: "They both mutually give themselves one to the other, and mutually accept each other [mutuo se concedunt unus alii, et mutuo se suscipiunt]" (lib. IV, 4, 1 [*Augustinus de fide pactionis et consensus*] [1234]).

29. "Ubi vincit uxor, nisi affectu fidei, affectu coniugii, affectu sincerioris castiorisque caritatis"? (*Sermones* 51:16, 26).

that he goes on to indicate what it is that distinguishes the married relationship—that is, the fact that it involves a man and a woman not in any mere ordinary friendship, but in a procreative society.[30] We have already noted above passages of the same work which can rightly be termed personalist. Let us also recall the terms in which, in *De civitate Dei*, he envisions marriage in Eden: "A faithful covenant between the spouses based on love and mutual respect."[31]

St. Augustine and Conjugal Sexuality

This brings us to a second aspect of St. Augustine's thought. Although the goodness of marriage has been questioned and relativized in modern times, the goodness of sex seems paradoxically to have become unquestioned and absolutized. Even to suggest, however qualifiedly, that "there is something wrong with sex" is likely to provoke an outburst of wrath at what is considered a revived Puritanism. And if I were to suggest (which I do) that St. Augustine holds there *is* something wrong with sex, the reply would surely be immediate: "See, you grant the truth of the criticism about St. Augustine's negative attitude toward sex, which is clearly a vestige remaining from his Manichean phase."

Was St. Augustine's view of sexuality—especially in its conjugal context—negative, or does it contain insights that can provide a more positive understanding of how sexuality is meant to be, and to remain, an expression of married love?

St. Augustine's extraordinary sense of the holiness and majesty of God undoubtedly intensified his sense of man's sinfulness. If we feel that he exaggerates the latter, perhaps it is because we

30. "Sociale quiddam est humana natura, magnumque habet et naturale bonum vim quoque amicitiae. . . . Prima itaque naturalis humanae societatis copula vir et uxor est. . . . Consequens est connexio societatis in filiis, qui unus honestus fructus est, non coniunctionis maris et feminae, sed concubitus. Poterat esse in utroque sexu, etiam sine tali commixtione . . . amicalis quaedam et germana coniunctio" (*De bono coniugali*, 1).

31. "Inter se coniugum fida ex honesto amore societas" (XIV, 26).

are deficient in the former. Further, if Augustine sees and weighs man's littleness, he does so precisely in the light of God's infinite majesty and redemptive mercy. This explains why he is not pessimistic about man's possibilities and dignity—rather, just the contrary. This optimism of St. Augustine about man's calling and destiny—about the ultimate value of human life—explains how his thought has attracted and inspired countless numbers over the centuries. His optimism is all the more attractive and evident to those who understand the realism upon which it is so firmly grounded.

Augustinian realism has a special application to human sexuality. Here we repeat that any accusation of pessimism in the Catholic Augustine is firmly to be rejected. His struggle with his own sexual impulses was long and difficult, and such a sensitive personality combined with a Manichean background must have witnessed many temptations to lapse into pessimism. Yet Augustine was victorious in his struggle to control his sexuality, and to my mind he also conquered any pessimistic view of sexuality in general. He was not pessimistic about sex but was not optimistic either. Rather, he was realistic.

Here distinctions must be drawn and followed with the greatest care. In the first place it should be noted that it was not in his polemics against the Manicheans that Augustine maintained there is something wrong with our sexual instinct (the Manicheans thought it not so much wrong as unimportant), but in his later controversy with the Pelagians. Precisely because in the maturity of his thought he considered sexuality to be God-given and noble, he felt it so important to point out any negative element that may have affected sexuality. Catholic thought (largely under the influence of St. Augustine) has always defended the proposition that "sex is good." But to hold that "sex is good" is not the same as to affirm "there is nothing wrong with sex." The Catholic church defends the first proposition and rejects the second. Its overall view of creation in general and of man in particular is that, as God's work, both are good. But the church views the good work of creation as threatened by evil, often from within, and especially by the evil which man himself can freely design or choose. Between the goodness of creation and the need for redemption lies the reality of the fall of man. So the church, which holds that human nature is good, also holds that something has gone wrong with human nature, and that if this malady is not understood, taken into account, treated, and (if possible) remedied, it can frustrate and destroy man's development as man. Further, while this "something wrong" makes its presence felt in all aspects of human activity, it especially troubles the area of sexuality.

This "something gone wrong" is a strange tendency of man to center on created things, especially on himself, as if his happiness and fulfillment were to be found in created and perishable goods, and not in the uncreated good.[32] St. John, warning against the power of this potentially fatal attraction, distinguishes its three aspects: "The lust of the flesh, the lust of the eyes, and the pride of life" (1 Jn 2:16). St. Augustine is acutely aware of all three, but it is his understanding of the lust or concupiscence of the flesh ("*concupiscentia carnis*") that concerns us in particular. For it is indeed true that his thinking on this concept has had a profound effect in providing to Catholic understanding of sexuality its powerful and demanding realism.

Just as Augustine fought the negative views of the Manicheans, so he resisted the overly optimistic views of the Pelagians in a controversy where his purpose was to defend a Christian understanding of sexual morality against a naturalistic exaltation of sex. The Pelagian controversy forced Augustine to expound the de-

32. Aquinas, *Summa Theologiae* I–II, q. 82, a. 3.

fects of the *present* condition of sexuality. He has great difficulty in accepting that sexuality, as we now experience it, corresponds to the order created by God. He finds a disorder—that of concupiscence—in sexuality, and regards it, not as instituted by God, but as the result of sin.[33] This controversy and its subsequent effect on Catholic morality hinges on a proper understanding of the notion of concupiscence, and it is vital to understand the quite different positions sustained by the Pelagians and by Augustine. The former maintained that concupiscence is a natural good[34] and is evil only in its excesses,[35] while Augustine holds that it is in itself a disease or disorder which accompanies us as a consequence of original sin.[36]

The present imperfections of man are seen by Augustine in the light of the perfection of man's first creation and of his eternal destiny. The concupiscence of the flesh is but one aspect of that broader concupiscence—an unwanted law perverting man's values—experienced by Augustine (and all men). In his teaching on concupiscence, St. Augustine was of course following in the footsteps of St. Paul, who so bitterly complained to the Romans about the sin-engendered concupiscence which held him captive, and who so forcefully expressed his longings to be freed from the law of sin that dwelt in his members.[37] St. Augustine, like St. Paul, expresses neither Manicheism nor pessimism but revealed and realistic doctrine when he affirms that "our body weighs heavily on our soul."[38] Again like Paul, he looks for deliverance. He particularly senses that sexual nature is out of harmony with its original plan, and he longs for that situation of paradise where sexual desire

33. See *Contra duas epistolas Pelagianorum*, I, 17, 34 [hereafter "*Contra Pelag.*"]; *Contra Julianum* IV, 13, 63.

34. *Contra Julianum* IV, 21.   35. *De nupt. et conc.*, 2, 19, 34.

36. Ibid., 2, 32, 55; *Contra Jul. Pel.* V, 39.

37. Rom 7:8 and 7:23–24; Gal 5:17.

38. "Ubi quid intellecturi sumus, nisi quia corpus quod corrumpitur, aggravat animam?" (*De nupt. et conc.*, 1, 31, 35; cf. Rom 7:24).

and activity would not have been subject to libido,[39] and where
it would have been possible to engage in marital relations without the tendency of instinct to dominate over mind and will and
love. Augustine continually repeats that concupiscence is an evil in
itself, an evil nevertheless that has a good use—one only—which
is within marriage, in married intercourse directed to procreation.
He maintains that an evil is present in that licit use of marriage,
an evil which chaste spouses use well.[40] These are strong opinions
about concupiscence, and certainly they lend themselves to be
wrongly understood if they are taken out of context and above all
if there is a lack of proper understanding of what concupiscence
consists in, why it is evil, and how it is to be distinguished from a
healthy sexual and married instinct.

Augustine and Sexual Pleasure

In the first place, one must acknowledge that some looser
expressions found in St. Augustine's statements regarding concupiscence seem to imply that its simple presence involves a certain
personal guilt. This is not the case. What he holds is that concupiscence can only be regarded as sinful inasmuch as it comes from sin
and induces to sin, but it is not a sin in itself. This is clear enough
from the terms in which he defines it: concupiscence is a certain
bad inclination or quality.[41] This is clear too from the various texts
where Augustine says that all sins are forgiven in baptism, concupiscence however remaining after its reception.[42] This is what
Thomas Aquinas teaches with his usual precision: concupiscence

39. Ibid., I, 27, 30; *De civitate Dei*, XIV, 23, 24; *Contra Jul. Pel.*, III, 25, 57; and *De Genesi ad Litteram* [hereafter "*De Gen. ad litt.*"], IX, 10, 18.
40. *De nupt. et conc.*, 2, 21, 36; *De peccato originali*, 37, 42; *De continentia*, 12, 27; and *Contra Jul. Pel.*, V, 16.
41. "Affectio est quaedam malae qualitatis" (*De nupt. et conc.*, 1, 28, 67).
42. *De peccatorum meritis*, 2, 4, 4 and 2, 28, 45; *De nupt. et conc.*, 1, 23, 25; *Contra Pelag.*, 1, 13, 27 [hereafter "*Contra Pelag.*"]; *Contra Julianum* 2, 9, 22; and *Imperfectum opus contra Julianum* [hereafter "*Imperfectum*"], 2, 226.

remains in us as a defect (*poena*) that accompanies our fallen state, and not as a moral fault (*culpa*).[43]

However, one must address the question of whether, in Augustine's mind, concupiscence is simply to be identified with sexual pleasure in itself; and, concretely in marriage, with that pleasure which accompanies the physical union between the bodies of the spouses when they engage in the marital act. Here we need to think things out gradually. First, let us not forget that the thought of great minds is in constant ferment; it progresses and matures, and at times it even changes radically, above all (something quite logical) in the case of persons who have experienced a drastic conversion, passing from one concept of life and of human nature itself to another that is totally different. Let us think of St. Paul, for example, and of so many notable figures of more modern times, especially since the mid-nineteenth century.

There is no more remarkable example of this than St. Augustine. For that reason, if we want to thoroughly appreciate his concept of concupiscence (which was certainly negative), it is necessary to ponder mainly the writings of his final years—the period of his maturity, if we can express it so—in which he studies and thoroughly analyzes the nature of concupiscence: the period of his anti-Pelagian writings. Here what especially stands out is his long debate with the Pelagian bishop, Julian of Eclanum, who in some sense deserves our gratitude because the dialectic between the two gave rise to Augustine's work, *De nuptiis et concupiscentia*, where his concern to clarify certain delicate aspects of his thought helps us immensely to grasp that thought with greater precision.

Julian had twisted Augustine's strictures on concupiscence, as though they implied a negative judgment on the attraction between the sexes or on sexual pleasure in conjugal relations. Augustine vig-

43. "Non est malum culpae, sed poena tantum, quae est inobedientia concupiscentiae ad rationem" (*Suppl.*, q. 49, a. 4, ad 2).

orously denies Julian's charges that he had ever condemned sexual differences or union or fruitfulness: "He asks us whether it is the difference in the sexes which we ascribe to the devil, or their union, or their very fruitfulness. We answer, then, nothing of these qualities, inasmuch as sexual differentiation pertains to the bodies of the parents, while the union of the two pertains to the procreation of children, and their fruitfulness to the blessing pronounced on the marriage institution. But *all these things are of God.*"[44] And in a later passage he repeats that he has nothing to object to Julian's praise (by which he seeks to lead the thoughtless astray) "of the works of God; that is, his praising of human nature, of human seed, of marriage, of sexual intercourse, of the fruits of matrimony: *which are all of them good things.*"[45] When Augustine condemns concupiscence, therefore, he condemns none of these divinely-given values of sexual nature. Now a further point needs to be noted. Augustine makes it clear that what he regards as the disorder of concupiscence is also not synonymous with sexual *pleasure*.

This point needs to be especially stressed because, given the vigor with which Augustine criticizes the yielding to concupiscence, a superficial reader might easily conclude that he is criticizing the actual seeking of pleasure itself in marital intercourse. A proper reading shows that this is not so. Already in *De bono coniugali*, in a passage where he compares nourishment and generation, he had insisted that sexual pleasure, sought temperately and rationally, is not and cannot be termed concupiscence.[46] Elsewhere he contrasts the lawful pleasure of the conjugal embrace with the unlawful pleasure of fornication.[47] In his debate with Julian, he

44. *De nupt. et conc.*, 2, 14, 21.   45. Ibid., 2, 26, 42.
46. "Et utrumque non est sine delectatione carnali, quae tamen modificata, et temperantia refrenante in usum naturalem redacta, libido esse non potest" (*De bono coniugali*, 16, 18).
47. "Delectant coniugales amplexus: delectant etiam meretricum. Hoc licite, illud illicite" (*Sermones* 159, 2, 2).

makes it clear that it is not pleasure which he criticizes, "because pleasure can also be honorable,"[48] and he is content with Julian's admission that pleasure can be both licit and illicit.[49]

One particularly interesting passage shows the methodical way in which Augustine deals with his adversary, declining to let him score debating points by reading ideas into Augustine's writings which he has not put there, or by accusing him of things he has not said. He will go along with Julian when the latter lists the God-made and therefore praiseworthy aspects of the sexual relationship, but he will not let himself be drawn further. When Julian affirms (as if Augustine had denied) that marital intercourse, with its intimacy, with its pleasure, and with its semination, are from God and therefore in their own way to be praised, Augustine rapidly ticks off these "non-arguments" which are irrelevant to their debate since Augustine is in full agreement that these are good things given by God. But, he goes on, Julian, who says all of this (making points which I had never called into question), does not mention precisely what I say is bad in intercourse: carnal concupiscence or *libido*.[50] His reserve, then, is not aimed at the goodness of marriage, nor at the intimacy and pleasure of conjugal intercourse, but rather the force and effect of *libido* or the *concupiscentia carnis* which, he says, "is not a good that proceeds from the essence of marriage, but an evil which is the accident of original sin."[51]

---

48. *De nupt. et conc.*, 2, 9, 21.

49. "Satis est nobis, quod confitearis aliam esse illicitam, aliam licitam voluptatem. Ac per hoc mala est concupiscentia quae indifferenter utrumque appetit, nisi ab illicita voluptate licita voluptate frenetur" (*Contra Jul. Pel.* 6, 16, 50; and 4, 2, 7).

50. The passage reads: "'Ista,' inquit, 'corporum commixtio, cum calore, cum voluptate, cum semine, a Deo facta, et pro suo modo laudabilis approbatur' . . . Dixit 'cum calore'; dixit 'cum voluptate'; dixit 'cum semine': non tamen dicere ausus est, cum libidine: quare, nisi quia nominare erubescit, quam laudare non erubescit?" (*De nupt. et conc.*, 2, 12, 25). For the evolution of Augustine's thought on concupiscence and libido, see Schmitt, "Le mariage chrétien," 94–105.

51. *De nupt. et conc.*, 1, 17, 19.

Concupiscence in Marriage

What then, for Augustine, is carnal concupiscence, if it is not the pleasure of sexual intercourse?[52] It is that "disobedience of the flesh" as a result of which the human will "has lost all proper command for itself over its own members,"[53] "that carnal appetite which impels man to seek feelings because of the pleasure they give, *whether the spirit opposes or consents to this.*"[54] It is that disordered aspect of sexual desire which breaks away from man's will and from the rational ordering of the sex appetite, thus making him often experience sexual desire when satisfaction of that desire is either impossible or illicit, blurring his moral sense and inspiring actions that his mind reproves, that are to be judged *non concupiscendo, sed intelligendo.*[55] In a word, concupiscence is the compelling tendency to seek pleasure in a sidetracking of both reason and will.

We would repeat that, in dealing with our present subject, it is necessary to define terms with the greatest possible precision. In our opinion, it seems more accurate to describe sexual concupiscence as "a lack of control on the part of the intellect and the will over the movements of the sexual organs"[56] than simply as "the passionate, uncontrolled element in sexuality."[57] Man's passions form part of his nature in its original state. It is not the passionate, but the uncontrolled, element that characterizes concupiscence.

One would expect few to quarrel with Augustine if he had illustrated the presence of concupiscence or lust by pointing to such phenomena as fornication or adultery. But we cannot and should

52. This presumes that it is also not the *rational* desire for pleasure.
53. *De nupt. et conc.*, 1, 6, 7; and *De Gen. ad litt.*, 9, 10, 16.
54. *Contra Jul. Pel.*, 4, 14, 65.
55. *Imperfectum*, 4, 69.
56. Schmitt, "Le mariage chrétien," 95.
57. Gerald Bonner, *St. Augustine of Hippo* (Norwich: Canterbury Press, 1986), 375.

not want to pass over the fact that he speaks of concupiscence within marriage itself, in the exercise of conjugal relations. One of his frequently repeated ideas is that even in the lawful use of marriage there is an *evil* present, an evil which chaste spouses use well.[58] For some people this idea alone justifies the charge against Augustine of a negative and Manichean approach to sex. Yet I think that his position can be shown not only to be truly Christian but to contain deep insights for the guidance of the married and the single.

Part of Augustine's argument is that no one is ashamed of what is totally good,[59] and he uses this point to show that some element of disorder accompanies the marriage act, in both its preparation and its consummation. He argues that, even though people think it fitting to perform their upright actions in the broad light of day, this is not so with the conjugal act, which—although upright—spouses would be ashamed to perform in public: "Why so, if not because that which is by nature fitting and decent, is so done as to be accompanied with a shame-begetting penalty of sin?"[60] Why is it that normal married couples, who are not ashamed to give public expression to their mutual affection by means of a glance or a smile, would nevertheless be embarrassed to perform the marital act before others, even (once again the example is Augustine's) before their own children?

The explanation no doubt lies partly in the imperious nature of the sexual urge, as a result of which an ambivalent element easily enters even into marital sexuality. The ambiguity appears in the very marriage act itself inasmuch as what should be wholly an act of love may be merely an act of selfishness. What should be the greatest physical expression of self-giving and dedication to an-

58. *De nupt. et conc.*, 2, 21, 36; *De peccato originali*, 37, 42; *De continentia*, 12, 27; *Contra Jul. Pel.*, 5, 16; etc. See Aquinas, *Suppl.*, q. 41, a. 3, ad 4.

59. "Cum debeat neminem pudere quod bonum est" (*De nupt. et conc.*, 2, 21, 36).

60. *De civitate Dei*, 14, 18; and *Contra Pelag.*, 1, 16, 33.

other—filled therefore with gentleness and consideration—can be reduced to an essentially selfish act, intent on satisfying a powerful urge to that pleasure which resides in the mere physical possession of the other. So it should be clear that, even within marriage, seeking to satisfy one's concupiscence in a self-seeking way (and therefore without genuine love), with the intention of *using* one's spouse as an object to be subjected to one's carnal longings and without the desire to give oneself lovingly to him or her, constitutes an offense against the essence of marital respect and self-donation.

Spouses who sincerely love each other are aware of this element in their relationship which requires purification.[61] They sense the need to temper or restrain the force drawing them together in a way that they can be united in an act of true mutual giving and not one of mere simultaneous taking. Their intimacy is therefore not something to which they can too lightly abandon themselves, for they are put to the test in it, at least before each other's eyes.[62] It is natural that they do not want that test to be subject to the scrutiny of others.

A further point is that the sexual urge, besides being imperious, tends to be indiscriminate. It easily disconnects itself from

---

61. That there is something to purify in marital sexuality is expressly recalled by the Second Vatican Council when it speaks of how the Lord has "healed [*sanare*], perfected and elevated" conjugal love, also in its physical expressions (GS, no. 49; see FC, no. 3). One should recall again the strong statements in CCC (in the section entitled "Marriage under the regime of sin"): "Every man experiences evil around him and within himself. This experience makes itself felt in the relationships between man and woman. Their union has always been threatened by discord, a spirit of domination, infidelity, jealousy, and conflicts that can escalate into hatred and separation" (no. 1606). "According to faith the disorder we notice so painfully does not stem from the *nature* of man and woman, nor from the nature of their relations, but from *sin*. As a break with God, the first sin had for its first consequence the rupture of the original communion between man and woman. Their relations were distorted by mutual recriminations; their mutual attraction, the Creator's own gift, changed into a relationship of domination and lust" (no. 1607).

62. A test that Pope John Paul II does not hesitate to describe as "the test of life and death" (Audience of June 27, 1984; TB, 376).

love and draws a person in a direction that love cannot or ought not to go. Such is the case, for instance, of the single person who feels a powerful attraction towards the husband or wife of a friend. The fact of marrying does not necessarily eliminate these difficulties. A married person too can be suddenly beset by an unwanted and perhaps apparently uncontrollable sexual desire for a third person. Within married life itself, as between husband and wife, desire may come at a moment when it cannot be lovingly satisfied, or go in a direction which may not be properly followed. The husband who cares for his wife will at times find himself drawn into this conflict. He realizes that his wife perhaps does not want intercourse, and yet he does: or, more accurately, his instinct does. He would wish to have his sexual nature readily obedient to the call of his will, to the control of reason, yet finds that his instinct does not easily obey. He has to master it. This difficulty which he experiences, this "struggle between will and libido,"[63] this threatening presence (even within marriage) of sexual selfishness constitutes the evil of concupiscence which, according to Augustine, married people must learn to use well.

Conjugal Chastity

This disorder of concupiscence, which in our present state accompanies the goodness of marriage, is redeemed by the virtue of chastity. Here Augustine's thought can be condensed in a single phrase, where he distinguishes "the goodness of marriage from the evil of carnal concupiscence, which is well used by conjugal chastity."[64] What Augustine means by married chastity emerges from his commentary on the Genesis account of Adam and Eve's behavior before and after the fall. Before the fall, they were naked and yet felt no shame (Gen 2:25) "not because they could not see, but

63. *De civitate Dei*, 14, 23, 3.
64. *De nupt. et conc.*, 2, Preface; *Imperfectum*, Preface.

because they felt nothing in their members to make them ashamed of what they saw."[65] In that state of integrated nature, Adam and Eve sensed nothing disordered—no element of selfishness—in the conjugal attraction between them. Not mere instinct, but their mind and will, would have determined the occasions of having marital relations, which would have corresponded fully and effortlessly to their own sense of mutual donation in the exercise of their generative power. "If there had been no sin, man would have been begotten by means of the organs of generation, not less obedient than his other members to a quiet and normal will."[66]

Augustine dwells on our first parents' reaction when, after sinning, they discovered that sexual desire seemed to have broken loose from conjugality: a sense of shame made them cover their members, and they clothed themselves. It is important to bear in mind that this shame was just between the two of them: who, after all, were husband and wife, and were alone. It was precisely into their mutual relationship that shame had entered. They were not ashamed to be husband and wife, nor to express their conjugal affection, but they were ashamed at a new element that threatened the purity which they had experienced in their original relationship.

Here we see both the effect of concupiscence and the natural reaction to it. Its effect is to make man and woman become too immediately absorbed with the exterior physical aspects and attraction of sex, preventing them from reaching, "seeing," and understanding the inner meaning and real substance and value of sexual differences and complementarity. Our first parents had that deeper and fuller vision in their state of original creation, and so could look with undisturbed joy on one another's nakedness without having sexual attraction or sexual understanding—sexual en-

65. *De nupt. et conc.*, I, 5, 6.
66. Ibid., 2, 7, 17; 22, 37; and 31, 53.

richment—perturbed by an excessive corporal impact. The covering of their nakedness after the fall was a natural reaction designed to defend the clarity of their vision, their ability to see each other's sexuality in its full "nuptial" meaning and not to run the risk of being blinded by its physical aspect alone.[67]

In the reaction of Adam and Eve we see the *pudicitia coniugalis*: a certain modesty or reserve as between husband and wife born of their vigilance toward what each senses is a tendency not to honor the mystery of their reciprocal sexuality, and not to act according to the laws which their mind discovers in it, that is, a tendency which is a temptation to use, and not to respect, the other. Adam and Eve—the only couple to experience sexuality as it was before the fall—give the first example of married chastity, taking precautions so as to preserve their mutual love from the selfishness of that urge "which is not readily obedient to the will of even chaste-minded husbands and wives."[68] The action of Adam and Eve exemplifies that sense of shame which, given the present state of our nature, is now natural to all men and women.[69] Their action also provides a clear lesson: if married people do not observe a certain modesty or restraint in their conjugal relations, this can undermine the mutual respect that should characterize their love as well as the true freedom with which their reciprocal spousal donation should be made. Not only before their marriage, but also within it, love itself should inspire the spouses to protect and strengthen that freedom. Pope John Paul II refers to "that interior freedom of the gift, which of its nature is explicitly spiritual and

67. See Pope John Paul II, *General Audience*, January 2, 1980 (TB, 57–58).

68. *De nupt. et conc.*, 2, 35, 59.

69. "This expression of chastity, this need for shame is certainly inborn in everyone, and is in some way enjoined by the laws of nature in such a way that even chaste spouses feel some shame in this matter [Hoc pudoris genus, haec erubescendi necessitas certe cum omni homine nascitur, et ipsis quodammodo naturae legibus imperatur, ut in hac re verecundentur etiam ipsa pudica coniugia]" (*Contra Pelag.*, 1, 16, 33).

depends on a person's interior maturity. This freedom presupposes such a capacity of directing one's sensual and emotive reactions as to make self-donation to the other possible, on the basis of mature self-possession."[70]

If modern man does not see that something is wrong—fallen and broken—in the relations between the sexes, he will not see the importance of chastity, the key to sexual salvation. We could express this in another way by saying that whoever values sex more than love will become more and more subject to the dominion of the former, and less and less capable of experiencing and expressing the latter. The exaltation of sex necessarily involves a depreciation of love and, in the long run, the loss of the very capacity for love. There is no one who does not realize this truth deep in his or her heart, and I think there are few who do not in some way long to achieve or recover the capacity of a more human, truer, and purer sexual love. Augustine's cry could well be theirs: "Lord, make me chaste, though not yet,"[71] the cry of a spirit divided between the slavery of the flesh—whose relentless force it at least recognizes—and the longing for a clean love that remains in each person until the end, however depraved he or she may seem to be. One can therefore understand that not only St. Augustine's doctrine but above all his life—narrated with such sincerity in his *Confessions*—continues to be a source of inspiration and hope for those who, in a world inundated by eroticism, come to know it.

Catholic Tradition and the Wrong Use of the Body

Perhaps the closest parallel to the experience of Adam and Eve is that of the teenage boy and girl in whom an initial attraction of idealistic love suddenly becomes aware of the disturbing element

70. *General Audience*, November 7, 1984 (TB, 414); see also in particular his reflections on shame and nakedness in earlier audiences of 1979–80 (TB, 63–117).

71. *Confessionum*, VIII, 7, 17.

of the flesh. They should realize that this new attraction between them is also natural, while at the same time recognizing that not everything about it is good. Just as, at a later stage, the young man and woman preparing to marry can be convinced that not everything is good in the instinct drawing them so powerfully to one another and can remain so convinced even when they recognize the goodness of the union to which it draws them. It is not bad to be drawn to that union; yet it is not good to be drawn to it against one's better judgment.

Most modern "sex education" is in effect trying to instill into young minds the idea that there is no such thing as a good or bad use of sexuality: that all use of the body is in fact indifferent. Augustine, along with the whole Catholic tradition of moral teaching, insists that it is precisely because the body is good that it can be used wrongly. In a characteristic passage, he contrasts the virtuous use of the evil of *libido* (that is, the ordered use of sexuality despite the disorder of concupiscence) by married people, and the sinful misuse of the good of the body by the unchaste.[72] Concupiscence constantly threatens to dominate both the married and the single person; it has, as Augustine says, "to be mastered by the chaste,"[73] and chastity, further, is "a gift of God."[74] Continuous pressure is being exercised on young people today to behave as if it were immodesty, and not modesty, which is natural: as if a man or a woman, a boy or a girl, felt no natural reproach from within at certain ways of talking or dressing or acting, as if passion were never selfish and grasping and in need of being so judged and resisted. All of this can lead, through a progressive dulling of the

72. "Bonum opus est bene uti libidinis malo, quod faciunt coniugati, sicut e contrario malum opus est, male uti corporis bono, quod faciunt impudici" (*Imperfectum*, 5, 12).

73. *De nupt. et conc.*, 2, 35, 59. Aquinas says that continence "involves the resistance of reason to evil concupiscences" (*Summa Theologiae* II–II, q. 155, a. 4).

74. *De bono viduitatis*, 4, 5; *De nupt. et conc.*, 1, 3, 3.

moral sense, to the unnatural and inhuman situation where the atmosphere reigning between the sexes becomes one of suspicion, distrust, or fear, and where lack of respect acts as a powerful inhibitory factor on the growth and maturing of tenderness and love.

In this context, it should be emphasized that awareness of the presence of a selfish element in the realm of sexuality is not the result of formal religious training. On the contrary, it is natural for each person to be aware of this problem,[75] just as it is natural for each one to be aware of "something wrong" with his or her nature, which Christians have traditionally called original sin, and which prompts "desires against which the faithful also have to battle."[76] The church does not accept that it is being negative in urging people to fight against the bad tendencies of fallen nature. This is realism, not negativism or pessimism. It would be pessimism to believe (as Augustine believed for a long time) that it is not possible to win in the fight. The church proclaims that we can win with Christ's help, and cannot win without him.[77] At the other extreme, to say that there is no fight to be fought is unrealistic and a form of Pelagianism.

The faithful readily recognize the truths behind the church's teaching. They may well wish that there were no need to struggle: "There is indeed no Christian seeking holiness who would not wish to free the spirit from the bad desires of the flesh that war against it."[78] But faced with the inevitability of the fight, they welcome positive guidance about the nature of the war which all of us must wage, and about the spiritual means offered to us (prayer and the sacraments, above all) so as not to be defeated in the struggle,

75. F.-J. Thonnard, "La notion de concupiscence en philosophie augustinienne," *Recherches Augustiniennes* 3 (1965): 95.

76. "Desideria, contra quae dimicant et fideles" (*Contra Jul. Pel.*, 2, 3, 5).

77. "I can do all things in him who strengthens me" (Phil 4:13).

78. "Nullus quippe sanctorum est, qui non velit facere ne caro adversus spiritum concupiscat" (*Imperfectum*, 6, 14).

or so as to remedy the defeats that may come, and so ensure eventual victory. It is in this sense that Augustine recalls St. Paul's experience of the temptations of the flesh and the remedy he found for them. Augustine takes up that heartfelt cry, "Wretched man that I am! Who will deliver me from this body of death?" (Rom 7:24)—words of one who fights in anguish but learns to win—and comments that we too need to understand these words and apply them to ourselves because, like Paul, we are involved in the same battle and have the same means to conquer that he had.[79]

Truth in Sexual Knowledge

Space does not permit more than a brief reference to a question that occupied St. Augustine (although from quite a different point of view to the one outlined here): why Adam and Eve did not (as it seems) have intercourse in paradise.[80] It was after the fall that they, to use the biblical term, *knew* each other.[81] Canon law places personal consent at the heart of the constitution of the matrimonial covenant, and insists that no human power can replace this consent (c. 1057). It does not seem necessary to suppose that divine power, God's will, replaced the human consent of Adam and Eve. One can surely say rather that they, knowing they had been created by God to be husband and wife, joyfully accepted and ratified this divine choice. If they did not have intercourse in paradise, however, this was no doubt because they were not yet "ready for it"; they were still, we might say, in a period of courtship, in the process of getting to know each other spousally. The act of intercourse—as involving the fullness of spousal donation, self-revelation, and knowledge—would, at that stage, not yet have made sense.[82]

79. *Contra Julianum*, lib. 6, 23, 70.
80. Aquinas, *Summa Theologiae* I, q. 98, a. 2, ad 2.
81. Gen 4:1.
82. If one supposes (although the position is not free from difficulties) that

The tendency towards sexual union when this "does not make sense" is the practical expression of carnal concupiscence, present in both single and married people. Intercourse for those not joined in marriage makes no sense: they cannot share the spousal knowledge of each other implied in intercourse, which thus becomes a non-sensical act for them. For husband and wife, intercourse makes sense, but it only makes full sense if the act implies a ratification of the procreative orientation of the married relationship. That is why contraceptive marital intercourse again makes no sense, as it "contradicts the *truth* of conjugal love"[83] and is therefore a sign of the domination of carnal concupiscence. That is also why intercourse restricted to the infertile periods without due reason makes little sense; whereas restriction to those periods, with sufficient reason, makes sense, and shows the full dominion of reason over instinct.

The Imperfection of Non-Procreative Marital Intercourse

What should we think of Augustine's frequently expressed opinion that married intercourse is justified only if it is intended to be procreative, and has an element of imperfection or venial fault if carried out solely for pleasure?[84] Augustine was basing himself on 1 Corinthians 7:5–7, where St. Paul, advising spouses not to abstain too long from intercourse, adds that he says this "*secundum veniam*" (the Vulgate says "*secundum indulgentiam*"). Since Paul is evidently speaking of what can be allowed to married couples, one

---

their consent to be husband and wife came at a later time, the matter is clearer still: intercourse—the act of spousal knowledge—when they had not yet consented to be spouses, would have made no sense.

83. Pope John Paul II, Address of September 17, 1983, *Insegnamenti di Giovanni Paolo II*, VI, 2 (1983), 563.

84. *Sermones* 51, 13, 22; see *De bono coniugali*, 6, 6; *De nupt. et conc.*, 1, 14, 16; *Contra Jul. Pel.*, V, 16, 63; *Imperfectum*, I, 68; etc.

can certainly quarrel with Augustine's exegesis that he is imputing a sin to them. It seems to me that, between Paul and Augustine, there is a difference of emphasis but also an indication of the close connection in their thought, as shown in the proposition that for spouses to seek intercourse—consciously disconnected from its procreative finality—is excusable self-seeking (Paul), but is still self-seeking (Augustine), and in this latter sense a venial fault. No doubt it is hard nowadays to subscribe to such a view, which seems to pass over the aspect of human solace ("*humanitatis solatium*") in marriage. Some would reject it out of hand as ignoring the unitive power and function which marital intercourse has in itself. This latter point merits some consideration.

Augustine, if he were alive today (and Aquinas with him), might draw our attention to the essential teaching of *Humanae Vitae*—that the unitive and the procreative meanings of the marriage act are inseparable—and ask us to ponder whether one can actually say that intercourse has a unitive meaning "in *itself*," without reference, that is, to its procreative meaning.[85] If *Humanae Vitae* tells us that the two meanings of the act are inseparable, does it not follow that the exclusion of the procreative meaning—even on the merely intentional level—frustrates the act's unique power to express and effect union? As we will seek to show in the next chapter, the unitive meaning of conjugal intercourse consists precisely in this sharing of reciprocal procreativity; one can find nothing else in it that makes it truly expressive of the uniqueness of the conjugal relationship.

If spouses are not consciously seeking the unitive experience of sharing their complementary procreativity, what else is it but pleasure (divorced from meaning) that they are seeking? I do not maintain that they do wrong in seeking this pleasure; all I suggest

85. See Samek, "Sessualità," 271.

is that the mutual sharing of pleasure alone is a very imperfect substitute for the truly unitive experience. It is only in open-to-life intercourse that each spouse confirms the other as a totally unique person in their life. Married chastity is necessarily based on understanding and respecting the procreative orientation of the conjugal act. Augustine points out how concupiscence is moderated by "parental affection" and says that "a certain gravity or depth of meaning is given to the intense pleasure of intercourse when husband and wife reflect that their union tends to make them father and mother."[86] Once again we see that he has nothing to say against pleasure, but insists on the need to reflect on the *meaning* lying behind an act as pleasurable as intercourse.[87]

St. Augustine's insistence that marital sex is truly rational only if it is open to procreation may seem, at first sight, to have neglected the personalist value of sexuality. A closer analysis, however, should lead us to ask whether there is any true personalism that is anti-procreative, that is, whether sex deliberately separated from its procreative orientation has rational and personalist conjugal meaning. We mentioned earlier the passage of *De bono coniugali* where St. Augustine states that the pleasure of married sexual intercourse, kept by temperance within its "natural use," is not concupiscence.[88] I am convinced that Augustine, if he were alive today, would thoroughly understand and readily accept the analyses that recent magisterium has made of the personalist aspect of the marital union. I am of the opinion moreover that he would enlarge his way of expressing himself so as to admit and maintain that the married act and its concomitant pleasure are realized and

86. *De bono coniugali*, 3, 3.
87. St. Thomas too indicates that if there is a defect in conjugal intercourse this lies not in the intensity of the pleasure accompanying it (which he defends), but in the fact that this pleasure tends not follow the guide of reason; see *Suppl.*, q. 49, a. 4, ad 3.
88. *De bono coniugali*, 16, 18.

experienced according to their natural use when what moves the spouses is the desire to reaffirm their spiritual and interpersonal love through this corporal union, without this necessarily being accompanied on their part by an actual desire to engender offspring.

But Augustine would be firm, as is the contemporary magisterium, that the spouses, when they seek and experience that joyous corporal union, in order to protect themselves against the self-enclosing effect of concupiscence, must respect the integral nature of the married act without denaturalizing it artificially by contraceptive means. With the broader and more mature outlook that time would have given him, I believe that St. Augustine would maintain that the pleasure which accompanies authentic "*affectus maritalis*" is not concupiscence. But he too, like the magisterium, would put a condition *sine qua non*: that it should be a genuine marriage act by which the spouses effectively become *una caro*, which only happens when they do not artificially separate the procreative from the unitive aspect of the act.[89] Perhaps it takes a nature as deep and sensitive as Augustine's to appreciate fully the threat to human dignity and love posed by the loss of rational and spontaneous control over sexual appetite. A constant effort is called for in order to endow the relationship between the sexes— and between husband and wife—with the respect due between persons. Human life, for the single or the married, is disturbed when this effort is not made, and it is in danger of quick deterioration when the effort itself is scorned.

89. "In the sexual relationship between man and woman *two orders meet: the order of nature,* which has as its object reproduction, and *the personal order,* which finds its expression in the love of persons and aims at the fullest realization of that love. We cannot separate the two orders, for each depends upon the other. . . . Sexual relations between a man and a woman in marriage have their full value as a union of persons only when they go with conscious acceptance of the possibility of parenthood" (Karol Wojtyla, *Love and Responsibility* [San Francisco: Ignatius Press, 1993], 226–27).

Realistic Christian Optimism

In any case, without attempting to force the mind and texts of St. Augustine, it could well be asked if there is not a tendency today to leave married people with the impression that nothing in their mutual physical relationship calls for restraint, that their mutual love is in no way endangered by the element of selfishness operative in sexuality. Proper guidance for the married should surely help them to distinguish that aspect of self-seeking which can be present in their intimate relations, and which tends to be more present the more the conjugal act itself is intentionally severed from its procreative orientation. In Augustine's teaching, conjugal chastity keeps spouses on the right side of the *"limes mali,"*[90] the boundary of evil, beyond which lies the area of moral fault. If spouses allow pleasure to matter too much to them, they are in danger of taking rather than of giving and thus of losing the sense of mutual donation. Conjugal chastity will help them keep the truly personalist values of intercourse paramount in their minds—that is, the reaffirmation by its means of their spousal relationship, shown in the sharing of open-to-life procreativity. These higher motives express and preserve their good will. And then, as Augustine says, the good will of the spouses leads and ennobles the ensuing pleasure (which is had and enjoyed), but their good will is not led and dominated by that pleasure.[91]

When we enter into contact with the thought of others, we tend to be most struck by that in it which harmonizes with, or is repugnant to, our own ideas and outlook. This no doubt is why contact with a mind as rich as St. Augustine's produces such diverse

90. *Contra Jul. Pel.*, IV, c. 8, n. 49.

91. "Bona voluntas animi, sequentem ducit, non ducentem sequitur corporis voluptatem" (*De nupt. et conc.*, 1, 12, 13). We could remark here on how the Catholic attitude towards pleasure is boldly brought out by Thomas Aquinas. He teaches that in the state of innocence the pleasure of marital intercourse would have been even greater due to a purer nature endowed with a more sensitive body (*Summa Theologiae* I, q. 98, a. 2, ad 3).

reactions, and why he has been interpreted in such different keys. Regarding sexuality in general, I do not think that Augustine in his mature thought was pessimistic, though I do think that some of his commentators were or are, and that their commentaries as well as their selective quotations from his works reflect this pessimism. Could it be that they are in fact imbued with some of the Manichean tendencies that St. Augustine eventually shook off?

St. Augustine had to combat both Manichean pessimism (in which he had shared) and Pelagian over-optimism. His battle with the Manicheans led to his encomium of marriage, to that analysis of its greatness, its essential values, that has never been superseded. His struggle with the Pelagians fostered his realism about sexuality, also in marriage, and about the need for a constant effort if sexuality is not to become less than human. The contemporary western attitude to marriage ranges from simple loss of esteem, to pessimism, to downright contempt. A return to St. Augustine's analysis of the *bona* provides a broad and solid basis for a reappraisal of matrimony in all its human value and appeal. A precondition for this return is the overcoming of clichés about the *bona* representing an outdated institutional view of marriage, and to understand that, in consonance with the harmony of God's work, St. Augustine's analysis singles out precisely those aspects of the institution that have most human and personalist appeal.

Our contemporaries profess to have a simple view of sex. More than simple, it is simplistic, and ultimately destructive. Positive in appearance, it tends in reality to negativity and pessimism. Pelagian in origin, it ultimately leads to Manicheism. Sex is a much more complex reality which can influence each life for great good or great evil depending on whether its true human significance is understood and whether the power of its instinctual demands is submitted to its rational purpose—that of perpetuating both the love of life and the life of love.

7

The Inseparability of the Unitive and Procreative Aspects of the Conjugal Act

We have entered an age in which it has become commonplace to reject the concept and conviction of a natural, necessary, and sacred connection between sexual intercourse and marriage. The generalized collapse of this conviction, which had characterized civilization after civilization throughout human history, could be considered a central consequence of the "sexual revolution" of the 1960s. But the progressive disassociation of sex and marriage from the 1960s onward is in itself a consequence of the movement in the earlier part of the twentieth century to dissociate sexual intercourse within marriage from any necessary relationship to procreation. Right up to the twentieth century, all religious denominations regarded artificial birth control as a grave perversion of the marital relationship.[1] The first change in this stance came from

1. Many secular psychologists concurred with this assessment. Consider, for instance, the judgment of Sigmund Freud: "It is a characteristic common to all the [sexual] perversions that in them reproduction as an aim is put aside. This is actually the criterion by which we judge whether a sexual activity is perverse—if it departs from reproduction in its aims and pursues the attainment of gratification independently" (*Introductory Lectures on Psychoanalysis* [London: Allen & Unwin, 1952], 266).

the Anglican church, which at the Seventh Lambeth Conference (1930) sanctioned the use of birth control by married couples.[2] This led to the strong reaction of Pope Pius XI who, in his encyclical *Casti Connubii* of the same year, declared that the use of contraceptives in marriage is "against nature and intrinsically wrong."[3] It is our purpose in this chapter to advance the anthropological arguments that show that the use of contraceptives in marriage is both unnatural and hence intrinsically wrong.[4] For reasons that will immediately become evident, our thesis will be developed along personalist lines.

The mid-twentieth century argument for conjugal contraception claimed to speak in personalist terms and can be summarized as follows. The marriage act has two functions: a biological or procreative function, and a spiritual-unitive function. However, while it is only potentially a procreative act, it is actually and in itself a "love act": it truly expresses conjugal love and unites husband and wife. Now, while contraception frustrates the biological or procreative potential of the marital act, it fully respects its spiritual and unitive function, and in fact facilitates it by removing tensions or fears capable of impairing the expression of love in married intercourse. In other words, according to this perspective, while contraception suspends or nullifies the procreative aspect of marital intercourse, it leaves its unitive aspect intact.

Until quite recently, the core argument presented by Catholic moralists against non-natural birth control was that the sexual act is naturally designed for procreation, and therefore it is wrong to

2. One loses perspective unless one bears in mind that up to the 1960s the issue of the use of and access to contraceptives was debated in terms of the their use *within marriage*. Many legislations prohibited such use. It was only in 1965 that the Supreme Court of the United States declared such laws unconstitutional, on the grounds that they violated the "right to marital privacy" (*Griswold v. Connecticut*, 381 U.S. 79 [1965]).

3. AAS 22 (1930): 559.

4. It is scarcely necessary to say that this applies *a fortiori* outside marriage.

frustrate this design because it is wrong to interfere with man's natural functions. Many were not altogether convinced by this argument, which does seem open to rather elementary objections. After all, we do interfere with other natural functions, for instance when we use earplugs or hold our nose, etc., and no one has ever argued that to do so is morally wrong. Why then should it be wrong to interfere for good reasons with the procreational aspect of marital intercourse? The defenders of contraception in any case habitually dismissed this traditional argument as mere "biologism," as an understanding of the marital act that fails to go beyond its biological function or possible biological consequences and thus ignores its spiritual function, that is, its function in signifying and effecting the union of the spouses.

Those advancing this defense of marital contraception—couched in apparently personalist terms—feel that they are on strong and positive ground. If an effective answer is to be offered to this position that shows its radical defectiveness, I suggest that we too need to develop a personalist argument based on a true personalist understanding of sex and marriage. The contraceptive argument outlined is evidently built on an essential thesis: that the procreative and the unitive aspects of the marital act are separable, that the procreative aspect can be nullified without this in any way vitiating the conjugal act or making it less a unique expression of true marital love and union.

This thesis is explicitly rejected by the church. In 1968, the teaching of *Casti Connubii* was reaffirmed by Pope Paul VI in his Encyclical *Humanae Vitae*. There, as the main reason why marital contraception is totally unacceptable to a Christian conscience, he proposes the *"inseparable connection*, established by God . . . between the unitive significance and the procreative significance which are both inherent to the marriage act."[5] While Paul VI af-

5. HV, no. 12.

firmed this inseparable connection, he did not go on to explain why these two aspects of the marital act are in fact so inseparably connected or why this connection is such that it is the very ground of the moral evaluation of the act. I think that reflection matured by the ongoing debate of more than forty years and particularly by the anthropological analyses of John Paul II can enable us to set forth the reasons why this is so, why the connection between the two aspects of the act is in fact such that the destruction of its pro-creative reference necessarily destroys its unitive and personalist significance. In other words, if one deliberately destroys the power of the conjugal act to give life, one necessarily destroys its power to signify love, that is, the love and union proper to marriage.

The Marital Act as Unitive

Why is the act of intercourse called *the* conjugal act? Why is it regarded as the most distinctive expression of marital love and self-giving? Why is this act, which is but a passing and fleeting thing, particularly regarded as an act of union? After all, people in love express their love and desire to be united in many ways: sending letters, exchanging looks or presents, holding hands, etc. What makes the sexual act unique? Why does this act unite the spouses in a way that no other act does? What is it that makes it not just a physical experience but an experience of love?

Is it the special pleasure attaching to it? Is the unitive meaning of the conjugal act contained just in the sensation, however intense, that it can produce? If intercourse unites two people simply because it gives special pleasure, then it would seem that one of the spouses could at times find a more meaningful union outside marriage than within it. It would follow too that sex without pleasure becomes meaningless, and that sex with pleasure, even homosexual sex, becomes meaningful.

This is not the case. The conjugal act may or may not be accompanied by pleasure, but the meaning of the act does not consist in its pleasure. The pleasure provided by marital intercourse may be intense, but it is transient. The *significance* of marital intercourse is also intense, but it is not transient; it lasts.

Why should the marital act be more significant than any other expression of affection between the spouses? Why should it be a more intense expression of love and union? Surely because of what *happens* in that marital encounter, which is not just a touch, not a mere sensation (however intense), but an act of communication, an offer and acceptance, an exchange of something that uniquely represents the gift of oneself and the union of two selves.

Here, of course, it should not be forgotten that while two persons in love want to give themselves to one another, to be united to one another, this desire of theirs remains (humanly speaking) on a purely volitional level. They can bind themselves to one another, but they cannot actually give themselves. The greatest expression of a person's desire to give himself is to give the seed of himself.[6] Giving one's seed is much more significant, and in particular is much more real, than giving one's heart. "I am yours, I give you my heart" remains mere poetry to which no physical gesture can give true body. But, "I am yours; I give you my seed" is not poetry, it is love. It is conjugal love embodied in a unique and privileged physical action whereby intimacy is expressed—"I give you what I give no one"—and union is achieved. "Take what I have to give. United to you, this will be a new *you-and-me*, the fruit of our mutual knowledge and love." In human terms, this is the closest one can come to giving one's self conjugally and to accepting the conjugal self-gift of another, and thus achieving spousal union.[7]

---

6. "Seed" is intended here to refer equally to the male or the female generative element.

7. In a 1974 essay, Karol Wojtyla wrote: "When a person gives himself or herself by making a gift of self or by doing something in which this gift is expressed, a condi-

Therefore, what makes marital intercourse express a unique relationship and act of union is not the sharing of a sensation but the sharing of a power, of an extraordinary creative physical sexual power. In a true conjugal relationship, each spouse says to the other: "I accept you as somebody like no one else in my life. You will be unique to me and I to you. You and you alone will be my husband; you alone will be my wife. The proof of your uniqueness to me is the fact that with you, and with you alone, I am prepared to share this God-given life-oriented power." In this consists the singular quality of intercourse. Other physical expressions of affection do not go beyond the level of a mere gesture; they remain a symbol of the union desired. But the conjugal act is not a mere symbol. In true marital intercourse, something real has been exchanged, with a full gift and acceptance of conjugal masculinity and femininity. And there remains, as witness to their conjugal relationship and the intimacy of their conjugal union, the husband's seed in the wife's body.[8]

If one deliberately nullifies the life-orientation of the conjugal act, *one destroys its essential power to signify union*. Contraception in fact turns the marital act into self-deception or into a lie. "I love you so much that with you, and with you alone, I am ready to share this most unique power." But *what* unique power? In contraceptive sex, no unique power is being shared, except a power to produce pleasure, but then the uniqueness of the marital act is reduced to pleasure; its significance is gone. Contraceptive intercourse is an exercise in meaninglessness. It could perhaps be compared to going through the actions of singing without letting

---

tion of the functioning of the gift, a condition of its realization in an interpersonal relationship or relationships, is the genuine reception of the gift or of the act through which the gift of the person is expressed" (*Person and Community*, 322).

    8. In this way the uniqueness of the decision to marry a particular person is in fact reaffirmed in each marital act. By every single act of true intercourse, each spouse is *confirmed* in the unique status of being husband or wife to the other.

any sound pass one's lips. Love duets, once popular in Hollywood films, depict two lovers who (together and in opera style) express their mutual love in song. How absurd it would be if they were to sing *silent* duets: going through the motions of singing, but not allowing their vocal chords to produce an intelligible sound. Rather, such duets would create meaningless reverberations, a flurry of movement signifying nothing.

Contraceptive intercouse is very much like that. Contraceptive spouses involve each other in bodily movements, but their "body language" is not truly human. They refuse to let their bodies communicate sexually and intelligibly with one another. They go through the motions of a love-song, but there is no song. Contraception is not just an action without meaning; it is an action that contradicts the essential meaning of true conjugal intercourse, which signifies total and unconditional self-donation.[9] Instead of accepting each other totally, contraceptive spouses reject each other in part, because fertility is part of each of them. They reject part of their mutual love: its power to be fruitful.

A couple may say: we do not want our love to be fruitful. But if that is so, there is an inherent contradiction in their trying to express it by means of an act which of its nature implies fruitful love; and there is even more of a contradiction if, when they engage in the act, they deliberately destroy the orientation to fertility from

---

9. "Contraception contradicts the full *truth* of the sexual act as the proper expression of conjugal love" (*Evangelium Vitae*, no. 12); cf. FC, no. 32, and TB, 398. Bonaventure makes an interesting comment (which could also be pertinent to the question of whether a contraceptive act consummates a marriage): "Some have intercourse *according to truth*, some have intercourse *according to appearance*. If they are joined in marriage, then the bond between them is not dissolved, because in their case there was true intercourse and a true bond. If they are joined in appearance, then the bond is dissolved—but this simply means that there was no prior [matrimonial] bond between them at all [aliqui copulantur *secundum veritatem*, aliqui copulantur de facto et *secundum apparentiam*. Si sint matrimonialiter copulati, non solvuntur, quia vere fuit ibi copula et vinculum; si secundum apparentiam, solvuntur; sed illud solvere nihil aliud est quam ostendere prius non fuisse]" (*Sent. Lib. IV*: d. 31, dubium 2).

which derives its capacity to express the uniqueness of their love. In true marital union, husband and wife are meant to experience the vibration of human vitality in its very source.[10] In the case of contraceptive "union," the spouses experience sensation, but it is drained of real vitality. The anti-life effect of contraception does not stop at the "no" which it addresses to the possible fruit of love. It tends to take the very life out of love itself. Within the hard logic of contraception, anti-life becomes anti-love. Its devitalizing effect devastates love, threatening it with early aging and premature death.

At this point it is important to anticipate the possible criticism that our argument so far is based on an incomplete disjunction, inasmuch as it seems to affirm that the conjugal act is either procreative or else merely hedonistic. Spouses using contraception might respond with the sincere affirmation that, in their intercourse, they are not merely seeking pleasure; they are also experiencing and expressing love for one another. Let us clarify our position on this point. We are not affirming that contraceptive spouses may not love each other in their intercourse, nor—insofar as they are not prepared to have such intercourse with a third person— that it does not express a certain uniqueness in their relationship. Our argument is that it does not express *conjugal* uniqueness. Love may somehow be present in their contraceptive relationship, but conjugal love is not expressed by it. Conjugal love may in fact soon find itself threatened by it. Contraceptive spouses are constantly haunted by the suspicion that the act which they share could in-

10. This still remains true even in cases where the spouses are infertile. Their union in such cases, just as the union of a fertile couple during the wife's pregnancy, draws its deepest meaning from the fact that both their conjugal act and the intention behind it are "open to life," even though no life can actually result from the act. It is their basic openness to life which gives the act its meaning and dignity. Just as the absence of this openness is what undermines the dignity and meaning of the act when the spouses, without serious reasons, deliberately limit their marital intercourse to the infertile periods.

deed be, for each of them, a privileged giving of pleasure, but could also be a mere selfish taking of pleasure. It is logical that their love-making be troubled by a sense of falseness or hollowness, for they are attempting to found the uniqueness of the spousal relationship on an act of pleasure that tends ultimately to close one in on oneself. They are refusing to found that relationship on the truly unique, conjugal dimension of loving co-creativity capable, in its vitality, of opening each of them out not merely to one another but to the whole of life and creation.

Sexual Love and Sexual Knowledge

The mutual and exclusive self-donation of the marriage act consists in its being the gift and acceptance of something unique. This is not just the seed (this indeed could be "biologism") but also the fullness of the sexuality of each spouse. It was in the context of its not being good for man to be alone that God made him sexual. He created man in a duality—male and female—with the potential to become a trinity. The differences between the sexes speak therefore of a divine plan of complementarity, of self-completion and self-fulfillment through self-perpetuation. It is not good for man to be alone because man, on his own, cannot fulfill himself; he needs others. He especially needs another: a companion, a spouse. Union with a spouse, giving oneself to a spouse—sexual and marital union in self-donation—are normally a condition of human growth and fulfillment for spouses.

Marriage, then, is a means of fulfillment through union. Husband and wife are united in mutual knowledge and love, a love which is not just spiritual but also bodily; a knowledge supporting their love which is likewise not mere speculative or intellectual knowledge. It is bodily knowledge as well. Their marital love is also meant to be based on carnal knowledge; this is fully human and fully logical. How significant it is that the Bible, in the original

Hebrew, refers to marital intercourse in terms of man and woman "knowing" each other. Adam, Genesis says, knew Eve, his wife (Gen 4:1). What comment can we make on this equivalence which the Bible draws between conjugal intercourse and mutual knowledge? What is the distinctive knowledge that husband and wife communicate to one another? It is the knowledge of each other's integral human condition as spouse. Each "discloses" a most intimate secret to the other: the secret of his or her personal sexuality. Each is revealed to the other truly as spouse and comes to know the other in the uniqueness of that spousal self-revelation and self-gift. Each lets himself or herself be known by the other and surrenders to the other, precisely as husband or wife.

Nothing can undermine a marriage so much as the refusal to fully know and accept one's spouse or to let oneself be fully known by him or her. Marriage is constantly endangered by the possibility of one spouse holding something back from the other; keeping some knowledge to oneself that he or she does not want the other to possess.[11] This can occur on all levels of interpersonal communication: physical as well as spiritual. In many modern marriages, there *is* something in the spouses and between the spouses, that each does not want to know, does not want to face up to, or wants to avoid—namely, their sexuality. As a result, since they will not allow each other full mutual carnal knowledge, they do not truly know each other sexually, humanly, or spousally. This places their married love under a tremendous existential tension that can tear it apart.

In true marital intercourse each spouse renounces protective self-possession so as to fully possess and be fully possessed by the other. This fullness of true sexual giving and possession is only

---

11. Obviously we are not referring here to those occasions in which, out of justice to a third party, one of the spouses is under an *obligation* to observe some secret, e.g., of a professional nature. Fulfillment of such an obligation is in no way a violation of the rights of married intimacy.

achieved in marital intercourse open to life. Only in procreative intercourse do the spouses exchange true "knowledge" of one another, speak humanly and intelligibly to one another, and truly reveal themselves to one another in their full human actuality and potential. Each offers and accepts full spousal knowledge of the other. In the bodily language of intercourse, each spouse utters a "word" of love that is both a self-expression, an image of each one's self, as well as an expression of his or her longing for the other. These two words of love meet and are fused into one concept. As this new unified word of love takes on flesh, God shapes it into a person, the child, which is the incarnation of the husband's and wife's sexual knowledge of one another and sexual love for one another.

Contracepting spouses will not let the "word" which their sexuality longs to utter unite in one concept and take on flesh. They will not even truly speak the word to each other. They remain humanly impotent in the face of love, sexually dumb and carnally speechless before one another. Sexual love is a love of the whole person, body and spirit. Love is falsified if body and spirit do not "say" the same thing. This happens in contraception. The bodily act speaks of a presence of love or of a degree of love that is denied by the spirit. The body says, "I love you totally," whereas the spirit says, "I love you reservedly." The body says, "I seek you," whereas the spirit says, "I will not accept you, not all of you." Contraceptive intercourse is disfigured body language; it expresses a rejection of the other. By it, each says: "I do not want to know you as my husband or my wife; I am not prepared to recognize you as my spouse. I want something from you, but not your sexuality; and if I have something to give to you, something I will let you take, it is not my sexuality."[12]

12. If it is not sexuality that each spouse in contraceptive intercourse gives to or takes from the other, what does each one in fact actually take or give? In what might be

Here we can develop a point mentioned earlier. The negation enacted by a contraceptive couple is not directed just towards children, or life, or the world. They address a negation directly towards one another. "I prefer a sterile you," is equivalent to saying, "I do not want all that you offer me. I have calculated the measure of my love, and it is not big enough for that; it is not able to accept all of you. I want a "you" that is cut down to the limited measure of my love." The fact that both spouses may concur in accepting a cut-rate version of each other does not save their love or their lives—or their possibilities of happiness—from the effects of such radical human and sexual devaluation.

Normal conjugal intercourse fully asserts masculinity and femininity. The man asserts himself as man and husband, and the woman equally asserts herself as woman and wife. In contraceptive intercourse, only a deficient sexuality is asserted. In the truest sense sexuality is not asserted at all. Contraception represents such a refusal to let oneself be known that it simply is not real carnal knowledge. A deep human truth underlies the theological and juridical principle that a contraceptive sexual act does not consummate marriage. Contraceptive intercourse, then, is not real sexual intercourse at all. That is why the disjunctives offered by this whole matter are insufficiently expressed by saying that if intercourse is contraceptive, it is merely hedonistic. This may or may not be true. What is true at a much deeper level is that if intercourse is contraceptive, then it is not sexual. In contraception there is an "intercourse" of sensation, but no real sexual knowledge or sexual love, no true sexual revelation of self or sexual communication of self or sexual gift of self. The choice of contraception is in fact the rejec-

---

termed the better cases, it is a form of love divorced from sexuality. In other cases, it is merely pleasure, also—be it noted—divorced from sexuality. In one case or the other, contraceptive spouses always deny themselves sexuality. Their marriage, deprived of a true sexual relationship, suffers in consequence.

176 ASPECTS OF THE CONJUGAL ACT

tion of sexuality. The distortion of the sexual instinct from which modern society seems to suffer represents not so much an excess of sex, as a lack of true human sexuality. True conjugal intercourse unites; contraception separates. It not only separates sex from procreation, but also separates sex from love. It separates pleasure from meaning, and body from mind. Ultimately it separates wife from husband and husband from wife.

Contraceptive couples who stop to reflect realize that their marriage is troubled by some deep malaise. The alienations they are experiencing are a sign as well as a consequence of the grave violation of the moral order involved in contraception. Only a resolute effort to break with contraceptive practices can heal the sickness affecting their married life. This is why the teaching of *Humanae Vitae* as well as subsequent papal magisterium on the matter, far from being a blind adherence to an outdated position, represent a totally clear-sighted defense of the innate dignity and true meaning of human and spousal sexuality.

Why Does Only Procreative Sex Fulfill?

Our argument thus far is that contraceptive marital sex does not achieve any true personalist end. It does not bring about self-fulfillment in marriage, but rather prevents and frustrates it. However, one may still ask: does it follow that open-to-life marital sex alone leads to the self-fulfillment of the spouses? I think it does, and the reason lies in the very nature of love. Love is creative. God's love (if we may put it this way) "drove" him to create. Man's love, made in the image of God's, is also meant to create. If it deliberately does not do so, it frustrates itself. Love between two persons makes them want to do things together. While this is true of friendship in general, it has a singular application to the love between spouses. A couple truly in love want to do things together; if possible, they want to do something "original" together. Nothing is more original to a couple in love than their child: the image and fruit of their love and their union. That is why the "marital thing" is to have children; and other things, as substitutes, do not satisfy conjugal love. Procreative intercourse fulfills also because only in such intercourse are the spouses open to all the possibilities of their mutual love, ready to be enriched and fulfilled not only by what it offers to them, but also by what it demands of them.[13]

Further, procreative intercourse fulfills because it expresses the human person's desire for self-perpetuation.[14] It does not contradict this desire as contraception does. When a normal married couple have a child, they pass their child joyfully to each other. If their child dies, there is no joy; rather, there are tears. Spouses should weep over a contraceptive act: a barren, desolate act which rejects the life that is meant to keep love alive, and would kill the life their love naturally seeks to give origin to. There may be physical satisfaction, but there can be no joy in passing a dead seed, or in passing a living seed only to kill it. The vitality of sensation in sexual intercourse should correspond to a vitality of meaning (remembering, as we have said, that sensation is not meaning). The very explosiveness of sexual pleasure suggests the greatness of the creativity of sex. In each conjugal act, there should be something of the magnificence—of the scope and power—of Michelangelo's depiction of creation in the Sistine Chapel. It is the dynamism not just of a sensation, but of an event: of something that happens, of

13. "A 'communio personarum' always requires the affirmation of parenthood in conjugal intercourse—at least potential parenthood. The spouses in their sexual relations must bring to this act both an awareness and a readiness that expresses itself as 'I could become a father,' 'I could become a mother.' *The rejection of such an awareness and readiness endangers their interpersonal relationship*, their 'communio personarum'" (Karol Wojtyla, *Person and Community*, 331; emphasis added).

14. Pope John Paul II, in the context of the "one flesh" of Gen 2:24, says: "In this way a great creative perspective is opened. It is precisely the perspective of man's existence, which is continually renewed by means of procreation, or, we could say, self-reproduction" (TB, 74).

a communication of life. A lack of true sexual awareness character-izes the act if the intensity of pleasure does not serve to stir a fully conscious understanding of the greatness of the conjugal experi-ence. I am committing myself, my creative life-giving power, not just to another person but to the whole of creation: to history, to mankind, to the purposes and design of God.[15] In each act of con-jugal union, teaches Pope John Paul II, "there is renewed, in a way, the mystery of creation in all its original depth and vital power."[16]

The question that we are considering is of course tremendous-ly complicated by the very strength of the sexual instinct. Never-theless, the strength of this instinct should itself point toward an adequate understanding of sexuality. Basic common sense says that the power of the sexual urge must correspond to deep human aspi-rations or needs. It has been traditional to explain the sexual urge in cosmic or demographic terms: just as we have an appetite for food to maintain the life of the individual, so we have a sexual ap-petite to maintain the life of the species. This explanation makes sense, as far as it goes, but it clearly does not go far enough. The strength of the sexual appetite corresponds not only to cosmic or collectivist needs, but also to personalist needs. If man and woman feel a deep longing for sexual union, it is also because they have a deep longing for all that is involved in true sexuality: complemen-tarity, self-giving, self-realization, and self-perpetuation in spousal union with another.

The experience of such complete spousal sexuality is filled with many-faceted pleasure in which the simple physical satisfac-tion of a mere sensory instinct is accompanied and enriched by the personalist satisfaction of the much deeper and stronger longings involved in sex, and not marred and soured by their frustration.

15. See Smith, "Conscious Parenthood," 934.
16. General Audience of November 21, 1979 (TB, 50).

If continuous and growing sexual frustration is the main consequence of contraception, this is also because the contraceptive mentality deprives the very strength of the sexual urge of its real meaning and purpose, and then tries to find full sexual experience and satisfaction in what is little more than a physical release.

Same-Sex Marriages

Whatever one wishes to make of same-sex unions, the concept of a same-sex marriage makes no sense within any Christian or even natural view of matrimony. Marriage essentially involves one man and one woman, two human beings with a masculine and a feminine nature respectively, who can complement one another psychologically and physically to the extent of becoming "one flesh," also as the united principle (parenthood: paternity-maternity) of the family, the first natural cell from which a love-based society can be built up. A "same-sex marriage" fails on all counts to fit into this natural and logical scheme.[17]

Our argument in this chapter has been that contraceptive intercourse between husband and wife denies the truth of conjugal love by radically falsifying the very act which should give the fullest bodily expression to that love. The same reasoning underlines the hollowness of the idea of a "homosexual marriage." Homosexual acts can appease physical desire but they can never even remotely signify the self-giving of two persons. Nor can they effect their union; the two are simply not made "one flesh." Homosexual

17. In consequence, "legal recognition of homosexual unions or placing them on the same level as marriage would mean not only the approval of deviant behavior, with the consequence of making it a model in present-day society, but *would also obscure basic values which belong to the common inheritance of humanity*" (Congregation for the Doctrine of the Faith, "Considerations Regarding Proposals to Give Legal Recognition to Unions Between Homosexual Persons" [June 3, 2003]; http://www.vatican.va/roman_curia/congregations/cfaith/documents/rc_con_cfaith_doc_20030731_homosexual-unions_en.html).

acts are an exercise in emptiness, satisfying individual passion but leaving the persons as separate as before; nothing in the act unites them. Only a dualistic culture that chooses to see no natural and intrinsic connection between body and soul could wish to describe a homosexual relationship as a marriage.

8

An R.I.P. for the *Remedium Concupiscentiae*

The length of this final chapter is, I hope, justified by the nov-
elty and importance of the theses it proposes. An initial resumé
of the overall argument may facilitate its reading. The term *remedium concupiscentiae*, presented up to 1983 as a "secondary" end
of marriage, has been seriously misapplied over the centuries. In
practice it has been taken to imply that marriage gives a lawful
outlet to sexual concupiscence (or lust) and hence married couples can yield to it, since it is now "legitimized." The consequences
go further: if concupiscence was "remedied" by the fact of being
married, then it was either automatically purified of whatever self-
centered (and hence anti-love) elements it entails; or, if these elements remain, they (in theory) present no obstacle to the life and
growth of married love. As regards the conjugal act itself, the only
moral proviso was that its procreative orientation be respected;
given this proviso, there was an implicit suggestion that spouses
can give concupiscence free rein, without this posing any moral or
ascetical difficulties for the development of a full Christian life in
their marriage.

While the expression "*remedium concupiscentiae*" is occasionally found in the writings of Augustine and Thomas Aquinas, it was not used by them in the sense that it later acquired. St. Thomas especially speaks of marriage as a "remedy *against* concupiscence," inasmuch as it offers graces to overcome the self-seeking that concupiscence involves. The subsequent reduction of the term to "remedy *of* concupiscence" led to the loss of this understanding. My purpose in what follows is (1) to stress that while the acceptance in ecclesiastical thinking of marriage as a "remedy" or legitimation of concupiscence has for centuries impeded the development of a positive and dynamic notion of marital chastity, Pope John Paul II's "Catecheses on Human Love" (1979–84), if assimilated in depth, lead into a totally new way of thinking and presents this chastity as the safeguard to conjugal love and a means to its growth; (2) to show that sexual desire and sexual love are, or should be, good things, not to be confused with sexual concupiscence or lust in which self-seeking operates to the detriment of love; and (3) to show that these insights give the basis for effectively overcoming the mindset which regards marriage as a second-class Christian way, and for seeing it as God has wished it to be: a full vocation to holiness precisely to be attained in and through the married state.

Human Nature and Concupiscence

Christianity is the religion of God's greatness and love, and of man's potential, as well as of his frailty, misery, redemption, and elevation. In the Christian view, man is a fallen masterpiece of creation, capable indeed of sinking lower but actually ransomed and strengthened to rise higher. As a result of original sin, says the *Catechism* (no. 405):

Human nature has not been totally corrupted: it is wounded in the natural powers proper to it, subject to ignorance, suffering and the dominion of death, and inclined to sin—an inclination to evil that is called 'concupiscence.' Baptism, by imparting the life of Christ's grace, erases original sin and turns a man back towards God, but the consequences for nature, weakened and inclined to evil, persist in man and summon him to spiritual battle.

Called to surpass ourselves and to attain divine heights, we are still drawn down by that tendency to lower things which goes by the name of concupiscence. In Biblical and theological usage, concupiscence covers the unregulated tendency to pursue or adhere to created goods. "Etymologically, 'concupiscence' can refer to any intense form of human desire. Christian theology has given it a particular meaning: the movement of the sensitive appetite contrary to the operation of the human reason. The apostle St. Paul identifies it with the rebellion of the 'flesh' against the 'spirit' (Gal 5:16ff.)" (no. 2515).

Drawing from the first epistle of St. John, Christian tradition has seen three forms of concupiscence arising from self-enclosing attachment to created things. Two of these come from the sensitive appetite, the third from the intellect. "All that is in the world, the lust of the flesh and the lust of the eyes and the pride of life, is not of the Father but is of the world. And the world passes away, and the lust of it; but he who does the will of God abides for ever" (1 Jn 2:16–17). The pride of life consists in taking self-centered satisfaction in one's own talents and excellence, and springs from intellectual appetition. Thus the spirit too has its lusts, for not all its desires are upright; many are vain, mean, vengeful, and egotistic, thereby tending to distort the truth. Hence man and woman are threatened not only by the rebellion of the flesh, but also by that of the spirit.

After these introductory remarks we go on to the more limited scope of this chapter: the theological and human evaluation of (carnal) concupiscence in marriage. Our study is divided into three main sections: (1) the history, and also the utility and indeed the validity of the notion that marriage is, and is intended to be, a "remedy for concupiscence"; (2) a deeper analysis of concupiscence as it relates to married love; and (3) the new perspective, for the sanctification of married life, that is opened up by this analysis.

Concupiscence and Marriage: Theological Positions

The "*remedium concupiscentiae*" as an End of Marriage

Prior to the Second Vatican Council, the phrase *remedium concupiscentiae* ("remedy for concupiscence") was customarily used in ecclesial writing to describe one of the ends of matrimony. The Code of Canon Law of 1917, crystallizing this view in c. 1013, distinguished between a single primary end of marriage and a twofold secondary end: "The primary end of matrimony is the procreation and education of offspring; the secondary end is mutual help and the remedy of concupiscence."[1] It is worth bearing in mind that, although this structured presentation of the ends of marriage had been common in theological writing for many centuries, the 1917 Code was the first magisterial document to use the terms "primary" and "secondary" in relation to these ends, thus proposing them as hierarchically structured.[2]

The fifty years following the promulgation of the Pio-Benedictine Code witnessed a growing debate regarding the ends of marriage. The debate concerned the relative importance to be attached to procreation on the one hand, and to a rather (as yet) ill-defined "personalist" end seen as largely or wholly unconnected with pro-

1. "Matrimonii finis primarius est procreatio atque educatio prolis; secundarius mutuum adiutorium et remedium concupiscentiae."

2. "However surprising it may seem, the fact is that c. 1013 (CIC 1917) is the first document of the Church to list the ends [of marriage] and to set them out in an hierarchical order. . . . This canon is also the first document of the Church to use the terminology of 'primary' and 'secondary'" (U. Navarrete, SJ, "Structura iuridica matrimonii secundum Concilium Vaticanum II," *Periodica* 56 [1967]: 368); see A. Sarmiento, *El Matrimonio Cristiano* (Pamplona: EUNSA, 2001), 360.

creation, on the other. In chapter 3 we summarized the main lines of this debate, and so we pass on here to the presentation of the ends of marriage in the Second Vatican Council and in post-conciliar magisterium.

Gaudium et Spes is the main conciliar document which treats of marriage. The only specific end of matrimony mentioned in the Constitution is the procreation-education of children.[3] It indeed says that marriage "has various ends" (no. 48), and adds that the natural ordering of marriage towards procreation should not be taken as "underestimating the other ends of marriage."[4] Surprisingly, as we noted earlier, these other ends are nowhere specified. It may be that the council fathers did not want to foreclose the ongoing debate about the ends of marriage, and they may have also prudently felt that further ecclesial reflection would be necessary before a general consensus might be reached on new ways of expressing the various ends of marriage and their mutual relationship.

Peculiarly, it seems to have been as the result (initially at least) of canonical more than of theological reflection that a new and very precise expression of the ends of marriage finally emerged. This becomes less peculiar when one recalls that Pope John XXIII's convocation of the Council was accompanied by the decision to elaborate a new code of canon law. Revising the 1917 Code so that it would more faithfully reflect conciliar thinking about the life of the church and of the faithful became a major post-conciliar undertaking. This work of revision, done in depth and without haste, lasted more than fifteen years, resulting in the 1983 Code of Canon Law, described by Pope John Paul II at its promulgation as "the last document of the Council."[5]

The revision carried out by the Pontifical Commission en-

---

3. "By their very nature, the institution of matrimony itself and conjugal love are ordered to the procreation and education of children" (GS, no. 48, repeated in no. 50).

4. "Non posthabitis ceteris matrimonii finibus" (GS, no. 50).

5. Address to the Roman Rota, January 26, 1984 (AAS 76 [1984]: 644).

trusted with the task was guided not merely by the terms of canon law, but also—and very deliberately—by theological considerations. This was in conformity with the directive of the Council that canon law should be presented in the light of theology and of the mystery of the church.[6] One of the novelties of the 1983 Code is in fact the inclusion of canons which are simply theological statements of doctrine.[7] Hence, whenever these canons use modified or new terms in presenting the church's law, one can legitimately look to them for a possible development in theological and magisterial thinking.

With this in mind, let us turn to the opening canon in the section of the *Code* which deals with marriage.[8] Canon 1055 states: "The matrimonial covenant, by which a man and a woman establish between themselves a partnership of the whole of life, *is by its nature ordered toward the good of the spouses and the procreation and education of offspring*; this covenant between baptized persons has been raised by Christ the Lord to the dignity of a sacrament" (emphasis added). Our attention centers on the italicized words. We read, without surprise, that one end of matrimony is the procreation and upbringing of children. However, when we turn to the other end specified—the *bonum coniugum*, or the "good of the spouses"—we see here that an altogether new term is used in a magisterial document to describe an end of marriage. This novel way of expressing the ordering or purposes of marriage was accepted and given further authority nine years later in what may be considered an even more important magisterial document, the *Catechism*, which repeats (no. 1601) the above canon word for word.[9] Notably, no. 2363 expresses this specifically in terms of *ends*: "the

6. See Vatican II Decree, *Optatam totius* 16.
7. See, e.g., cc. 747ff. in Book 3; and cc. 849, 879, 897, 959, 998, 1008 in Book 4.
8. Book 4, *The Sanctifying Office of the Church*; Part 1, title 7.
9. See also CCC, nos. 2201 and 2249.

twofold end of marriage: the good of the spouses themselves and the transmission of life."[10]

Undoubtedly one of the most important issues brought up by this new formulation of the ends of marriage is the nature of the *bonum coniugum*. We have studied this matter in chapters 3 and 4 and written on it extensively on other places.[11] This is not an easy question, especially when we bear in mind that the term *bonum coniugum* is of very recent coinage. It is scarcely ever to be found in ecclesial writing prior to the Second Vatican Council. Only in 1977 was it first used by the Pontifical Council for the Revision of the Code to describe an end of marriage. But scarcely less noteworthy is the fact that neither the 1983 Code nor the 1992 *Catechism* express the ends of marriage any longer in terms of a hierarchy, but place them together as, so it seems, of equal standing. My impression is that we have moved into a new stage where the church wishes to emphasize not any possible ranking of the ends, but the *interconnection* between them. With regard to the *mutuum adiutorium*, a former secondary end, it is not my purpose to study its place in the present scheme of the ends of marriage. There seems to be little if any disagreement among authors that, even if not specifically mentioned in these recent magisterial texts, "mutual assistance" is to be included within the proper meaning of the "good of the spouses."[12]

A particular point of interest for the present study is the absence, in the documents of the Second Vatican Council and in subsequent church magisterium, of any direct or indirect mention of the former *remedium concupiscentiae* or "remedy of concupis-

10. "Duplex matrimonii finis." This point of the *Catechism*, we can note in passing, confirms that the expression "is ordered to" (in the *Code* or in CCC, no. 1601) is simply equivalent to "has as an end."

11. "The "*bonum coniugum*" and the *bonum prolis*," 704–13; and "Progressive Jurisprudential Thinking," 437–78.

12. Burke, "Progressive Jurisprudential Thinking," 459.

cence."[13] That this omission was deliberate cannot be doubted. Moreover, though the other secondary end, the *mutuum adiutorium*, fits simply enough within the new concept of the *bonum coniugum*,"[14] this is not so of the *remedium concupiscentiae*. Rather than suggest (as has been done) an implicit presence of the *remedium concupiscentiae* within the new scheme of the ends of marriage—and thus attempt to show a certain continuity of ecclesial thinking—I prefer to submit that, despite the long presence it has enjoyed in much of ecclesial writing and its acceptance over fifty years in the 1917 Code, the concept of the *remedium concupiscentiae* (1) lacks theological and anthropological substance (and, contrary to generalized opinion, has little if any backing in the thought of St. Augustine or St. Thomas), and (2) its currency, over centuries, has accompanied (and possibly explains in large part) the failure of moralists to develop a theological and ascetical consideration of marriage as a way of sanctification.

As I seek to develop my argument, I would ask the reader to bear two things in mind. The first is that sexual concupiscence or lust, as I use the term, is not to be taken in the sense of simple sexual attraction or indeed the desire for marital intercourse and the pleasure that accompanies it. Lust or bodily concupiscence is the *disordered* element that in our present state tends to accompany marital intercourse, threatening the love it should express with self-centered possessiveness. On that supposition, my main point is that the use (however longstanding) of the term *remedium concupiscentiae* to signify an end of marriage has had a profoundly

13. As late as 1977, the Pontifical Commission for Revising the 1917 Code of Canon Law did consider a draft in which the *remedium concupiscentiae* appeared among the ends of marriage (*Communicationes* [1977], 123). This passing nod to traditional terminology did not however prevent the Consultors from dropping the notion completely when it came to the final draft of the new Code, approved and promulgated six years later.

14. The biblical juxtaposition of *bonum* and *adiutorium* in the Jahwist account of the divine institution of marriage is evident in Gen 2:18.

negative effect on married life, inasmuch as it suggests that lust or concupiscence is "remedied" or at least "legitimized" by marriage; in the sense either of automatically disappearing or else of being no longer a self-centered element to be constantly taken into account if married love is to grow. To my mind the faulty reasoning behind this has been a major obstacle to understanding how love in marriage stands in need of constant purification if it is to achieve its human fullness and its supernatural goal of merging into love for God. I will endeavor to justify my position on both points.

Concupiscence: An Evil Present in Marriage?

It is impossible to study the development of Christian thought on marriage without reference to St. Augustine. The many-faceted and nuanced character of Augustinian thinking in this field is probably to be attributed not so much to Augustine's personal experience in sexual matters as to his having been involved over some forty years in varied controversies concerning matrimony. As we have seen in chapter 6, the earlier part of his Catholic life saw him engaged in conflict with the pessimism of the Manicheans; in his later years he combated the naturalistic optimism of the Pelagians. The Manicheans saw marriage and procreation as major expressions of material and bodily creation and hence as evil, while Augustine defended the goodness of both. The Pelagians, in their excessive optimism about man's present state, took little or no account of the disordered element strongly present in sex that is also found in conjugal sexuality, and Augustine sought to alert people to this disorder.

St. Augustine and the *bona* of Marriage

St. Augustine's greatest legacy in this field is his doctrine of the matrimonial *bona*.[15] He sees marriage as essentially charac-

---

15. Inevitably, for the sake of developing our argument here clearly and cogently, we will briefly repeat some points made in an earlier chapter, and will also quote again some key passages of St. Augustine.

terized by three principal elements or properties, each of which shows the goodness and greatness of the marital relationship.[16] So convinced is he that each of these characteristics underpins the goodness of marriage that he refers to each not just as a "property" or "characteristic," but as a *bonum*, as something *good*, as a uniquely positive value: "Let these nuptial goods be the objects of our love: offspring, fidelity, the unbreakable bond. . . . Let these nuptial goods be praised in marriage by him who wishes to extol the nuptial institution."[17] This doctrine of the *bona* is without a doubt St. Augustine's main contribution to the analysis of marriage in its divinely instituted beauty which has come down to us through fifteen centuries of unbroken tradition.[18] In particular, St. Augustine's teaching about the presence and effect of concupiscence in all sexual activity, including marital intercourse between spouses themselves, is the aspect of his thought which interests us here.

Saint Augustine and "Putting Bad to Good Use"

One of many seminal ideas in Augustinian thought is that "bad can be used to good purpose."[19] God, he points out, makes positive use of those aspects of creation which seem to have gone wrong, and we should learn to do likewise. The idea is repeatedly expressed: "God uses even bad things well"; "God knows how to put not only good things, but also bad things, to good use"; "Al-

16. In Augustine's view offspring was certainly the purpose or end of marriage: "Cum sint ergo nuptiae causa generandi institutae" (*De coniugiis adulterinis*, 12). Nevertheless this was not his major point of focus and interest. He took the end of marriage for granted; his interest and arguments were directed at defending its goodness.

17. "In nuptiis tamen bona nuptialia diligantur, proles, fides, sacramentum. . . . Haec bona nuptialia laudet in nuptiis, qui laudare vult nuptias" (*De nupt. et conc.*, I, 17, 19; and 21, 23).

18. See B. Alves Pereira, *La doctrine du mariage selon saint Augustin* (Paris: Beauchesne, 1930); A. Reuter, *Sancti Aurelii Augustini doctrina de bonis matrimonii* (Rome, 1942).

19. Of course, this is not the same as saying that one can *do* bad so as to achieve good.

mighty God, the Lord of all creatures, who, as it is written, made everything very good, so ordered them that he could make good use both of good things and of bad"; "Just as it is bad to make bad use of what is good, so it is good to make good use of what is bad. . . . Good is used well by whoever vows continence to God, while good is used badly by whoever vows continence to an idol; evil is used badly by whoever indulges concupiscence through adultery, while evil is used well by whoever restricts concupiscence to marriage."[20]

In his writings on marriage, Augustine refers this principle particularly to the presence of concupiscence in conjugal intercourse. Such intercourse is good, but the carnal concupiscence or lust which accompanies it is not. Nevertheless spouses in their intercourse use this evil well,[21] and he wants them to be aware of this. "So let good spouses use the evil of concupiscence well, just as a wise man uses an imprudent servant for good tasks"; "I hold that to use lust is not always a sin, because to use evil well is not a sin"; "as for the warfare experienced by chaste persons, whether celibate or married, we assert that there could have been no such thing in paradise before [man's] sin. Marriage is still the same, but in begetting children nothing evil would then have been used; now the evil of concupiscence is used well"; "this evil is used well by faithful spouses."[22]

20. "*Deus utitur et malis bene*" (*De civitate dei*, XVIII, 1, 51); "Non solum bonis, verum etiam malis bene uti novit [Deus]" (ibid., 14.27); "Deus omnipotens, Dominus universae creaturae, qui fecit omnia, sicut scriptum est, bona valde, sic ea ordinavit, ut et de bonis et de malis bene faciat" (*De agone christiano*, 7); and "Sicut autem bono male uti malum est, sic malo bene uti bonum est. Duo igitur haec, bonum et malum, et alia duo, usus bonus et usus malus, sibimet adiuncta quattuor differentias faciunt. Bene utitur bono continentiam dedicans Deo, male utitur bono continentiam dedicans idolo; male utitur malo concupiscentiam relaxans adulterio, bene utitur malo concupiscentiam restringens connubio" (*De peccatorum meritis*, 1.57).

21. *De nupt. et conc.*, 1.9, 1.27, 2.34, and 2.36; *De continentia*, 27; *Contra Julianum*, 3.53, 4.35, 4.65, 5.46, and 5.66; *Imperfectum*, Preface, 1.65, 2.31, 4.29, 4.107, 5.13, 5.20, and 5.23; *Contra Pelag.*, 1.33; *De gratia Christi et de peccato originale* [hereafter "*De gratia*"], 2.42; *De Trinitate*, 13.23; etc.

22. "Sic utantur coniuges boni malo concupiscentiae, sicut sapiens ad opera

For Augustine, lust is an evil. Nevertheless, spouses can use it well in their truly conjugal intercourse, whereas unmarried people yield to sin by using this evil badly.[23] It follows, within this logic, that the married person who engages in illicit intercourse uses lust badly and therefore sins. Illicit intercourse obviously comprises adultery, and there is no doubt that in Augustine's thought it also covers contraception. Augustine goes further still and proposes an opinion that clashes directly with modern views on married sexuality. He holds that married intercourse is "excusable" (and wholly conjugal) only when it is carried out for the conscious purpose of having children.[24] If it is engaged in just for the satisfaction of concupiscence, it always carries with it some element of fault, at least of a venial type.

In his view, the intention of spouses in intercourse should not be pleasure for its own sake but rather procreation, adding that if in their intercourse the spouses intend more than what is needed for procreation, this evil (*malum*), which he refuses to consider as proper to marriage itself, remains excusable (*veniale*) because of the goodness of marriage itself.[25] Elsewhere he puts this position even more clearly: if pleasure-seeking is the main purpose of

---

utique bona ministro utitur imprudente" (*Contra Julianum*, 5.60); see also "Ego enim dico, uti libidine non semper esse peccatum; quia malo bene uti non est peccatum" (ibid.); "bellum quod in se casti sentiunt, sive continentes, sive etiam coniugati, hoc dicimus in paradiso, ante peccatum nullo modo esse potuisse. Ipsae ergo etiam nunc sunt nuptiae, sed in generandis filiis tunc nullo malo uterentur, nunc concupiscentiae malo bene utuntur" (ibid., 3.57); "hoc enim malo bene utuntur fideles coniugati" (ibid., 3.54); and ibid., 4.1, 4.35, 5.63, etc.

23. "With shameful lust to have licit intercourse, is to use an evil well; to have it illicitly, is to use an evil badly [pudenda libidine qui licite concumbit, malo bene utitur; qui autem illicite, malo male utitur]" (*De nupt. et conc.*, 2.36).

24. "Sexual intercourse necessary for begetting is free from blame, and it alone is [truly] nuptial [Concubitus enim necessarius causa generandi, inculpabilis et solus ipse nuptialis est]" (*De bono coniugali*, 11); and "Only for the cause of procreating is the union of the sexes free from blame [Sola enim generandi causa est inculpabilis sexus utriusque commixtio]" (*Sermones* 351).

25. *De bono viduitatis*, 4, 5.

spouses in their intercourse, they sin, but only venially on account of their Christian marriage.[26] In support of this view Augustine repeatedly cites the passage in 1 Corinthians 7 where St. Paul "allows" Christian spouses to refrain from conjugal intercourse by mutual consent and for a time, but recommends that it not be for too long, "lest Satan tempt you through lack of self-control," adding that this advice of his is given not as a command, but *secundum indulgentiam*, or, as Augustine translates it, *secundum veniam*.

St. Paul and 1 Corinthians 7:1–9

The first verses of 1 Corinthians 7 have had extraordinary (and possibly disproportionate) importance in the development of Christian moral thought concerning conjugal relations. Bringing the full text before our mind can help us consider to what extent Augustinian and parallel subsequent interpretations are justified. Augustine of course wrote in Latin, so for key passages we will reproduce parenthetically the Latin version which has been in common use over the ages, the Vulgate translation of his contemporary, St. Jerome:

It is well for a man not to touch a woman. But because of the temptation to immorality, each man should have his own wife and each woman her own husband. The husband should give to his wife her conjugal rights, and likewise the wife to her husband. For the wife does not rule over her own body, but the husband does; likewise the husband does not rule over his own body, but the wife does. Do not refuse one another except perhaps by agreement for a season, that you may devote yourselves to prayer; but then come together again, lest Satan tempt you through lack of self-control. I say this by way of concession, not of command [*Hoc autem dico secundum indulgentiam, non secundum imperium*]. I wish that all were as I myself am. But each has his own

---

26. *De nupt. et conc.*, 1:27; *Contra Julianum*, 3.43, 4.33; and *Contra Pelag.*, 1.33 and 3.30.

special gift from God, one of one kind and one of another. To the un-married and the widows I say that it is well for them to remain single as I do. But if they cannot exercise self-control, they should marry. For it is better to marry than to be aflame with passion [*Melius est enim nubere quam uri*].

Our attention for the moment centers on the words "*Hoc autem dico secundum indulgentiam, non secundum imperium.*" We note that Augustine translates as *secundum veniam* what St. Jerome renders as *secundum indulgentiam*, and understands *venia* in the sense of pardon or forgiveness for what carries guilt.[27] Augustine's argument in fact rests wholly on this rendering, for he holds that if something requires a *venia* it necessarily involves a fault that quali-fies as a sin.[28]

It is not clear however that Augustine is justified in his render-ing. If so, his whole argument can of course be questioned. To sug-gest that in this passage St. Paul proposes to condone sin seems to alter the original text. The Greek word used by St. Paul, *suggnome*, has in fact the meaning of allowance or concession.[29] St. Paul's meaning is surely not that concession can be made to people so as to sin, but rather that allowance can be made to follow a less per-fect way. This is precisely what he goes on to say in the following verse: "I wish that all were as I myself am. But each has his own spe-cial gift from God, one of one kind and one of another." It is clear that Paul regards the celibacy he has chosen as a more desirable

27. Nowhere in the New Testament does the Vulgate employ "*venia*" in this sense; in the Old Testament four occurrences are to be found (Num 15:28; Wis 12:11; and Sir 3:14–15, 25:34). "*Indulgentia*" appears three times in the Old Testament (Jdt 8:14; and Isa 61:1, 63:7); and once, in the passage we are considering, in the New Testament.

28. "Secundum veniam, non secundum imperium, concedit Apostolus. Evi-denter quippe dum tribuit veniam, denotat culpam" (*De gratia*, 2.43). See also *Contra Pelag.*, 1:33; *De nupt. et conc.*, 16; *Contra Julianum*, 2.20 and 5.63; *Imperfectum*, 1:68; etc.

29. In the Revised Standard Version: "I say this by way of concession, not of com-mand"; the New American Bible (1986) also uses "concession," where the Jerusalem Bible renders the whole passage more loosely: "This is a suggestion, not a rule."

way; at the same time however he presents marriage too as a "gift of God." The thrust of St. Paul's thought seems rather to pass from a simple ascetical counsel for married people (it could be good to abstain for a time from conjugal relations), to a clarification that he regards his own choice of celibacy for God as higher than the married state, to the concession (with an "indulgent" outlook) that those who choose marriage also choose a gift of God.

If we turn to St. Thomas, we find that he reads this passage (1 Cor 7:6) according to the Vulgate as *secundum indulgentiam* and not *secundum veniam* but, at least in one place, seems to interpret the passage in much the same way as St. Augustine.[30] Elsewhere, however, he modulates his position. Quietly observing that the Apostle appears to be expressing himself "carelessly" or "improperly" (*inconvenienter*), inasmuch as he would seem to imply that marriage is sinful,[31] Aquinas comes up with two possible readings. In the first, *secundum indulgentiam* would refer to a permission not for sin but for what is less good; that is, Paul says it is good to marry, but less good than to remain celibate.[32] This seems to me the better interpretation. However, St. Thomas does allow another

30. The spouse who seeks married intercourse simply because he or she will otherwise not be continent sins venially: "if he intends to avoid fornication, this shows something beyond what is reasonable, and in this there is venial sin. For marriage was not instituted for this purpose, except by way of forgiveness, which relates to venial sins [si intendat vitare fornicationem in se, sic est ibi aliqua superfluitas; et secundum hoc est peccatum veniale: nec ad hoc est matrimonium institutum, nisi secundum indulgentiam, quae est de peccatis venialibus]" (*Super Sent.*, lib. 4, d. 31, q. 2, a. 2, ad 2).

31. "The Apostle seems to express himself improperly here; after all forgiveness can only refer to what is sinful. Hence in saying that matrimony is allowed by way of forgiveness, he appears to imply that matrimony is a sin [videtur apostolus inconvenienter loqui; indulgentia enim non est nisi de peccato. Per hoc ergo quod apostolus, secundum indulgentiam se dicit matrimonium concessisse, videtur exprimere quod matrimonium sit peccatum]" (*Super I Ep. ad Corinthios lectura*, cap 7, lect. 1).

32. "The Apostle here condones, that is, permits matrimony, which is less good than virginity, which is not mandated but is a greater good [apostolus hic indulget, id est, permittit matrimonium, quod est minus bonum quam virginitas, quae non praecipitur, quae est maius bonum]" (ibid.).

reading where sin may be present in marital intercourse, that is, when it is engaged in out of lust, though such lust is at least restricted to one's spouse. In this case there is venial sin, which would become mortal if one were indifferent whether the object of one's lust were one's spouse or not.[33]

From Marriage Affected by Concupiscence to Concupiscence "Remedied" by Marriage

How and when did the notion of marriage being directed to the "remedy" of concupiscence emerge in church thinking? While roots of the idea can be found in St. Augustine and St. Thomas, I do not consider that either of them held or proposed it in the sense of the concept as used in the centuries prior to the Second Vatican Council—a sense advanced and established by writers of those intervening centuries.

Both Augustine and Thomas are conscious of a sullying and negative effect of concupiscence in general and in married intercourse. Both try to show that the conjugal act is nevertheless "justified"[34] through its natural connection with the *bona* of marriage. For St. Augustine it is fundamentally the *bonum prolis* that justifies conjugal intercourse. St. Thomas is broader in his outlook and relates this justification also to the good of fidelity[35] and to the unique unbreakable nature of the married bond.[36] It is clearly

33. "Indulgence can be understood in another way in reference to culpability. . . . In this sense indulgence is referred to the conjugal act inasmuch as it has a venial fault attached to it; that is, when a man is stirred to the conjugal act out of concupiscence which he nevertheless restricts to the limits of marriage, in such a way that he is content to have intercourse only with his wife. At times this can be a real mortal sin, for instance when concupiscence is not limited to marriage, because he seeks intercourse with his wife, but would as readily or more readily seek it with another woman" (ibid.); see also *Suppl.*, q. 40, a. 6.

34. "Justified," as used by these two authors, would seem to have a much more positive meaning than modern parlance attributes to it. It is not merely that the act is "excused" but that it is rendered *just* in the biblical sense, i.e., holy and pleasing to God.

35. *Super Sent.*, lib. 4, d. 31, q. 2, a. 2 co.

36. Ibid., q. 2, a. 1 co.

one thing to hold that the concupiscence of marital intercourse is "justified" or "excused" by marriage, and another to hold that it is "remedied" thereby. My reading of these two doctors is that the notion of marriage being a *remedium* of concupiscence is not directly proposed by either. Hence it should rather be considered a subsequent development.

The idea of marriage as a "remedy" appears only once or twice in St. Augustine's writings, while he never uses the actual phrase *remedium concupiscentiae*. We have quoted earlier one of his most appealing passages in defense of the goodness of marriage, where he writes: "The goodness of marriage is always a good indeed. In the people of God it was at one time an act of obedience to the law; now it is a remedy for weakness, and for some a solace of human nature."[37] It is true that in another of his works, where he combats Pelagian viewpoints, one may claim to find a more direct reference to marriage considered as a remedy to *libido* or disordered sexual desire. The Pelagian bishop Julian of Eclanum had written that holy virginity, in its readiness to fight greater battles, had ignored the "remedy" of marriage. Augustine seizes on this point, and asks Julian: against what disorder do you regard marriage as a remedy? Obviously, he answers, against the disorder of lust. Then, concludes Augustine, we are both agreed that marriage is a remedy; so why do you defend the very disorder of lust against which this "conjugal remedy" is directed?[38] The weight of this passage is debatable, but the context certainly countenances the view that the idea of mar-

37. "Nuptiarum igitur bonum semper est quidem bonum; sed in populo Dei fuit aliquando legis obsequium; nunc est infirmitatis remedium, in quibusdam vero humanitatis solatium" (*De bono viduitatis*, 8.11; see *De Gen. ad litt.*, 9.7).

38. "Dixisti enim: "Sanctam virginitatem confidentia suae salutis et roboris contempsisse remedia, ut gloriosa posset exercere certamina." Quaero quae remedia contempserit? Respondebis: Nuptias. Quaero: Ista remedia contra quem morbum sunt necessaria? Remedium quippe a medendo, id est a medicando, nomen accepit. Simul itaque videmus ambo remedium nuptiarum: cur tu laudas libidinis morbum . . . , si non ei resistat aut continentiae retinaculum, aut coniugale remedium?" (*Contra Julianum*, 3.21.42).

riage as a remedy, carelessly put forward by Julian, is used by Augustine rather to score a point against Pelagian logic than to propose his own considered mind on the subject.

Regarding St. Thomas, we find him twice briefly expressing the notion that matrimony exists also for the *remedium concupiscentiae*.[39] But particular attention should be directed to another passage where his position is more precisely articulated. To the suggestion that marriage does not confer grace but is simply a "remedy," he replies, "this does not seem acceptable; for it implies that marriage is a remedy of concupiscence, either inasmuch as it curbs concupiscence, which cannot be without grace; or inasmuch as it satisfies concupiscence in part, which it does from the very nature of the act independently of any sacrament. Besides, concupiscence is not curbed by being satisfied but is rather increased, as Aristotle says in his *Ethics*."[40] Here there is not the slightest hint of marriage being simply in itself a remedy *of* concupiscence. He insists rather that either the remedy in question lies in the *curbing* of concupiscence—which is not possible without grace—or else it is to be taken in the sense of the simple satisfaction of concupiscence, and then it is not a remedy at all, but tends rather to its increase. Later, again on the issue of whether marriage confers grace, he clinches his argument. Taking up again the objection that marriage, precisely because it tends to increase concupiscence, cannot be a vehicle of grace, he turns the objection around and says that grace is in fact conferred in marriage precisely to be a remedy *against* concupiscence, so as to *curb* it at its root (that is, its self-absorbed tendency).[41] Clearly, to curb or repress concupiscence is not quite the same as to "remedy" it.

39. *IV Sent.*, d. 33, q. 2, a. 1, ad 4; *Super I Cor.*, c. 7, lect. 1.

40. *IV Sent.*, d. 2, q. 1, a. 1.

41. "It can offer a remedy against concupiscence . . . in order to curb it in its very root; and so marriage offers a remedy through the grace that it confers" (*IV Sent.*, d. 26, q. 2, a. 3, ad 4).

The attribution to Augustine and Aquinas of the teaching that marriage is directed to the remedy *of* concupiscence therefore lacks a solid basis. Augustine regards concupiscence as an evil factor affecting human life that married persons can nevertheless use well in intercourse oriented to procreation. Having given a broad description of marriage as a remedy for weakness, Augustine accepts that it is also a remedy against concupiscence. On a couple of occasions and speaking in general terms, Aquinas does apply the phrase *remedium concupiscentiae* to marriage, but his more precise formulations indicate that for him marriage is meant to be a remedy *against* concupiscence. He clearly shares Augustine's conviction that concupiscence is a negative element, also in married love, and one to be resisted. Expounding upon the sense in which each sacrament is given as a remedy against the deficiency of sin, he says that marriage is given as a "*remedium contra concupiscentiam personalem*," a remedy against concupiscence in the individual.[42] Concupiscence remains an enemy of personal holiness; each Christian has to fight against it. Marriage, especially in its sacramental nature, helps the Christian to fight this enemy. Nowhere in Thomas's teaching do we find any suggestion that concupiscence or lust is "neutralized" and less still "emancipated" by the fact of getting married. It remains a threat to married as well as single Christians. Those who marry do have a special grace to fight against this threat so as to purify their marital intercourse of self-seeking and turn it more and more into an act of loving self-donation. But concupiscence remains a negative reality, a *malum* or evil to be used in a purified way.

In the century before Thomas Aquinas, Hugo of St. Victor (1096–1141) follows Augustine in presenting the "good" of marriage as countering the "bad" of concupiscence,[43] while Peter

---

42. *Summa Theologiae* III, q. 65, a. 1; see *IV Sent.*, d. 2, q. 2; and d. 26, q. 2.
43. *De sacramento coniugii* 2:11 (PL 176:494).

Lombard (1100–1160) simply says that marriage is *ad remedium* or *in remedium*, without specifying the operation of this remedy.[44] St. Bonaventure (1217–74) is as precise as his contemporary St. Thomas in his teaching: "The use of marriage . . . acts as a remedy *against* concupiscence, when it checks it as a medicine."[45] However, already before Bonaventure, Alexander of Hales (1170–1245) had written: "Matrimony is a remedy of lustful concupiscence."[46] This, rather than the precision of St. Thomas, is the line that will be followed in later centuries.[47] Theologians, without qualification or comment, state matter-of-factly that marriage exists (also) for the "remedy of concupiscence." In the seventeenth century, the Jesuit Busenbaum writes that the spouses are united "*ad remedium concupiscentiae*."[48] St. Alphonsus Liguori (1696–1787), the patron of moral theologians, teaches: "The accidental intrinsic ends of marriage are two: the procreation of offspring, and the remedy of concupiscence."[49]

By the nineteenth and twentieth centuries, this form of expression is firmly established. The manuals of moral theology in most common use before the Second Vatican Council unanimously propose the *remedium concupiscentiae* as one of the secondary ends of marriage without subjecting the idea to any true critical analysis. One finds this not only in all of the Latin manuals,[50] but also in

44. *IV Sent.*, d. 26 (PL 192:908–9).

45. "Est usus matrimonii . . . in remedium contra concupiscentiam, dum illa refrenat ut medicamentum" (*IV Sent.*, d. 26, a. 1, q. 1).

46. "Coniugium . . . quod est in remedium libidinosae concupiscentiae" (*Glossa in IV Libros Sententiarum*: In lib. IV. 457).

47. One of the few exceptions is Bellarmine: "The third end is that marriage be a remedy against concupiscence [Tertius finis est ut sit coniugium in remedium contra concupiscentiam]" (*De Sacramento*, 1.10).

48. H. Busenbaum, SJ, *Medulla Theologiae Moralis*, tract. 6 (1645); see *De matrimonio*, c. 2.

49. "Fines [matrimonii] intrinseci accidentales sunt duo, procreatio prolis, et remedium concupiscentiae" (St. Alphonsus Liguori, *Theologiae Moralis* [Bassano-Remondini, 1785], lib. 6, 881).

50. It is worth giving an extensive, though not exhaustive, list: A. Ballerini, SJ,

the best-known vernacular texts. Thomas Slater's manual speaks of "a lawful outlet for concupiscence" as does the even better-known manual of Henry Davis.[51] The *Dictionary of Moral Theology* says that "the secondary end is the remedy of concupiscence."[52]

Bernard Häring's *The Law of Christ*, although supposedly updated in the light of the Second Vatican Council, repeats the same: "The sacrament of matrimony has a secondary or subordinate end or function (*finis secundarius*): the healing of concupiscence (*remedium concupiscientiae*)."[53] The 1967 *New Catholic Encyclopedia*[54] restates this traditional doctrine, as does the University of Salamanca's *Biblia Comentada*.[55] The 1963 edition of the Ford-Kelly *Contemporary Moral Theology* lists the "remedy of concupiscence" among the essential ends of marriage.[56] The authors observe: "The remedy for concupiscence is now beginning to be called, or at least partially explained as the sexual fulfillment of the partners,

---

Opus theologicum morale (Prati: Ex Officina Libraria Giachetti, Rilii et Soc., 1892), 6:167; Giovanni Bucceroni, SJ, *Institutiones theologiae moralis secundum doctrinam S. Thomae et S. Alphonsi* (Rome, 1898), 2:334; C. Marc, CSSR, *Institutiones morales Alphonsianae* (Lugduni, 1900), 2:447; Christinaus Pesch, SJ, *Praelectiones dogmaticae* (9 vols.) (Freiburg: Herder, 1900); "De Sacramentis," pars 2, n. 691; Augustinus Lehmkuhl, SJ, *Theologia moralis* (Freiburg: Herder, 1914), 2:616; F. M. Cappello, SJ, *Tractactus canonico-moralis* (Rome, 1927), 3:39; L. Wouters, CSSR, *Manuale theologiae moralis* (Bruges: Carolus Beyaert, 1932), 2:542; E. Genicot, SJ, *Institutiones theologiae moralis* (Brussels, 1936), 2:410; J. Aertnys, CSSR, and C. A. Damen, CSSR, *Theologia moralis* (2 vols.) (Turin, 1950), 2:473; H. Noldin, SJ, *Summa theologiae moralis* (Innsbruck: F. Rauch, 1962), 429; B. H. Merkelbach, OP, *Summa theologiae moralis* (Bruges, 1956), 3:759; E. F. Regatillo and M. Zalba, SJ, *Theologiae moralis summa* (Madrid: Biblioteca de Autores Cristianos, 1954), 3:582; G. Mausbach, *Teologia morale* (Alba, 1956), 3:144; and A. Tanquerey, *Synopsis theologiae moralis et pastoralis* (Paris, 1955), 381.

51. T. Slater, SJ, *A Manual of Moral Theology* (New York: Benzinger, 1925), 200; H. Davis, SJ: *Moral and Pastoral Theology* (New York: Sheed and Ward, 1958), 4:69.

52. Francesco Roberti, *Dictionary of Moral Theology* (Westminster, Md.: Newman Press, 1962), 732.

53. *The Law of Christ* (Cork: Mercier Press, 1967), from the 7th German edition of *Das Gesetz Christi* (1963).

54. (Washington, D.C.: The Catholic University of America Press, 1967), 9:267.

55. *Biblia Comentada* 6:403 (Madrid: BAC, 1965).

56. John C. Ford, SJ, and Gerald Kelly, SJ, *Contemporary Moral Theology* (Westminster, Md.: Newman Press, 1963), 2:48 and 2:75.

thus giving it a more positive content."[57] They add: "Sexual activity and sexual pleasure are now considered by theologians to have positive values. Formerly the attitude toward sex was negative and disparaging. Sexual expression even in marriage was somewhat reluctantly given its place. It needed to be "excused" by the *tria bona* of marriage. Today Catholic theologians attribute positive values to sex which would have surprised St. Augustine, if not St. Thomas."[58] Nevertheless, the authors state that they prefer to continue using the traditional expression *remedium concupiscentiae.*[59]

It is fair to remark that, rather than in specific teachings of St. Augustine or St. Thomas, this century-old view has sought its justification in the difficult phrase, "*melius est nubere quam uri,*" used by St. Paul (1 Cor 7:7–9) and mentioned earlier. Paul first remarks, "I wish that all were as I myself am [i.e., celibate]. But each has his own special gift from God, one of one kind and one of another," and then addresses those who are not married: "To the unmarried and the widows I say that it is well for them to remain single as I do. But if they cannot exercise self-control, they should marry, for it is better to marry than to burn [with passion]." The last sentence of this passage seems clearly addressed to particular persons: not to the unmarried generally, but to those among them who lack sexual self-control. Nevertheless a whole tradition of moral thinking zeroed in on these words and, taking them out of their limited Scriptural context, used them to sustain a broad and generalised doctrine with a twofold implication: marriage is for those who lack self-control,[60] hence self-control in marriage, at

57. Ibid., 2:48.
58. Ibid., 2:97. Augustine might have been surprised at this comment, which fails to grasp the distinction he makes between sexual pleasure (which is a good accompaniment of marital intercourse) and lust (its bad accompaniment).
59. Ibid., 2:75 and 2:99.
60. The 1950 edition of a much-used manual thus explains the purpose of the *remedium concupiscentiae* as an end of marriage: "So that those who are conscious of their

least in the spouses' sexual relations, is not of special importance.

It is hard to say which of these two propositions should be considered more harmful. The former supported the mindset which regarded marriage as a sort of second-class Christian option. The latter was arguably the strongest obstacle to the development of a properly conjugal asceticism or spirituality, that is, a spiritual approach for married persons powerful and deep enough to help them seek perfection within and not despite the peculiar conditions of their proper way of life.

Over the centuries, the church has suffered from a disregard of and neglect toward the spiritual possibilities of marriage. The scant number of married persons among declared saints (extraordinarily few in proportion to celibates) reflected or perhaps provoked the widespread idea that "getting married" was the normal alternative to "having a vocation." Marriage was not for those who were called; it was rather for the disadvantaged.

Furthermore, the main handicap that those who chose to marry apparently suffered from—their lack of self-control—was considered either to be automatically remedied by the act of marrying, or in any case to be no longer of great account. It was not that to marry stopped the "burning" of lust or concupiscence, but that once married one could yield unconcernedly to this "burning" whose satisfaction is legitimized by marrying. In this view, conjugal relations, justified by being oriented to procreation, were exempt from any further moral or ascetical issue of control or purification. Lust, having been "remedied," is no longer a troublesome force for married people, nor need one consider it as a source of imperfection, or an enemy to the growth of their married love and their sanctification before God. In practice, the idea that mar-

---

weakness, and do not want to sustain the attack of the flesh, can use the remedy of matrimony in order to avoid sins of lust" (Aertnys and Damen, *Theologia moralis*, 2:473).

riage was the *remedium concupiscentiae* seemed to suggest to many that concupiscence in marriage could be indulged quite freely. The only requirement laid down for the satisfaction of sexual desire in marriage was that the procreative orientation of the conjugal act be respected. If that condition was fulfilled, neither morality nor spirituality had further guidelines to offer.

It seems to me that the moral evaluation of concupiscence remained stuck in this standpoint: the indulgence of sexual concupiscence, being always seriously sinful outside marriage, is legitimate for spouses provided that the procreative orientation of the marriage act is respected. This appears as the almost universal moral analysis of sexual concupiscence: there is only one proper and licit place for its indulgence, and that is marriage. In other words, *marriage legitimizes sexual concupiscence or lust*. This is the understanding of the *remedium concupiscentiae* which has established itself among Catholic theologians and moralists to the point of being considered almost axiomatic. Concupiscence in marriage is therefore appraised not as a force to be resisted, but as something simply "remedied" by marriage itself. This, I maintain, was the common attitude as late as the middle of the twentieth century, when the idea of "married spirituality" was being seriously proposed. Further, despite the clear teaching of the Second Vatican Council on the universal call to holiness, including married people in particular, the attitude remains prevalent today.

The Twentieth Century: Unrealistic Optimism
and Pessimistic Realism?

In the twentieth century, signs appeared of a desire to renew theological and ascetical reflection on marriage. As noted in chapter 3, early "personalist" writers such as Herbert Doms and Bernard Krempel sought to underline the human value of intercourse as an expression of conjugal love, though on a very inadequate level of anthropological analysis. Doms saw the essence of marriage in the physical union of the spouses, and its end as their fulfillment and realization as persons. He rejected the idea that in order to be unitive, married intercourse must retain its intrinsic orientation to offspring, and rather maintained that "the conjugal act is full of meaning and carries its own justification in itself, independently of its orientation towards offspring."[61] Krempel ignored offspring as an end of marriage; rather, its end is the "life-union" of man and woman of which the child is simply an expression.[62]

These theses show personalism working at a very superficial level. Perhaps it was in reaction that Pope Pius XI's encyclical *Casti connubii* of 1930, while giving new prominence to the importance of love in marriage, insisted that "love" is secondary to the main end of procreation. In line with the accepted tradition, the encyclical teaches that the satisfying of concupiscence is an end which the spouses may seek but does not broach the issue of the relationship between concupiscence itself and marital love. In matrimony, it says, "there are also secondary ends, such as mutual aid, the cultivating of mutual love, and the satisfying [*sedatio*] of concupiscence which husband and wife are not forbidden to consider so long as the due ordination of intercourse to the primary end is respected."[63]

As the twentieth century progressed, it ushered in a new (and perhaps not sufficiently qualified) emphasis on the dignity of the physical sexual relationship in marriage. This no doubt left many moralists not too happy with the earlier opinion that there is venial sin in having conjugal intercourse just for pleasure. Rather than seeking a possible solution of the matter through a deeper analysis

---

61. Doms, "Conception personnaliste," *Revue Thomiste* 45 (1939): 763.
62. See A. Perego, "Fine ed essenza della società coniugale," *Divus Thomas* 56 (1953): 357.
63. Denz., no. 2241.

of the relationship between love and the sexual urge, the tendency was to side-step the issue. So we read in the last pre-Vatican II edition of a widely-used manual: "In practice there is no need to worry spouses if they exercise the conjugal act in an ordinary and upright way without actually thinking of a particular end. The reason is that the conjugal act performed in a natural way fosters marital love and this love favors the good of offspring—in view of which, as all the authors teach, conjugal intercourse is licit."[64] This begs the question of whether intercourse, in order to be a truly natural expression of marital love, needs to be purified as far as possible from the concupiscence that accompanies it.

By contrast, late-twentieth-century magisterium offers startlingly new perspectives on this issue. Pope John Paul II opened his pontificate with a lengthy and surprising weekly catechesis on "Human Love in the Divine Plan," now commonly known in English as his theology of the body. This extended from September 1979 to November 1984. It offered an extraordinarily profound view of the purpose and dignity of human sexuality and the conjugal union, and also dwelt on the presence and dangers of lust within marriage. In July 1982, treating of both virginal celibacy and marriage as "gifts of God," Pope John Paul II took up those difficult passages in St. Paul's first letter to the Corinthians: "It is well for a man not to touch a woman. But because of the danger of incontinence, each man should have his own wife and each woman her own husband," and "to unmarried persons and to widows I say, it is good for them to remain as I am. But if they cannot live in continence, let them marry. It is better to marry than to burn."[65] The Pope posed the question:

64. D. M. Prümmer, OP, *Manuale theologiae moralis* (Freiburg: Herder, 1961), 3:504.

65. 1 Cor 7:1–2 and 8–9. St. Thomas, it should be noticed, is quite critical of St. Paul's phrase, "It is better to marry than to burn," which he considers an "abusive" way of putting things: "One must note here that *the Apostle uses the comparison abusively*;

Does the Apostle in First Corinthians perhaps look upon marriage exclusively from the viewpoint of a remedy for concupiscence, as used to be said in traditional theological language? The statements mentioned ... would seem to verify this. However, right next to the statements quoted, we read a passage in the seventh chapter of First Corinthians that leads us to see differently Paul's teaching as a whole: "I wish that all were as I myself am, but each has his own special gift from God, one of one kind, and one of another" (1 Cor 7:7). Therefore even those who choose marriage and live in it receive a gift from God, his own gift, that is, the grace proper to this choice, to this way of living, to this state. The gift received by persons who live in marriage is different from the one received by persons who live in virginity and choose continence for the sake of the kingdom of God. All the same, it is a true gift from God, one's own gift, intended for concrete persons. It is specific, that is, suited to their vocation in life. We can therefore say that while the Apostle, in his characterization of marriage on the human side ... strongly emphasizes the reason concerning concupiscence of the flesh, at the same time, with no less strength of conviction, he stresses also its sacramental and charismatic character. With the same clarity with which he sees man's situation in relation to concupiscence of the flesh, he sees also the action of grace in every person—in one who lives in marriage no less than in one who willingly chooses continence.[66]

The least that can be said from a reading of this passage is that John Paul II, while not explicitly rejecting the concept of *remedium concupiscentiae*, suggests that the traditional teaching on the matter has remained one-sided precisely because of a failure to weigh the sacramental implications of marriage.

Some months later in 1982, the Pope's catechesis turned more directly to the sacramentality of marriage. Once again he showed

---

for to marry is good, even if less so [than virginity], while to burn [with lust] is bad. It is better therefore, that is, more to be countenanced, that a man should choose what is less good, than that he should fall into the evil of incontinence" (*Super I Cor.*, c. 7, lect. 1; emphasis added).

66. TB, 295.

a clear reserve regarding the concept of marriage as a remedy for concupiscence, insisting rather that the sacramental grace of marriage enables the spouses to dominate concupiscence and purify it of its dominant self-seeking. "These statements of St. Paul [quoted above] have given rise to the opinion that marriage constitutes a specific remedy for concupiscence. However, as we have already observed, St. Paul teaches explicitly that marriage has a corresponding special "gift," and that in the mystery of redemption marriage is given to a man and a woman as a grace." Within this mystery of redemption, as the pope sees it, the sacramental graces of marriage, sustaining conjugal chastity, have a special effect in achieving the redemption of the body through the overcoming of concupiscence:

As a sacrament of the Church, marriage . . . [is] a word of the Spirit which exhorts man and woman to model their whole life together by drawing power from the mystery of the "redemption of the body." In this way they are called to chastity as to a state of life "according to the Spirit" which is proper to them (see Rom 8:4–5; Gal 5:25). The redemption of the body also signifies in this case that hope which, in the dimension of marriage, can be defined as the hope of daily life, the hope of temporal life. On the basis of such a hope the concupiscence of the flesh as the source of the tendency toward an egoistic gratification is dominated. . . . Those who, as spouses, according to the eternal divine plan, join together so as to become in a certain sense one flesh, are also in their turn called, through the sacrament, to a life according to the Spirit.[67] This corresponds to the gift received in the sacrament. In

67. Here Pope John Paul II places the concept of "two in one flesh" in the context of "the mystery of the *redemption of the body*." St. Augustine, as we saw earlier, affirms in his *De bono coniugali* that "the *bodies* of the spouses are *holy*" insofar as they live marriage according God's plan. Two notable statements, separated by some 1,500 years, which might yield matter for further interesting research, especially if we consider the following: when dealing with the traditional analysis of "form" and "matter" in relation to the sacrament of matrimony, moralists of many centuries past seemed hesitant to put too much "corporality" into the concept of "matter." Using a contractualist ap-

virtue of that gift, by leading a life according to the Spirit, the spouses are capable of rediscovering the particular gratification which they have become sharers of. As much as concupiscence darkens the horizon of the inward vision and deprives the heart of the clarity of desires and aspirations, so much does "life according to the Spirit" (that is, the grace of the sacrament of marriage) permit man and woman to find again the true liberty of the gift, united to the awareness of the spousal meaning of the body in its masculinity and femininity.[68]

This dense passage teaches in summary that through the specific grace of matrimony, spouses can purify the conjugal act of the grasping and self-centered spirit inherent in concupiscence and thus recapture the truly donative experience and pleasure of marital intercourse. This marks a step forward of extraordinary significance in magisterial teaching. We will return to this catechesis below.

Meanwhile, the magisterium of recent decades continues to present new stances and insights on our topic. They show that while the church is expressing a deepened appreciation of the dignity of sexual intercourse in marriage as an act of love-union and mutual self-giving, it has not weakened its teaching that our whole nature, and sexual desire in particular, were seriously impacted by the fall. The *Catechism* teaches clearly and emphatically that as a result of original sin, an operative evil is to be found in human nature, not least in the sexual attraction between man and woman, including within marriage. In a section entitled "Marriage under the regime of sin," the *Catechism* insists (nos. 1606–7):

---

proach, they tended to identify the matter with a simple "right over the body" (see, for instance, Prümmer, *Manuale Theologiae Moralis*, 3:467–68). St. Josemaría Escrivá had no such hesitation. Consistent with his constant preaching that *all* the aspects of marriage enter fully into it as a way and vocation to holiness, he expresses the theological doctrine in all directness: "Marriage is a sacrament that makes one flesh of two bodies. Theology expresses this fact in a striking way when it teaches us that the matter of the sacrament is the bodies of husband and wife" (*Christ Is Passing By*, 45).

68. TB, 348–49.

Every man experiences evil around him and within himself. This experience makes itself felt in the relationships between man and woman. Their union has always been threatened by discord, a spirit of domination, infidelity, jealousy, and conflicts that can escalate into hatred and separation. . . . According to faith the disorder we notice so painfully does not stem from the nature of man and woman, nor from the nature of their relations, but from sin. As a break with God, the first sin had for its first consequence the rupture of the original communion between man and woman. Their relations were distorted by mutual recriminations; their mutual attraction, the Creator's own gift, changed into a relationship of domination and lust.

A relationship of lust: strong words indeed to describe a distortion that tends to affect relations between the sexes from adolescence to old age and even, as the context makes clear, in inter-spousal relations. As is evident, the *Catechism* gives no support to the idea that concupiscence is in some way "remedied," in the sense of being eliminated or reduced to non-importance, by the simple fact of getting married—rather, just the contrary.

With deliberate directness, the *Catechism* puts forward ideas not likely to gain easy acceptance among our contemporaries. Some may take them as showing that the church is still imbued with Augustinian (or Thomistic) pessimism about sexuality. That must be firmly contested: what is being taught here is not pessimism but realism. In pointing to real difficulties that accompany and can threaten sexual love, these texts rather call Christians to deeper reflection as to ways of solving these dangers, so that love itself can grow.

Concupiscence and Married Love: An In-Depth Analysis

Lust, Normal Sexual Desire, and Conjugal Desire

To distinguish between lust and "normal" sexual desire may provoke the reaction: surely normal sexual desire inevitably contains some element of lust? The objection itself points to the need for deeper analyses of sexuality, sexual reaction, and sexual attraction. The concept of "normal" bears reference not primarily to frequency but to order. Civil disorder may be frequent in certain situations, but only an improper use of language would classify it as normal. In most intersex relations concupiscent lust is just below the surface and ready to assert itself. Its constant presence suggests a disorder and indicates in fact a state of abnormality.

The modern difficulty in understanding the church's teaching on married sexuality stems in large part from a failure to distinguish between lust and what is (or should be) normal sexual desire, that is, between assertive and unregulated sexual desire, bent foremost on physical self-satisfaction, and simple sexual attraction, which can include a desire for union and is characterized by respect and regulated by love. The two are not to be equated. Pope John Paul II insists on the distinction: "The perennial call . . . and, in a certain sense, the perennial mutual attraction on man's part to femininity and on woman's part to masculinity, is an indirect invitation of the body. But it is not lust in the sense of the word in Matthew 5:27–28."[69]

Lust or sexual concupiscence is a disorder and hence always an evil. Sexual desire (just as sexual pleasure) is not an evil but a good, provided it is directed and subordinated to conjugal love and made a proper part of it. Sexual desire is part of conjugal love; concupiscence, though present also in marriage, is not. Hence their moral evaluation is totally different. The distinction should be evident if one carefully ponders and respects the propriety of terms.[70]

---

69. TB, 148

70. Michael Waldstein's new translation of *Theology of the Body* is much to be welcomed. However in one point of his rendering of John Paul II's text, there seems to be room for disagreement (I follow his comments given in an interview with Zenit, 1 June 2006; http://www.zenit.org/en/articles/retranslating-the-theology-of-the-body-part-2). He considers that the English translations hitherto in use are misleading in

Sexual Concupiscence

Lust or carnal concupiscence can be described as the engross-
ing urge for pleasure and exploitative possession which, in our present condition, almost always accompanies sexual desire and tends
to take it over. From the moral point of view, it is a negative force
and a powerful enemy of true human and spiritual growth. The
Christian idea of sexual concupiscence can only be understood in
the light of the fall. Christians hold that the original state of man
vis-à vis woman was one of joyous harmony, particularly in relation
to their reciprocal sexuality with its potential for mutual appreciation and enrichment, and for unitive and fruitful love. The mutual
attraction between man and woman naturally has its physical aspect and this too, as the *Catechism* says, is part of "the Creator's
own gift" (no. 1607). Sin corrupted this harmonious peace of the
man-woman relationship. After the fall, says the *Catechism*, "the
harmony in which they [Adam and Eve] had found themselves,
thanks to original justice, is now destroyed: the control of the soul's
spiritual faculties over the body is shattered" (no. 400). This disor-

---

speaking of "lust," when simple sexual desire is closer to Pope John Paul II's thought
("Desire can be good or bad; lust is a vice," he rightly says). As a particular example he
adduces precisely the passage in Mt 5:28. Translations up to now have followed the Revised Standard Version according to which Jesus says, "Whoever looks at a woman lustfully has already committed adultery with her in his heart." Waldstein considers that
"John Paul II's translation is much closer to the Greek original; it has 'Whoever looks
at a woman to desire her.'" It is seldom that translations are not debatable. In this case I
would not agree with Michael Waldstein. The Friburg Greek Lexicon gives three shades
of meaning (and three Biblical examples) for the Greek word used here, *epithumeo*:
"(1) gener. of a strong impulse toward someth. *desire, long for* (Lk 16.21); (2) in a good
sense, of natural or commendable desire *long for, earnestly desire* (Lk 22.15); (3) in a bad
sense, of unrestricted desire for a forbidden pers. or thing *lust for* or *after, crave, covet*
(Mt 5.28; Acts 20.33)" (see *BibleWorks* commentary). Surely it is indisputable that in this
passage Jesus is speaking of desire which is gravely disordered; otherwise how explain his
judgment that the look is equivalent to having "already committed adultery with her in
his heart"? It is clear that Pope John Paul II himself, in his General Audience of September 17 and October 8, 1980, proposes this understanding (TB, 148 and 157).

der can extend to the marital relationship itself: "The union of man and woman becomes subject to tensions, their relations henceforth marked by lust and domination" (no. 409).

Normal Sexual Attraction

Sexual concupiscence cannot be equated simply with physical sexual attraction or even with a desire for genital union. The romantic or idealistic love between a teenage boy and girl (frequently still to be found even in our modern sensualized world) may also be accompanied by a desire to show bodily affection—a desire filled with a tenderness and respect that operate as a powerful curb, not only on lust if it seeks to assert itself but also on bodily expressions of love which would not be true to the real existential relationship between the couple. This is part of the chastity natural to incipient adolescent sexuality. Its power should not be underestimated, as natures fresh to sexuality can have a purer sense of the mystery of the body and a spontaneous understanding of the true relationship of bodily actions to human love.

Sexual Attraction (Desire) and Conjugal Attraction

In virtue of their complementarity, the sexes naturally experience an attraction to each other that does not always take the form of physical desire (though, as we have mentioned, unbalanced desire may in our present state be just below the surface). Ability to appreciate and admire well-developed masculine or feminine characteristics is a sign of growing human maturity. As young people meet in the context of normal social friendships between men and women, more particularized one-to-one relationships develop in response to what could be called the "conjugal instinct" or attraction. In its essence this "instinct" is more spiritual than physical; in the Christian understanding it corresponds to the natural desire for forming a committed and exclusive lifelong partnership with a spouse.[71] As the conjugal instinct inspires two persons in preparation for marriage, it leads them to avoid any physical relations which would express a permanent union that they have not yet freely and mutually ratified. This is the human and anthropological sense of pre-marital chastity. Once they are married, then their physical conjugal union becomes *the* conjugal act which, when realized in a human way, gives true and unique expression to their spousal relationship. In participating in it in its full significance, they express their marital chastity.

When Love and Lust Collide

We mentioned above the pure air of an adolescent's first love. Unfortunately sexual attraction finds it more and more difficult to keep breathing that air. Love needs to be very strong indeed if it is to remain pure and delicate, generous in gift and not grasping in possession—even when, ultimately, it has the right to possess. This applies to the whole of pre-marital friendship between the sexes, to courtship, and to marriage itself. Normal friendship between a teenage boy and girl can only be sincere and grow if they are on guard against lust. When the attraction between a boy and girl or a young man and woman takes the form of a more particularized love, then it is even more important to keep love free from lust. Clarity of mind and firmness of purpose are needed to achieve this. If love is sincere, there is little difficulty in noting the issues or differences that may arise. On the one hand, the indiscriminate instinct of lust with its promptings to seek satisfaction with the first appealing person available; on the other, the particularized

71. A rotal sentence quotes St. Thomas, "Man is naturally made for marriage. Hence the conjugal bond, or marriage, is natural" (*Suppl.*, q. 41, art. 1), and adds: "Marriage as proposed by the Church corresponds to the natural understanding which man and woman have of that exclusive, permanent and fruitful union with a member of the other sex to which one is naturally led by the human conjugal instinct" ("Sentence *coram* Burke," *Rotae Romanae Decisiones* 86 [December 12, 1991], 747).

human instinct (the conjugal instinct already present) urging to keep the gift of sexuality for one person and to respect that "one" when found but without there yet being a mutual conjugal commitment. No one will say that this instinct of respect is easy to follow; but if true love is there, the instinct too will be there.

Man and woman united in marriage is the fullest setting for human love.[72] It is in marriage that the collision of love and lust can be most dramatic, with so much depending on its outcome. We recall the title, "Marriage under the regime of sin," under which the *Catechism* insists that the harmony and ease of the original communion between man and woman have been ruptured by a "disorder [that] we notice so painfully": the disorder of concupiscence which takes over when mutual sexual attraction, instead of being filled with respect and love, is "changed into a relationship of domination and lust" (no. 1607).

Here our thoughts go naturally back to St. Augustine and the terms in which he described this disorder: the evil of lust that spouses need to "use well" (that is, to turn to good use), but which can frustrate and separate them if they use it badly. St. Augustine's view is nuanced and complex, but our reflections may help us see that it is neither pessimistic nor characterized by an anti-sex spirit.[73] One might perhaps give a modern personalist expression to

72. Conjugal union is a matter of both body and spirit. To be attracted by the body of one's spouse and to want to be united in body with the spouse, is indeed part of normal conjugal desire. But it is even more part of that conjugal desire to be attracted by the *person* of the other and to want to have a union of persons. The importance of this double aspect becomes clearer if we think in terms of love and not just of attraction or desire. Human spousal love is directed not mainly to the body but above all to the person of the other. The two loves—for the body and for the person—should ideally be in perfect harmony. In practice they often are not. In fact they can be in opposition, i.e., when desire for the body detaches itself from love for the person. That this can happen is nothing new; but it is certainly disturbing and a matter to be taken clearly and firmly into account.

73. I am seeking to develop an argument in personalist terms, and St. Augustine can scarcely be classified as a personalist in the modern sense. He nowhere distinguishes

his view by saying that spouses use the sexual attraction between them well when, through constant vigilance, they raise it to the level of conjugal vitality and keep it there, and use it badly when they let it decline toward the level of mere animal mating.

The contemporary magisterium insists time and again that each human being must be treated as a person and never as a thing. This is a rule for all human relationships, but for none as much as marriage. The conjugal instinct, as we have called it, wants to relate to one's spouse as a person and never as a mere object to be used for one's own physical satisfaction. Carnal concupiscence on the other hand, also present in marriage, tends in its self-centered forcefulness to disturb the loving relationship which should exist between husband and wife, and so can easily prevent marital sexuality from being completely at the service of love. Concupiscence wants to have and use the other person. Possession and satisfaction, not gift and union, are its concern. "In itself, concupiscence is not capable of promoting union as the communion of persons. By itself, it does not unite, but appropriates. The relationship of the gift is changed into the relationship of appropriation."[74]

A Comprehensive Moral Evaluation of Conjugal Intercourse

At this point in our study, the need for a deeper moral appraisal of conjugal sexuality is apparent. The hitherto prevalent

---

concupiscence from good sexual attraction, while some of his statements can indeed appear to equate concupiscence with simple sexual desire or with the pleasure accompanying marital intercourse. Nevertheless, as I have sought to show in Chapter Six, this is not his true mind: concupiscence for him does not mean the physical pleasure accompanying conjugal intercourse (which he defends) but rather the tendency to let the urge for that pleasure eclipse its true purpose and meaning. Those modern commentators who accuse Augustine of pessimism fail at least as much he does to distinguish between "good" and "bad" sexual desire. My wish is not to present Augustine as a personalist but rather to draw attention to the underappreciated depth and realism of his analysis.

74. TB, 127.

evaluation of conjugal intercourse, centered almost exclusively on its procreative function and finality, is both dated and deficient. Recent magisterial teaching has made it clear that the evaluation must be made also in view of the unitive function of the conjugal act, precisely bearing in mind that the two aspects, procreative and unitive, are inseparable (see *Humanae Vitae*, no. 12). A strong warrant for this broadened moral basis can be drawn from the personalist emphasis on the dignity of the person, the unity between body and soul, and the union between the spouses that is to be found in magisterial teaching over the past fifty years. This is noticeably present in *Gaudium et Spes*,[75] especially in the chapter devoted to marriage.[76] This text proposes a new and important principle governing the evaluation of the conjugal act: "The acts in marriage by which the intimate and chaste union of the spouses takes place are noble and honorable; the performance of these acts *in a truly human way* [*modo vere humano*] fosters the self-giving they signify."[77] The insistence that the conjugal act must be carried out "in a truly human way" raises the whole subject of conjugal intercourse above any merely corporal-physiological analysis. Intercourse is a physical corporal reality indeed, but depending on "the humanity" with which it is (or is not) performed, it will truly express, or may deny, the loving donation of the marital relationship.

The phrase from *Gaudium et Spes* has taken on new significance with the 1983 Code. These three words, *modo vere humano*, now qualify the juridical understanding of the consummation of marriage. A marriage is considered "consummated, if the spouses have *in a human manner* engaged together in a conjugal act in itself apt for the generation of offspring, to which act marriage is by its nature ordered, and by it the spouses become one flesh" (c. 1061).

75. See GS, nos. 12, 23, 26, 28–29, and 40–46.
76. GS, nos. 47–52.
77. GS, no. 49.

The qualifying phrase was not present in the corresponding canon of the 1917 Code (c. 1015) and pre-1983 rotal jurisprudence, in line with the general teaching of moral theology, tended to limit consideration of what constitutes "a conjugal act in itself apt for the generation of offspring" to the simple physical completion of intercourse through natural insemination. This is no longer adequate. The addition of the phrase "in a human manner" seems to preclude any consideration of the act limited exclusively to its physical aspect.[78] The determination of its value for the purposes of canonical jurisprudence poses no small problems, but independently of how canonists deal with these questions the phrase is very suggestive from the anthropological and ascetical points of view, clearly calling for an enriched understanding of the marital copula. The major implication would be that intercourse is not done "humano modo" just because it is open to procreation. The human nature of the act also lies in its being an act of intimate self-donation to, and of union with, one's spouse: a reconfirmation in the body of one's singular choice of him or her, a reconfirmation that is humanly expressed not only in the giving and receiving of pleasure but even more essentially in the care, respect, tenderness, and reverence accompanying the physical act.

We could already ask whether, in the present state of human nature, the sexual act tends spontaneously and easily to express all of this? Most people would agree that it does not, at least not easily. It can and should express it, but will only do so with an effort because, so to speak, much of the humanity of the conjugal act has been lost. It will be recovered only by those who consciously

78. It is clear that there is no consummation through a *copula* not carried out "humano modo," as verified for instance in the case of contraceptive intercourse where there is no real carnal *union*, no "*unio carnuum*" in any true sense. It is not so clear to what degree or at what point insistence (short of physical brute force) of one party overcoming the reluctance of the other to have intercourse, so "dehumanizes" the act that it can scarcely be considered any longer a physical expression of marital union.

exercise control over the self-absorbed mood that now tends to dominate it. However, we are anticipating conclusions that should come later, and so let us continue with the implications of "*modo vere humano exerciti*." The phrase itself suggests the disjunction: while conjugal intercourse can take place in a truly human way that gives it its dignity as a means of expressing and fostering conjugal love, it can also be performed in a way that, being less than truly human, neither properly expresses nor fosters spousal love.

The conjugal act is a physical-corporeal action charged with human significance which—it must be emphasized—derives from its unitive as well as its procreative aspects, both in inseparable connection. Anti-procreative measures destroy the unitive function of the act, but it is also true that anti-unitive practices or ways, even if the procreative orientation is respected, undermine the human significance of the act. A union effected in a mood of grasping appropriation gives poor expression to the mutual loving gift that should mark true conjugality, and the same is true of a union motivated mainly by self-seeking. Here we are touching upon the particularly human dimensions of conjugal intercourse. And the morality ("morality" here is as much as to say "the truly human quality") of the act must consider the special moral dimension that arises from the self-centeredness or the other-centeredness lived by each of the spouses in conjugal intercourse.

Biology alone is not capable of furnishing the true moral and human dimension of conjugal intercourse, which cannot be considered exclusively as a corporal act directed to biological procreation. It is a human act of spousal union indeed, not just of the spouses' bodies but also of their very persons. The bodily act should in every respect express the loving union of persons. As we read in *Familiaris Consortio* (no. 11):

Sexuality, by means of which man and woman give themselves to one another through the acts which are proper and exclusive to spouses, is by no means something purely biological, but concerns the innermost being of the human person as such. It is realized in a truly human way only if it is an integral part of the love by which a man and a woman commit themselves totally to one another until death. The total physical self-giving would be a lie if it were not the sign and fruit of a total personal self-giving.

The last sentence in this passage suggests the moral goal and challenge set before the spouses: that every aspect of their married life should be marked by loving participation, by generous giving and not by selfish taking.

What Makes the Conjugal Act Unitive

It is an extraordinary fact that right down to the present day there has been so little attempt to analyze and put in clear light what it is that turns sexual intercourse into a unique expression of conjugal love and self-giving. The formidable and widespread contraceptive movement of the last century, with its pretense that the conjugal act is fully and singularly expressive of marital love and union *even if* its procreative orientation is artificially excluded, called for a deeper anthropological analysis of why this is simply not so—an analysis which we have attempted in the previous chapter.

It may help if we briefly recall the main argument. The procreative design of the conjugal act is evident and undeniable. The contraceptive movement proposes various physical or chemical ways to cancel or negate this procreative design, claiming at the same time that this can be done without in any way rendering the act less expressive of the unique relationship of the partners as husband and wife (that is, less an act of spousal union). The inherent fallacy of this contraceptive argument is evident. What makes intercourse between spouses a unique expression of distinctive conjugal union is precisely the sharing in their mutual complementary procreative power. If the procreative orientation of the act is deliberately frustrated through contraception, then it no longer unites the spouses in any distinctively conjugal way. It is no longer *the* conjugal act, the most distinctive physical expression of full mutual surrender and permanent loving union. It is in fact no longer a sexual act in any true human sense, for there is no actual sexual intercourse or communication. The spouses refuse true carnal communication with one another, each rather using the other's body for pleasure. But a mere exchange of pleasure neither expresses nor achieves spousal union, for there is nothing in that pleasure which draws a person out of his or her solitude and draws each into a greater oneness with the other. This refusal of union, this voluntary remaining in solitariness, tends inexorably to the separation of the spouses. Contraception may be mutually gratifying but is no way unifying, tending rather to shut each spouse off in individual satisfaction. Hence it is not wholly exaggerated to speak of it as a mutual experience of solitary sex.[79]

Self-Centeredness, the Enemy of Conjugal Love

Love moves outward toward the loved one and seeks the good of the beloved. It is donative and, although it naturally tends toward union, the simple desire to possess or to take is not of the nature of true love. Hence the difficulty for the self-centered person (that is, all of fallen humanity) to learn to love, for he or she must strive to make other-centeredness take priority over self-centeredness. To love another with all one's heart is difficult; it is not in fact possible without a constant battle to purge one's actions and motives, since some element of self-seeking tends to remain in the best of them.

---

79. George Bernard Shaw was perhaps being crude, but not flippant nor cynical, when he commented that contraception amounts to "mutual masturbation."

This applies constantly in married life; it is in the small details that love is shown, that it grows or dwindles. If all aspects of conjugal relations need purification, is this not also true for the most intimate conjugal relationship of all?

If self-seeking predominates in sexual relations, then intercourse, even marital intercourse, is not primarily an expression of love. The natural satisfaction of the sexual urge is legitimate within marriage, but even there it may carry with it a degree of self-seeking that is contrary to love, hindering it rather than expressing or increasing it. As Pope John Paul II puts it, "disinterested giving is excluded from selfish enjoyment."[80] It is necessary to repeat that intercourse can and should be a maximum human expression of total conjugal love and donation. It ought to express full self-donation, centered (ideally) more on what the other receives than on what one gets. But it can be reduced to an act of mere selfish satisfaction. This has always been the central obstacle to be faced by conjugal spirituality and the pursuit of perfection in marriage. Lust is one of the most radically self-centered appetites. As such it impels toward a joining of bodies that in fact causes a separation of persons, because those who are carried away by it in their mutual relations are afterwards left more separated from one another than before. As a result of the fall, says Pope John Paul II, bodily sexuality "was suddenly felt and understood as an element of mutual confrontation of persons . . . as if the personal profile of masculinity and femininity, which before had highlighted the meaning of the body for a full communion of persons, had made way only for the sensation of sexuality with regard to the other human being. It is as if sexuality became an obstacle in the personal relationship of man and woman."[81]

We are brought back to the strong statements of the *Catechism*

---

80. TB, 130.   81. TB, 118–19.

regarding the distortion of the original communion between man and woman as a result of the fall, when their mutual attraction changed into "a relationship of domination and lust" (no. 1607). Pope John Paul II did not hesitate to express the matter in an even more startling manner. Commenting the words of Jesus about how adultery "in the heart" (Mt 5:27–28) is committed by the one who *looks* lustfully (without any further exterior action), he points out that this can apply to a man even in relation to his own wife:[82]

Adultery in the heart is committed not only *because* man looks in this way [lustfully] at a woman who is not his wife, but *precisely* because he looks at a woman in this way. . . . A man who looks in this way, uses the woman, her femininity, to satisfy his own instinct. Although he does not do so with an exterior act, he has already assumed this attitude deep down, inwardly deciding in this way with regard to a given woman. This is what adultery committed in the heart consists of. Man can commit this adultery in the heart also with regard to his own wife, if he treats her only as an object to satisfy instinct.

Is this an exaggerated statement?[83] Does it show a pessimistic or Manichean view of the married sexual relationship? Or is it a real possibility to be taken into account? Can a man *lust* after his wife, or vice-versa? If he or she can, is this a good or a bad thing for married life? Or is it something to be looked on with indifference? Is a spouse not meant to be the object of a different and nobler sort of desire than simple self-satisfaction? Should we be surprised then at St. Thomas's opinion that "*consentiens concupiscentiae in uxorem*" is guilty not of a mortal sin, but indeed of one that is venial?[84] One can see this as Manichean if one wishes; yet one can also see it as a

82. TB, 157.
83. Countless examples could be cited of the strong reaction that the Pope's words provoked in many quarters, revealing just how far our world is from appreciating the true challenges of married love.
84. *Super I Cor.*, c. 7, lect. 1.

challenge to love and virtue. To the extent that intercourse is dominated by lust, it is far from virtue. It becomes truly virtuous in the measure in which it is a genuine expression of self-giving. Concupiscence, with its self-absorbed desire for physical satisfaction, threatens the full authenticity of conjugal intercourse intended to be an expression of the love-union. Concupiscence has brought about, as Pope John Paul II puts it:

A violation, a fundamental loss, of the original community-communion of persons. The latter should have made man and woman mutually happy by the pursuit of a simple and pure union in humanity, by a reciprocal offering of themselves. . . . After breaking the original covenant with God, the man and the woman found themselves more divided. Instead of being united, they were even opposed because of their masculinity and femininity. . . . [They] are no longer called only to union and unity, but are also threatened by the insatiability of that union and unity.[85]

The presence of lust or concupiscence within marriage itself is undeniable. And at this stage in our study, far from being able to confirm that marriage offers a remedy for concupiscence, we realize that lust, inasmuch as it introduces an anti-love element into the sexual relationship, poses a threat to marriage and particularly to married love itself. How then, within a truly Christian understanding of marriage as a call of love and as a vocation to sanctity, should married persons treat the presence of concupiscence, that self-absorbed element present in their intimate union?

Abstinence

Up to now, spouses who really sought to live their conjugal relationship as God wished, to sanctify themselves in and through their marriage, received little orientation from the teaching of the church apart from the idea that a modicum of abstinence is a recommendable means not just of family planning but of positive

85. TB, 120.

growth in married sanctity.[86] Abstinence in this view often seemed to be presented as the ideal, or at least as the main means to union with God and the sanctification of one's life. One senses here (and this is the heart of the problem) a continuing underlying presumption that marital intercourse is something so "anti-spiritual" that spouses would do better and grow more in love for God by abstaining from it than by engaging in it. This presumption should be firmly resisted. If marriage is in itself a divine way of holiness, then all of its natural elements, including of course intimate conjugal relations, are a matter of sanctification. Certainly (as we will see below) these relations must be marked by temperance, yet total abstinence from such relations cannot be proposed as an ideal or ascetical goal for spouses.[87] Total abstinence as a means to counter the problem of lust is not a practical proposal for married people—yet lust must still be countered within marriage.

Married Love and Married Chastity
Rediscovering Conjugal Love as it Was
"In the Beginning"

The constant reference point for married life and vocation which Pope John Paul II presented throughout his 1979–84 weekly

---

86. Abstaining from or renouncing secular activities and the satisfactions or pleasures that may derive from them has been central to religious life since its inception in the early church. While the roots of this religious spirituality go back to Jesus's invitation to the rich young man (Mt 19:21), it is debatable whether it has offered the necessary inspiration and dynamism to guide lay people in general and married people in particular to the full goal of Christian life. It is true that Jesus said "whoever of you does not renounce all that he has cannot be my disciple" (Lk 14:33). Yet it is also clear that celibacy, whether in religious life or otherwise, is not the only Christian way; and indeed that, despite St. Paul's wish ("I wish that all were as I myself am"), God is not calling everyone to be celibate. Pope John Paul II recalls how Paul himself acknowledges that each one "has his own special gift from God."

87. There are various reasons why abstinence may enter periodically into conjugal life, but it would seem fundamentally flawed to propose abstinence as an ideal, or as a condition for holiness, in those called to Christian marriage. St. Paul's suggestion to spouses to abstain "for a time" (1 Cor 7:5) cannot be broadened into a general norm.

catechesis was "marriage constituted in the beginning, in the state of original innocence, in the context of the sacrament of creation," called to be a "visible sign of God's creative love."[88] That original human state was marked by a perfect harmony, within each one, of body and spirit.[89]

The Creator endowed the body with an objective harmony . . . [that] corresponded to a similar harmony within man, the harmony of the heart. This harmony, that is precisely purity of heart, enabled man and woman in the state of original innocence to experience simply (and in a way that originally made them both happy) the uniting power of their bodies, which was, so to speak, the unsuspected substratum of their personal union or *communio personarum*.[90]

That original harmony was short-lived, however; man and woman sinned and it was broken. With the sin of Adam and Eve concupiscence or lust made its appearance. It became present in their marriage (and is present in every subsequent marriage), posing a threat to married love and happiness.

In his "Catechesis on Human Love," Pope John Paul II made a lengthy examination of the discordant presence of lust in spousal relations.[91] Its fundamental effect is a loss or a limitation of the full freedom of love.

Concupiscence entails the loss of the interior freedom of the gift. The nuptial meaning of the human body is connected precisely with this freedom. Man can become a gift—that is, the man and the woman can exist in the relationship of mutual self-giving—if each of them exerts self-control. Manifested as a "coercion *sui generis* of the body," concu-

88. TB, 338 and 379.
89. Interpersonal harmony, between spirit and spirit, was not a necessary part of that state. Man and woman had freely to create that harmony between themselves, and each one with God. How in their first test they failed to do so, and then had to seek to restore it, forms the background to the whole human drama and to our present study.
90. TB, 204.
91. TB, 111–68.

piscence reduces self-control and places an interior limit on it. For that reason, it makes the interior freedom of giving in a certain sense impossible. Together with that, the beauty that the human body possesses in its male and female aspects, as an expression of the spirit, is obscured. The body remains as an object of lust and therefore as a "field of appropriation" of the other human being. In itself, concupiscence is not capable of promoting union as the communion of persons. By itself, it does not unite, but appropriates. The relationship of the gift is changed into the relationship of appropriation.[92]

Insatiable desire, appropriation instead of communion, taking instead of giving, possessive self-love overshadowing donative love toward the other; all are major disruptions which concupiscence now inflicts on the lost harmony of the sexual relationship. Is it possible for men and women to return to that original harmony and respect, or are they lost forever? They are not irreparably lost, for they can be recovered in hope and struggle. In the human person there always remains, however unconsciously, a longing for the respect inherent in pure love due to that which John Paul II refers to as "the continuity and unity between the hereditary state of man's sin and his original innocence" which remains a key to "the redemption of the body."[93] However, the recovery and maintenance of what can be repossessed of that original harmony is possible only through constant effort and with the help of prayer and grace.

A particularly striking part of Pope John Paul II's analysis is the place he gives to sexual shame in the work of recovering that harmony. He places shame among the "fundamental anthropological experiences"[94] though one which is beyond mere anthropology; rather, it is a mysterious fact, a sort of clue or pointer to

92. TB, 127.   93. TB, 34–35.
94. "Contemporary anthropology, which likes to refer to so-called fundamental experiences, such as the experience of shame" (TB, 52).

the reestablishment (however tentative) of that enviable and joyous sexual harmony and peace. In the present human condition, a certain instinct of shame acts as a guarantor of the mutual respect that is a *sine qua non* condition of true love between the sexes. The deeper and truer the love between a man and a woman, and especially between husband and wife, the more they will be prompted to pay heed to shame, to seek to understand it and to respond adequately to it. The consequence is a naturally modest behavior between them, a modesty that has its place even in the relationship of husband and wife.

In this sense each married couple should turn to the Bible, seeking the lessons of the divine narrative: not just imagining how the relationship of Adam and Eve must have been before the fall, but learning from their subsequent reactions, reactions that show a desire to preserve, in new and troublesome circumstances, the purity of that original attraction which they alone had experienced and which they could still recall. Before the fall, Adam and Eve were naked and not ashamed. As Pope John Paul II puts it, "the man of original innocence, male and female, did not even feel that discord in the body."[95] After the fall, shame appeared as a response to lust as a sort of protection against the threat which lust now offered to the simple joy and appreciation they had experienced in each other's sexuality "in the beginning." The importance of this sense of shame is powerfully brought out in the papal catechesis. On the one hand:[96]

If the man and the woman cease to be a disinterested gift for each other, as they were in the mystery of creation, then they recognize that "they

95. TB, 204. Pope John Paul II is at one with Augustine's analysis of the situation. Original nakedness provoked no untoward desire and hence no shame in Adam and Eve, "not because they could not see, but because they felt nothing in their members to make them ashamed of what they saw" (*De nupt. et conc.*, I, 5, 6).

96. TB, 74–75.

are naked" (Gen 3). Then the shame of that nakedness, which they had not felt in the state of original innocence, will spring up in their hearts. . . . Only the nakedness that makes woman an object for man, or vice versa, is a source of shame. The fact that they were not ashamed means that the woman was not an "object" for the man nor he for her.

He continues: "In the light of the biblical narrative, sexual shame has its deep meaning. It is connected with the failure to satisfy the aspiration to realize in the conjugal union of the body the mutual communion of persons."[97] The reaction of shame before the other, including shame that spouses experience with each other, betrays an awareness that the urge to bodily intercourse is not of the same human quality as the desire for the communion of persons, and cannot give this desire full effect.

On the other hand, while shame "reveals the moment of lust, at the same time it can protect from [its] consequences. . . . It can even be said that man and woman, through shame, almost remain in the state of original innocence. They continually become aware of the nuptial meaning of the body and aim at preserving it from lust."[98] The desire to preserve respect for the loved one is inherent in every genuine love. So in Pope John Paul II's analysis, the sense of shame becomes not only a guardian of mutual respect between husband and wife, but also a starting point for the recreation of a new spousal harmony between body and soul, between desire and respect, achieved on the basis of united purpose aided by prayer and grace. John Paul II does not suggest that this "re-creation" is in any way easy; it obviously is not. But his message for married people is that it should be attempted; their mutual love should see its need, and the sacramental graces of their marriage along with their personal prayer are the powerful means they have to achieve it.

97. TB, 121.
98. TB, 122.

The Purification of Conjugal Love from
Self-Absorbing Sensuality

In contrast to the effects of concupiscence, chastity and a right sense of shame protect and preserve the "freedom of the gift" proper to conjugal intercourse. Pope John Paul II insists that this interior freedom of the gift "of its nature is explicitly spiritual and depends on a person's interior maturity. This freedom presupposes such a capacity of directing one's sensual and emotive reactions as to make self-donation to the other possible, on the basis of mature self-possession."[99] This is the proper sense of chastity in marriage: the redirecting and the refinement of sensual appetite so that it is at the service of love and expresses it, along with the refusal to take advantage of the married relationship just for egoistic satisfaction. In a real sense, the task facing married couples is purification of sensual appetite, so that its satisfaction is sought not mainly for concupiscent self-centeredness but as an accompaniment to the donation of self that must underlie every true conjugal union. One can say that this task engages the couple in a constant humanizing of their marital love, facilitating the growth of mutual appreciation of each other as persons.[100]

True conjugal love is evidently characterized more by caring for and giving to the other than by wanting and taking for oneself. It is the classical distinction between *amor amicitiae* and *amor concupiscentiae*. Where the love of concupiscence dominates, the lover has not really come out of himself or overcome self-centeredness,

99. TB, 414; see also 75, 120–22, 127, 349, etc. Augustine emphasizes that the desires of concupiscence must be resisted, or they will dominate us: "There is therefore in us the concupiscence of sin, which must not be permitted to reign; there are the desires of concupiscence, which are not to be obeyed, lest they govern those obeying them [Est ergo in nobis peccati concupiscentia, quae non est permittenda regnare; sunt eius desideria, quibus non est oboediendum, ne oboedientibus regnet]" (*De continentia*, 8).

100. For the "depersonalizing" effect of concupiscence, see TB, 151–52.

and so gives himself at most only in part. "In the love of concupiscence, the lover, in wanting the good he desires, properly speaking loves himself."[101] The dominance of pleasure-seeking in marital intercourse means that there is too much taking of the body and not enough giving to the person; insofar as this imbalance is present, the true conjugal communion of persons is not realized.

In an age like ours, the difference between lust, sexual desire, and conjugal love has become progressively obscured. If, in consequence, many married couples do not understood or recognize the dangers of concupiscence and so do not endeavor to contain or purify it, it can dominate their relationship, undermining mutual respect and the very capacity to see marriage essentially as giving and not just as possessing, much less as simply enjoying, appropriating, and exploiting.

Thus we return to St. Augustine's invitation to married couples to purge their good marital intercourse of the evil that tends to accompany it: that evil which is not the pleasure of conjugal union but excessive and self-centered absorption with that pleasure. This is an inescapable task facing all married couples who in some way wish to restore the loving harmony of a spousal relationship filled with growing appreciation and respect. We spoke above of how abstinence or renunciation as a governing principle of religious life was often presented also to married couples wishing to grow spiritually, with the implicit or explicit invitation to apply it to their conjugal intercourse. We must add here that while renunciation is certainly a main gospel theme, it is not the only or even the dominant one. *Purification*, above all of one's inner intention and heart, is even more fundamental to the achievement of the ultimate Christian goal: "Blessed are the pure in heart, for they shall see God" (Mt. 5:8); "we know that when he appears we shall be like him, for we shall see him

101. Aquinas, *Summa Theologiae* I–II, q. 27, a. 3.

as he is. And every one who thus hopes in him purifies himself as he is pure" (1 Jn 3:2–3). These verses are of universal application.

This work of purification confronts married people in all aspects of their life. It is a particular challenge to them with regard to their intimate conjugal relations. To purify conjugal intercourse of the self-absorption that so easily invades it must be a major concern and point of struggle for spouses who wish their marriage to be marked by growing love and so also to become a way of sanctity.[102] Marital intercourse is purified when the urge for self-satisfaction plays a lesser part in it, intercourse being rather sought, lived, and felt as participation and particularly as other-centered donative love. Possession and pleasure will then be the *consequence* of generous self-giving. As Pope John Paul II says, "a noble gratification, for example, is one thing, while sexual desire is another. When sexual desire is linked with a noble gratification, it differs from desire pure and simple. . . . It is precisely at the price of self-control that man reaches that deeper and more mature spontaneity with which his heart, mastering his instincts, rediscovers the spiritual beauty of the sign constituted by the human body in its masculinity and femininity."[103]

One could note in passing that if pleasure is received with gratitude to God and to one's spouse, this is already a positive and significant step towards purifying it of self-centeredness, for gratitude is always a coming out of self and an affirmation of the other. On the other hand, if the seeking of pleasure is mainly self-centered, it may give momentary satisfaction but not real peace, that is, the peace that arises from the experience of true donative union. We could recall here how St. Thomas, invoking Galatians 5:17, explains

102. This certainly implies a restraint, but it is a restraint that should be an expression of love and consideration, just as when husband or wife restrains his or her temper out of consideration for the other.

103. TB, 173.

that a lack of interior peace is so often due to an unresolved conflict between what one's sense appetite wants and what one's mind wants.[104] The goal then, as indicated above, is that spouses *humanize* their intimate relations, rather than abstain from them. This is the work of purification proposed to them; this has to be the tone of married chastity.[105]

Sound Christian thinking has always been aware of the self-absorbing force of the urge to physical sexual satisfaction. The moral principle that to seek this satisfaction outside marriage is grievously wrong derives in part from the fact that this urge is so deeply egoistic. But there has been no parallel consideration of the possible effect on married life itself of this self-engrossed force. Moral theology has tended to ignore this question, which is today resurfacing as a major issue for theological and pastoral reflection. Simply to find reasons that "justify" marital sexual intercourse is an approach of the past. Also dated is the approach that would over-stress the idea of *abstention* from intercourse as a key to spiritual growth in marriage. What has to be put to spouses is the need to *purify* their intercourse so that they may more and more find in it the unmixed character of loving personal gift-acceptance that it would have had in Eden.

104. Aquinas, *Summa Theologiae* II–II, q. 29, a. 1.

105. "In earthly life, the dominion of the spirit over the body—and the simultaneous subordination of the body to the spirit—can, as the result of persevering work on themselves, express a personality that is spiritually mature" (TB, 241). This implies not a one-sided victory of the spirit over the body, but a perfect harmony between the two, so it "does not signify any disincarnation of the body nor, consequently, a dehumanization of man. On the contrary, it signifies his perfect realization. In fact, in the composite, psychosomatic being which man is, perfection cannot consist in a mutual opposition of spirit and body. But it consists in a deep harmony between them, in safe-guarding the primacy of the spirit" (ibid.). Pope John Paul II, applying the Pauline phrase about "discord in the body" (1 Cor 12:25) to the phenomenon of bodily shame resulting from original sin, insists on how a "transformation of this state" can be achieved "to the point of gradual victory over that discord in the body. This victory can and must take place in man's heart. This is the way to purity, that is, 'to control one's own body in holiness and honor'" (TB, 204–5).

Sensitive married couples who sincerely love each other are readily aware of this self-absorbed drive which detracts from the perfection of their physical conjugal union. They sense the need to temper or purify the force drawing them together so that they can be united in true mutual giving, and not in mere simultaneous taking. Their heart calls for this; insofar as they are mainly yielding to lust, a sense of cheating and of being cheated will always remain. Pope John Paul II reads this situation well: "I would say that lust is a deception of the human heart in the perennial call of man and woman to communion by means of mutual giving."[106] It is their very sensitivity to love which makes them troubled by this disorder they would like to remedy, but they have seldom been guided as to how to achieve this or as to why the endeavor and effort to do so is an integral part of their married calling to keep growing in love and so, ultimately, to attain sanctity.[107]

Chastity Gives Freedom to Conjugal Love

In our present condition, concupiscence (or the over-absorbing desires of the flesh) positions itself so easily against the "spirit," which also means against love and the desires of love. This is so before marriage, and remains so in marriage. Scripture insists on this, and so it is a truth that every Christian needs to ponder. At the start of our study we noted how the *Catechism* (no. 2525) identifies concupiscence with the *caro adversus spiritum* of Galatians: "The desires of the flesh are against the spirit, and the desires of the spirit are against the flesh" (Gal 5:17). Pope John Paul II opens the second part of his Catechesis on Human Love with a detailed consideration of this Pauline passage.

106. TB, 148.

107. Pope John Paul II has provided this clear and positive guidance, albeit in a dense catechesis, the very length of which may make it appear inaccessible to the ordinary reader. The "popularising" of his teaching in a form accessible to married couples and those preparing for marriage is a pastoral task of immense importance.

According to the Pope, Paul refers here to "the tension existing within man, precisely in his heart . . . [which] presupposes that
disposition of forces formed in man with original sin, in which every historical man participates. In this disposition, formed within
man, the body opposes the spirit and easily prevails over it."[108]
If we let the body prevail in this battle, we lose our freedom and
hence our very ability to love, for freedom is not true freedom unless it is at the service of love.[109] Only by using freedom truly and
well (and guarding against its false use) can the battle against concupiscence be gradually won; only in this way can we fulfill our
vocation to love in the freedom that Christ has won for us.

To understand the vocation to freedom in this way ("You were called
to freedom, brethren," Gal 5:13), means giving a form to the ethos in
which life "according to the Spirit" is realized. The danger of wrongly
understanding freedom also exists. Paul clearly points this out, writing
in the same context: "Only do not use your freedom as an opportunity
for the flesh, but through love be servants of one another" (Gal 5:13).
In other words, Paul warns us of the possibility of making a bad use
of freedom. Such a use is in opposition to the liberation of the human
spirit carried out by Christ and contradicts that freedom with which
"Christ set us free." . . . The antithesis and, in a way, the negation of this
use of freedom takes place when it becomes a pretext to live according
to the flesh. Freedom then . . . becomes "an opportunity for the flesh," a
source (or instrument) of a specific yoke on the part of pride of life, the
lust of the eyes, and the lust of the flesh. Anyone who lives in this way
according to the flesh, that is, submits . . . to the three forms of lust, especially to the lust of the flesh, ceases to be capable of that freedom for
which "Christ set us free." He also ceases to be suitable for the real gift
of himself, which is the fruit and expression of this freedom. Moreover,
he ceases to be capable of that gift which is organically connected with
the nuptial meaning of the human body.[110]

108. TB, 191.   109. TB, 197.
110. TB, 197–98.

John Paul II's warning here about "good" and "bad" uses of freedom brings to mind St. Augustine's distinction regarding the use of the body. In one of his sermons, Augustine invokes Galatians 5:17 in particular relation to chastity: "Listen well to these words, all you faithful who are fighting. I speak to those who struggle. Only those who struggle will understand the truth of what I say. I will not be understood by whoever does not struggle. . . . What does the chaste person wish? That no force should arise in his body resisting chastity. He would like to experience peace, but does not have it yet."[111] Augustine's words are directed to the married as much as to the unmarried. Both, he is convinced, will understand the truth he expresses if they are prepared to fight the constant warfare of Christian life. The church has not changed her doctrine regarding this battle. The Second Vatican Council teaches (in *Gaudium et Spes*, no. 37):

A monumental struggle against the powers of darkness pervades the whole history of man. The battle was joined from the very origins of the world and will continue until the last day, as the Lord has attested. Caught in this conflict, man is obliged to wrestle constantly if he is to cling to what is good, nor can he achieve his own integrity without great efforts and the help of God's grace.

The "Remedy" of Concupiscence: Chastity

As Karol Wojtyla puts it, "the problem for [sexual] ethics is how to use sex without treating the person as an object for use."[112] This is a perceptive observation which brings a properly human focus to bear on the question of the pleasure of marital intercourse. Pleasure should not be sought just for its own sake, since self-seeking (and "other-using") will then tend to dominate. But

111. *Sermones*, 128.
112. Wojtyla, *Love and Responsibility*, 60.

pleasure can and should be present as an important concomitant of the union achieved. This in the truest sense is what is implied in the remedying of concupiscence. It is a challenge to love and a work of chastity.[113] Earlier we quoted St. Thomas regarding the way in which grace is given in marriage as a remedy *against* concupiscence, so as to curb it in its root (that is, in its self-absorbed tendency),[114] and in chapter 2 we already suggested that one of the main graces bestowed by the sacrament of matrimony, as a "permanent" sacrament, is that of marital chastity in this precise sense. The goal cannot be *not* to feel pleasure or *not* to be drawn by it (both pertain to the instinct of conjugality), but not to be *dominated* by it (which is the very instinct of lust). St. Augustine points out the alternatives: "Whoever does not want to serve lust must necessarily fight against it; whoever neglects to fight it, must necessarily serve it. One of these alternatives is burdensome but praiseworthy, the other is debasing and miserable."[115]

Marital intercourse is indeed a unique way of giving physical expression to married love, but it is not the only way. There are moments in married life (sickness, for instance, or periods just before and after childbirth) when love will not seek intercourse but will still express itself in many other ways, also on the physical level. It is commonplace among marriage counselors or psychologists to assign as much or even more importance to these "lesser" physical expressions of affection and love as may be attached to the frequency of marital intercourse itself. Pope John Paul II does not pass over this point. With finely drawn distinctions, he differentiates "sexual excitement" from "sexual emotion" in man-woman relationships, and comments:

113. Concupiscence is an effect of original sin. What stems from sin, can only be remedied by virtue. So it is not marriage itself but marital chastity that remedies concupiscence.

114. *IV Sent.*, d. 26, q. 2, a. 3, ad 4.

115. *Contra Julianum*, 5:62.

Excitement seeks above all to be expressed in the form of sensual and corporeal pleasure. That is, it tends toward the conjugal act. . . . On the other hand, emotion . . . even if in its emotive content it is conditioned by the femininity or masculinity of the "other," does not *per se* tend toward the conjugal act. But it limits itself to other manifestations of affection, which express the spousal meaning of the body, and which nevertheless do not include its (potentially) procreative meaning.[116]

Men and women, married or single, who wish to grow in mutual love, cannot adapt themselves passively to the prevalent modern lifestyle which, especially as reflected in the media, is permeated with "sexual excitement" and serves as a constant stimulus to such excitement. Purity of heart, sight, and thought is essential if Christians are to keep sexual excitement within the limits of serving sexual emotion and genuine inter-sexual love. Their own intimate consciousness of the real nature of love will be the best incentive to help them keep firmly clear of all those external stimuli which necessarily subject a person more and more to the absorbing power of lust, and so lessen his or her capacity for a true, freely given, and faithful love.

Chastity Is for the Strong, as Is Growth in Love

Among the deceptions of marriage is the experience that what should so uniquely unite can also separate; it can be filled with tensions and disappointment rather than harmony and peace. The tensions come from the divisive force of concupiscence which can only be overcome and purified through a love that is truly donative rather than possessive. "It is often thought that continence causes inner tensions which man must free himself from. [But rather] continence, understood integrally, is the only way to free man from such tensions," as Pope John Paul II puts it.[117] In fact, the chastity proper to marriage unites the spouses, reduces tensions, increases respect, and deepens spousal love, thus leading this love

116. TB, 413.   117. TB, 411.

to its human perfection and preparing the spouses themselves for a love that is infinite and eternal. "The way to attain this goal," Pope Benedict XVI insists, "is not simply by submitting to instinct. Purification and growth in maturity are called for; and these also pass through the path of renunciation. Far from rejecting or 'poisoning' *eros*, they heal it and restore its true grandeur."[118]

Pope John Paul II states: "True conjugal love . . . is also a difficult love."[119] Love of another is always a battle against self-love. That division of the heart between self and spouse must be overcome: conjugal love gives unity to each heart and unites the two hearts in one love. Carnal concupiscence is not the only expression of self-love; but it so pervasively affects the most significant bodily expression of conjugal love that its tendency to dominate must be specially resisted, or love may not survive this battle. "The heart has become a battlefield between love and lust. The more lust dominates the heart, the less the heart experiences the nuptial meaning of the body. It becomes less sensitive to the gift of the person, which expresses that meaning in the mutual relations of man and woman."[120] The need for this battle, John Paul II insists, will be evident to those who reflect on the nature of conjugal-corporal love itself, who sincerely face up to the dangers it is subject to, and who wish to do whatever is necessary to ensure its protection and growth. "Purity . . . tends to reveal and strengthen the nuptial meaning of the body in its integral truth. This truth must be known interiorly. In a way, it must be felt with the heart, in order that the mutual relations of man and of woman—even mere looks—may reacquire that authentically nuptial content of their meanings."[121]

John Paul II is sure of the fundamental optimism and attraction of the understanding of married sexuality that he outlines. His anthropological analysis becomes moral teaching that is im-

118. *Deus Caritas Est*, 5 (2005).   119. TB, 290.
120. TB, 126.   121. TB, 213.

bued with human appeal. "Does not man feel, at the same time as lust, a deep need to preserve the dignity of the mutual relations, which find their expression in the body, thanks to his masculinity and femininity? Does he not feel the need to impregnate them with everything that is noble and beautiful? Does he not feel the need to confer on them the supreme value which is love?"[122]

However humanly true and appealing his analysis is, it is thoroughly enmeshed in the Christian framework of redemption. Love inspires generosity and sacrifice, but if these remain at the purely human level, they are not enough. The help of God, obtained especially through the sacraments and fervent prayer, is necessary to attain that conjugal chastity and mutual loving respect without which the best aspirations of love may fail. To illustrate this, Pope John Paul II resorts to two of the more "romantic" writings of the Old Testament, the Song of Songs and the book of Tobit. He sees the well-known verse of the former, "*fortis est ut mors dilectio*" ("love is as strong as death" or "as stern as death")[123] as perhaps over-idealized in the Canticle but expressed at the true level of spousal love and of humble human experience in Tobit.

It is the concupiscent approach which destroyed the previous marriages of Sarah. Tobiah is well aware of this and leads Sarah also to understand how prayer brings strength to pure love so as to enable it to overcome the deadening power of concupiscence. From the very first moment Tobiah's love had to face the test of life and death. The words about love "stern as death," spoken by the spouses in the Song of Songs in the transport of the heart, assume here the nature of a real test. If love is demonstrated to be as stern as death, this happens above all in the sense that Tobiah and Sarah unhesitatingly face this test. But in this test of life and death, life wins because, during the test on the wedding night, love, sup-

122. TB, 167–68.   123. Sg 8:6.

ported by prayer, is revealed as more stern than death; their love "is victorious because it prays."[124]

Those who love readily understand the human value and attraction of pure, chaste, and disinterested love. But to feel the human attraction is not enough. In the Christian view, chastity remains a gift of God, one that is only achieved through prayer. "Since I knew I could not otherwise be continent unless God granted it to me (and this too was a point of wisdom, to know whose the gift is), I went to the Lord and besought him."[125] Opening his work on continence (or chastity), St. Augustine insists that this virtue is a gift of God for both the single and the married, "Dei donum est,"[126] an idea that he stresses elsewhere with special reference to marriage: "The very fact that conjugal chastity has such power, shows that it is a great gift of God."[127]

Conclusion

We have studied the establishment and prevalence over many centuries of the notion that marriage is ordered to the "remedy of concupiscence." The practical effect of this, in our view, has been to create a certain idea that marriage "legitimizes" concupiscence, an idea which, if further analyzed, amounts to saying that "marriage legitimizes *disordered* sexuality." I believe that Christian life has suffered from these long-standing and widely held views which have regarded concupiscence not as a force to be resisted (and purified) in marriage, but as simply legitimized by marriage itself where, in consequence, it can be given free rein. The understanding of marriage as an outlet for concupiscence is, I claim, what seems to be implied in the simple phrase, *remedium concupiscentiae*, and what has

124. TB, 376.   125. Wis 8:21 (Vulgate).
126. *De continentia*, 1.
127. "Et si tantas vires habet ista pudicitia coniugalis, tantumque Dei donum est" (*Contra Julianum*, 3:43).

in fact been the well-nigh universal interpretation given to the term.

From the standpoint of pastoral theology, I have endeavored to show that the longstanding use of this term has propagated a narrow and impoverished view of marriage which has consistently ignored the consideration of matrimony as a sacrament of *sanctification*. If so, then the disappearance of the term should further facilitate the renewed theological and ascetical understanding of marriage as well as that of its *vocational* nature,[128] which has been emerging in the last three quarters of a century, and which current magisterium has so insistently fostered. In this renewed understanding, rather than as a "remedy" or even as an outlet for concupiscence, marriage should be seen and presented as a call to a particular growth in love—in an effort, with the help of grace, to recapture the purity and chaste self-donation of the original human sexual-conjugal condition.

A balanced Christian vision will avoid both naive optimism as well as radical pessimism about human nature. It will always see man as a sick creature made for a divine destiny. This balanced view is needed also because the pathologies of human nature can only be properly evaluated by those who both face up to the reality of sin and, being convinced of the goodness of creation and the nature of original health, know the means and effectiveness of the redemption worked by Christ which enables us, despite our ailments, to achieve something much greater still than the fullness of that original health.

---

128. From the moment he founded Opus Dei, Josemaría Escrivá insisted that marriage should be regarded and lived as a vocation in the fullest sense; see *Christ Is Passing By* (ch. 8) and "Marriage: A Christian Vocation." See also *Conversations with St. Josemaría Escrivá* (New York: Scepter Press, 2002), nos. 24, 91–92, 99, and 106. Particularly notable is his remark in the opening chapter of *The Way* (original Spanish edition published in 1939): "You laugh because I tell you that you have a 'vocation for marriage'? Well, you have just that: a vocation" (no. 27). For a critical-historical commentary on this remark, in its context of the 1930s, see *St. Josemaría Escrivá: Complete Works* (New York: Scepter Press, 2009), 1:225.

Bibliography

Abellán, P. M. *El fin y la significación sacramental del matrimonio desde S. Anselmo hasta Guillermo de Auxerre.* Granada, 1939.

Acta Apostolicae Sedis [AAS]. Vatican City, 1909–.

Acta Sanctae Sedis. Vatican City, 1865–1904.

Aertnys, J., CSSR, and C. A. Damen, CSSR. *Theologia moralis.* 2 vols. Turin, 1950.

Alexander of Hales. *Glossa in IV Libros Sententiarum.*

Alves Pereira, B. *La doctrine du mariage selon saint Augustin.* Paris: Beauchesne, 1930.

Anciaux, Paul. *Le sacrement du mariage: Aux sources de la morale conjugale.* Louvain: Nauwelaerts, 1961.

Aubert, J. M. "Foi et sacrement dans le mariage." *La Maison-Dieu* 104 (1970): 116–43.

Augustine of Hippo. *Confessionum.*

———. *Contra Adimantum Manichaei Discipulum.*

———. *Contra duas epistolas Pelagianorum.*

———. *Contra Faustum Manichaeum.*

———. *Contra Julianum.*

———. *De agone christiano.*

———. *De bono coniugali.*

———. *De bono viduitatis.*

———. *De catechizandis rudibus.*

———. *De civitate Dei.*

———. *De coniugiis adulterinis.*

———. *De continentia.*

———. *De Genesi ad Litteram.*

———. *De gratia Christi et de peccato originali.*

———. *De moribus Manichaeorum.*

———. *De nuptiis et concupiscentia.*

———. *De peccato originali.*

————. *De peccatorum meritis*.

————. *De Trinitate*.

————. *Imperfectum opus contra Julianum*.

————. *In Evangelio Joannis tractatus*.

————. *Sermones*.

Baldanza, G., SJ. "La grazia matrimoniale nell'Enciclica *Casti connubii*." *Ephemerides Liturgicae* 99, no. 1 (1985): 37–59.

Ballerini, Antonii. *Opus theologicum morale*. Prati: Ex Officina Libraria Giachetti, Rilii et Soc., 1892.

Barberi, P. *La celebrazione del matrimonio cristiano*. Rome, 1982.

Baudot, Denis. *L'inséparabilité entre le contrat et le sacrement de mariage: la discussion après le Concile Vatican II*. Rome: Pontifica Università Gregoriana, 1987.

Bellarmine, Robert. *De Sacramento Matrimonii*. Venice, 1721.

Bersini, F. *Il Nuovo Diritto Canonico Matrimoniale*. 3rd edition. Turin, 1985.

Biblia Comentada. Madrid: BAC, 1965.

Boissard, Edmond. *Questions théologiques sur le mariage*. Paris: Cerf, 1948.

Bonaventure. *Sent. Lib. IV.* Ed. Quaracchi, vol. IV.

Bonner, Gerald. *St. Augustine of Hippo: Life and Controversies*. Norwich: Canterbury Press, 1986.

Bucceroni, Giovanni, SJ. *Institutiones theologiae moralis*. Rome, 1898.

Burke, Cormac. "The *Bonum Coniugum* and the *Bonum Prolis*; Ends or Properties of Marriage?" *The Jurist* 49 (1989): 704–13.

————. "La Indisolubilidad Matrimonial y la Defensa de las Personas." *Scripta Theologica* 22 (1990): 145–55.

————. "Sentence *coram* Burke." *Rotae Romanae Decisiones* 86 (December 12, 1991): 746–55.

————. "Marriage: A Personalist or an Institutional Understanding?" *Communio* 19 (1992): 278–304.

————. "Personalism and the *bona* of Marriage": *Studia canonica* 27 (1993): 401–12.

————. "Marriage: A Personalist Focus on Indissolubility." *Linacre Quarterly* 61, no. 1 (1994): 48–56.

————. "Sexual Identity in Marriage and Family Life." *Linacre Quarterly* 61, no. 3 (1994): 75–86.

————. "La Indisolubilidad como expresión del verdadero amor conyugal." *Revista Española de Teología* 55 (1995): 237–50.

————. "Love and the Family in Today's World." *Homiletic and Pastoral Review* (March 1995): 20–29.

———. "Personnalisme et jurisprudence matrimoniale." *Revue de Droit Canonique* 45 (1995): 331–49.

———. *L'Oggetto del Consenso Matrimoniale: un'analisi personalistica.* Turin: Giappichelli, 1997.

———. "Personalism and the Essential Obligations of Marriage." *Angelicum* 74 (1997): 81–94.

———. "Personalism and the Traditional *Goods* of Marriage." *Apollinaris* 70 (1997): 305–14.

———. "Progressive Jurisprudential Thinking." *The Jurist* 58, no. 2 (1998): 437–78.

———. "Sentence *coram* Burke." *Rotae Romanae Decisiones* 90 (March 26, 1998): 259–81.

———. *Covenanted Happiness.* New York: Scepter Press, 1999.

———. *Man and Values: A Personalist Anthropology.* Nairobi, Kenya: Scepter Press, 2007.

———. *The Lawless People of God?* 2nd ed. Nairobi, Kenya: Scepter Press, 2009.

Busenbaum, H., SJ. *Medulla Theologiae Moralis.* 1645.

Cappello, F. M., SJ. *Tractatus canonico-moralis de sacramentis.* Rome, 1927.

The Catechism of the Catholic Church. Rome, 1992. Editio typica, 1997.

Codex Iuris Canonici. Rome: Libreria Editrice Vaticana, 1983.

Codex Iuris Canonici, fontium annotatione auctus. Rome: Libreria Editrice Vaticana, 1989.

Communicationes (Reports of the Pontifical Commission for the Revision of the Code of Canon Law). Rome: Libreria Editrice Vaticana, 1969–83.

Compendium of the Catechism of the Catholic Church. Rome: Libreria Editrice Vaticana, 2005.

Congregation for the Doctrine of the Faith. "Considerations Regarding Proposals to Give Legal Recognition to Unions Between Homosexual Persons." June 3, 2003. http://www.vatican.va/roman_curia/congregations/cfaith/documents/rc_con_cfaith_doc_20030731_homosexual-unions_en.html

Covi, D. "El fin de la actividad sexual según San Agustín." *Augustinus* 17 (1972): 47–65.

Davis, Henry, SJ. *Moral and Pastoral Theology.* New York: Sheed & Ward, 1958.

Denzinger, H. *Enchiridion Symbolorum.* Freiburg: Herder, 1937.

Dickens, Charles. *David Copperfield.* New York: Penguin, 2004.

Doms, Herbert. *Vom Sinn und Zweck der Ehe: eine systematische Studie.* Breslau: Ostdeutsche Verlagsanstalt, 1935.

———. "Conception personnaliste du mariage d'après S. Thomas." *Revue Thomiste* 45 (1939).

Durandus of Saint Pourçain. *Super quattuor Sententiarum.*

Enchiridion Vaticanum. Edizioni Dehoniane. Bologna, 1992–.

Escrivá, Josemaría. *Christ Is Passing By.* New York: Scepter Press, 1995.

———. *Conversations with St. Josemaría Escrivá.* New York: Scepter Press, 2002.

———. *The Way.* New York: Scepter Press, 2002.

———. *The Way* (Critical-Historical Edition). In *Complete Works*, vol. 1. New York: Scepter Publishers, 2009.

Favale, A. *Fini e Valori del Sacramento del Matrimonio.* Rome, 1978.

Finn, R. C. "Faith and the Sacrament of Marriage." *Marriage Studies*, vol. 3. Washington, D.C., 1985.

Flannery, Austin, ed. *Second Vatican Council: Documents.* Grand Rapids, Mich.: Eerdmans, 1984.

Ford, John C., SJ., and Gerald Kelly, SJ. *Contemporary Moral Theology.* Westminster, Md.: Newman Press, 1963.

Freud, Sigmund. *Introductory Lectures on Psychoanalysis.* London: Allen and Unwin, 1952.

Fumagalli Carulli, O. "La dimensione spirituale del matrimonio e la sua traduzione giuridica." *Ius* 27 (1980).

Genicot, E. *Institutiones theologiae moralis.* Brussels, 1936.

Gherro, S. *Diritto matrimoniale canonico.* Padua, 1985.

Häring, Bernard. *The Law of Christ.* Cork: Mercier, 1967.

Hervada, J. *Vetera et Nova.* Pamplona: 1991.

Hildebrand, Dietrich von. *Die Ehe.* München, 1929.

———. *Il Matrimonio.* Brescia, 1931.

Hugh of St. Victor. *De sacramento coniugii.*

International Theological Commission. *"Foedus matrimoniale"*; "The Sacramentality of Christian Marriage." *Enchiridion Vaticanum*, VI Edizione Dehoniane. Bologna, 1992: 352–97.

Langa, P. "Equilibrio agustiniano entre matrimonio y virginidad." *Revista Agustiniana* 21 (1980): 73–134.

Lawler, Michael G. "Faith, Contract, and Sacrament in Christian Marriage: A Theological Approach." *Theological Studies* 52, no. 4 (1991): 712–31.

Leclercq, Jean. *Le mariage Chrétien.* Paris: Cerf, 1950.

Lehmkuhl, Augustinus, SJ. *Theologia moralis.* Freiburg: Herder, 1914.

Liguori, St. Alphonsus. *Theologiae Moralis.* 3 vols. Bassano-Remondini, 1785.

Linden, Gulliermus van der. *Panoplia Evangelica.* Paris: 1564.

Maggiolini, S. *Sessualità umana e vocazione cristiana.* Brescia, 1970.

Marc, C., CSSR. *Institutiones morales Alphonsianae.* Lugduni, 1900.

Mausbach, G. *Teologia morale.* Alba, 1956.

May, William. "The 'Good of the Spouses' and Marriage as a Vocation to Holiness." October 3, 2004. http://www.christendom-awake.org/pages/may/marriage-2.htm.

Merkelbach, B. H., OP. *Summa theologiae moralis.* Bruges, 1956.

Migne, Jacques-Paul. *Patrologia Latina* [PL]. 217 volumes. Garnier: 1844–55.

Miralles, Antonio. *El Matrimonio.* Pamplona: EUNSA, 1993.

Navarrete, Urbano, SJ. "Structura iuridica matrimonii secundum Concilium Vaticanum II." *Periodica* 56 (1967): 356–83, 554–78.

———. "I beni del matrimonio: elementi e proprietà essenziale." In *La nuova legislazione matrimoniale canonica.* Rome, 1986.

New Catholic Encyclopedia. Washington, D.C.: The Catholic University of America Press, 1967.

Nicolas, M.-J. "Remarques sur le sens et la fin du mariage." *Revue Thomiste* 45 (1939).

Noldin, H., SJ. *Summa theologiae moralis.* Innsbruck: F. Rauch, 1962.

Oddie, William. *Chesterton and the Romance of Orthodoxy.* Oxford: Oxford University Press, 2008.

Ordo Celebrandi Matrimonium. Rome: Libreria Editrice Vaticana, 1970.

Pesch, Christianus, SJ. *Praelectiones dogmaticae.* 9 vols. Freiburg: Herder, 1900.

Palazzini, P. "Il Sacramento del Matrimonio." In *I Sacramenti.* Rome, 1959.

Perego, A. "Fine ed essenza della società coniugale." *Divus Thomas* 56 (1953).

Pfnausch, E. G. "The Good of the Spouses in Rotal Jurisprudence: New Horizons." *The Jurist* 56 (1996): 527–56.

Piolanti, A., ed. *I Sacramenti.* Florence: Libreria Editrice Fiorentina, 1959.

Pope Benedict XVI. *Deus Caritas Est.* 2005.

Pope Gregory IX. *Decretales.* 1234.

Pope John Paul II. *Insegnamenti di Giovanni Paolo II.* Rome: Libreria Editrice Vaticana, 1979–2005.

———. *Familiaris Consortio.* 1981.

———. *Addresses to the Roman Rota,* 1984, 1987.

———. "Address to Members of the American Psychiatric Association, Jan. 4, 1993." *Osservatore Romano* (English Edition). January 13, 1993.

———. *Letters to Families.* 1994.

———. *The Theology of the Body: Human Love in the Divine Plan*. Boston: Pauline Press, 1997.

Pope Leo XIII. *Arcanum*. *ASS* XII. 1880.

Pope Pius IX. *Acta SS.D.N. Pii PP. IX*. Rome: 1865.

Pope Pius XI. *Casti Connubii*. *AAS* XXII. 1930.

Prümmer, D. M., OP. *Manuale theologiae moralis*. 3 vols. Freiburg: Herder, 1961.

Regatillo, E. F., and Zalba, M., SJ. *Theologiae moralis summa*. Madrid: Biblioteca de Autores Cristianos, 1954.

Reuter, Amandus. *Sancti Aurelii Augustini doctrina de bonis matrimonii*. Rome, 1942.

Rincón-Pérez, T. "Fe y sacramentalidad del matrimonio." In *Cuestiones fundamentales sobre matrimonio y familia*. Pamplona, 1980.

Roberti, Francesco. *Dictionary of Moral Theology*. Westminster, Md.: Newman Press, 1962.

Rotae Romanae Decisiones. Rome: Libreria Editrice Vaticana, 1908.

Samek, L. E. "Sessualità, matrimonio e concupiscenza in sant'Agostino." *Studia Patristica Mediolanensia* 5. Milan: Università Cattolica del Sacro Cuore, 1976.

Sánchez, Thomas. *De sancto matrimonii sacramento*. Lugduni: 1739.

Sarmiento, A. *El Matrimonio Cristiano*. Pamplona: EUNSA, 2001.

Schmaus, Michael. *Katholische Dogmatik*. Münich: M. Hueber, 1957.

Schmitt, E. "Le mariage chrétien dans l'oeuvre de Saint Augustin." *Études Augustiniennes*. Paris, 1983.

Simon, René. "Sexualité et mariage chez saint Augustin." *Le Supplément* 109 (1974): 155–76.

Slater, T., SJ. *A Manual of Moral Theology*. New York: Benzinger, 1925.

Smith, Janet E. "Conscious Parenthood." *Nova et Vetera* (English ed.) 6, no. 4 (2008): 927–50.

Tanquerey, A. *Synopsis theologiae moralis et pastoralis*. Paris, 1955.

Thomas Aquinas. *In IV Sententiarum Libros*.

———. *Scriptum super Libros Sententiarum*; *In VIII Ethic*.

———. *Summa contra Gentiles*.

———. *Summa Theologiae, I, I–II, II–II*.

———. *Super I Ep. ad Corinthios lectura*.

———. *Supplementum*.

Thonnard, F.-J. "La notion de concupiscence en philosophie augustinienne." *Recherches Augustiniennes* 3 (1965): 259–87.

Wojtyla, Karol. *Love and Responsibility*. San Francisco: Ignatius Press, 1993.

———. *Person and Community: Selected Essays*. New York: Peter Lang, 1993.

Wood, Susan. "The Marriage of Baptized Nonbelievers: Faith, Contract, and Sacrament." *Theological Studies* 48, no. 2 (1987): 279–301.

Wouters, L., CSSR. *Manuale theologiae moralis*. Bruges: Carolus Beyaert, 1932.

Wrenn, Lawrence. "Refining the Essence of Marriage." *The Jurist* 46, no. 2 (1986): 537–45.

Index

Alexander of Hales, 200

American Psychiatric Association, 76n8

Anthropology, xxii, xxiii, xxv, 28, 69, 72, 76, 93, 130, 135, 165, 167, 188, 205, 214, 218, 220, 227, 239, 245

Apostolicam Actuositatem, 83

Aquinas, Thomas, 7, 9n13, 10, 40, 43, 51, 64, 65, 79–80, 111, 142, 144, 155n73, 157n80, 162n91, 182, 195, 199, 214n71, 224, 231, 233

Aristotle, 80, 198

Augustine, xiii–xiv, xxii, 28, 35, 78, 84, 91–92, 125–63, 182, 189–99, 208n67, 215, 228n95, 230n99, 231, 236, 237, 241; conjugal love, 131, 138–40; defender of the goodness of marriage, 130, 138, 140, 152, 190, 192, 197; sexual pessimist, 126–27, 140–47; 202

Augustinian *bona*, 28, 62, 70, 91–93, 129–38, 163, 189–90, 196

Bellarmine, Robert, 7n8, 9, 33, 38, 84n29, 200n47

Bonaventure, 21n41, 41n25, 51n2, 170n9, 200

Bonum coniugum. See Good of the Spouses

Bonum fidei, 92, 130, 133

Bonum prolis, 63, 66, 70, 80, 92, 93, 94–96, 100n43, 130, 133, 187n11, 196

Bonum sacramenti, 63, 92, 93, 130, 133

Busenbaum, H., 200

Carnal knowledge, 157, 172–75

Casti Connubii, 34, 42, 55, 57n16, 63, 75, 83, 84, 165, 166, 205

Children, 44, 49, 63, 65n27, 84, 92, 93–96, 99, 129, 137, 175, 177; supreme gift of marriage, 133

Church law, 100, 103; pastoral function, 104–5; and personal rights, 110–14; and Vatican II, 107, 108–10

Code of Canon Law of 1983, xxi, xxiv, 35, 50, 56, 69, 103, 185, 217; Code of 1917, 74n4, 184, 218

Code of Canon Law (individual canons), c. 213, 108; c. 273, 109n4; c. 277, 109n4; c. 284, 109n4; c. 762, 108; c. 1055, 57, 58n19, 59, 67, 74, 75, 83, 88n34, 91, 99, 186; c. 1057, 57, 74–75, 77n10, 85, 94, 98, 157; c. 1095, 57, 101, 102; c. 1098, 57, 100; c. 1101, 99; c. 1103, 57; c. 1134, 35; c. 1603, 123

Celibacy, 109, 136n26, 194, 195, 206, 225n86; and personalism, 136–37

Concupiscence (lust), 142–47, 158, 181–83, 216, 235; an anti-love factor, 224, 226; a "deception," 234, 238; in marriage, 148–54, 160–61, 184ff.; not the same as sexual desire, 182, 188, 210–11, 231

Conjugal act, 52, 53, 54, 64, 159, 181, 204, 214; abstinence from, 224–25, 231; by it the spouses become *una caro*, 161, 217, 219n67; what makes it unitive, 167–69, 209, 219–21;

251

Conjugal act (*cont.*)
  inseparability of procreative and
  unitive aspects, 54, 65, 68, 149, 162,
  164–79; 219
Conjugal chastity, 46–48, 151–54, 160,
  162, 182, 208, 214, 237, 240, 241; in
  John Paul II's *Catechesis on Human
  Love*, 182, 208, 230, 233, 234, 238,
  240
Conjugal instinct, 43–44, 213–16
Conjugal love, 43, 47, 49, 54, 59, 60,
  77, 84, 85, 87, 97, 131, 132, 134, 135,
  158, 168, 171, 182, 222, 225, 230, 239;
  and children, 177, 185n3; is a difficult
  love, 45, 63, 116, 139, 221, 239; purification of, xxvi, 150n61, 211, 219, 221,
  223n83, 230–34; St. Augustine and,
  138–40. *See also* Marital love
Contraception, 133, 158, 164–80, 192,
  218n78; does not actualize marital
  union, 169–72, 174–75, 221

Davis, Henry, 201
Doms, Herbert, 52, 65n26, 204

Ends of marriage, 24, 49–70, 71–102,
  187; hierarchy, 50, 53, 55, 59, 60, 67,
  68, 187; institutional or personalist
  view, 50, 53, 55, 60; 135; interconnection, 60–62, 67, 135, 187; primary
  and secondary, xiv, 50–51, 53, 59, 184
Escrivá, Josemaría, 39n21, 45n35, 209,
  242

Faith, and marriage as a sacrament, 1ff.
Familiaris Consortio, 6, 14, 25, 34, 97,
  220
Ford (John)-Kelly (Gerald), 201
Freedom, 47, 73, 98, 106, 107n3, 131,
  136n25, 153, 226, 227, 230, 234; right
  and wrong use, 235–236

Gaudium et Spes, 2n2, 34, 54, 57, 58, 63,
  73, 75, 83, 116, 136, 185, 217, 236
Genesis, Book of, 3, 61, 68, 78, 79, 81,
  82, 151, 173
Good of the spouses, xiv, 50, 57–60,
  62, 63, 67–69, 71, 116, 186–87; biblical roots, xxiv, 61, 81–82; end, not
  essential element, 89–90; a fourth
  augustinian *bona* 91–93; canonical
  observations (exclusion of; incapacity for), 98–102
Graces of the sacrament of matrimony,
  44–49

Häring, Bernard, 201
Hugo of St. Victor, 50n2, 81n22, 199
Humanae Vitae, 54, 65, 69, 159, 166,
  176, 217

Indissolubility, xxv, 28, 51, 63, 78, 92, 93,
  97, 99, 112–19, 123, 125, 131, 132, 135n24
Individualism, xxii, xxv, 73, 76, 87, 99,
  105–7, 136n25
International Theological Commission,
  12, 25

Jerome, St, 191, 194

Krempel, Bernard, 52, 204–5

Lambeth Conference and contracep-
  tion in marriage, 165
Law, law-truth-justice, 111–12
Lawler, Michael, 16n30, 18n36, 27
Liguori, Alphonsus, 200
Lombard, Peter, 200
Lumen Gentium, 30, 83, 108, 110
Lust (See Concupiscence)

Man and Values, xxiin2, 74n3, 131n1
Manicheans, 127–28, 135, 137, 140, 141,
  149, 163, 189, 223

Marital love, 40, 87–89, 166, 167, 172, 205, 206, 220, 230; and happiness, 115–18; is creative, 176–77

Marriage, canonical form, 7n9, 9, 13–14; as a "communion of persons," 76, 176–77, 210, 215n72, 216, 219, 224, 226, 229; consent, xxiv, 3n3, 6–7, 8, 9, 10, 11, 12, 13–14, 20, 23, 33, 34, 36, 42, 51, 54, 55, 57, 66, 72, 74–77, 86–87, 94, 98, 99, 100–101, 157; essence, xxin1, 16, 52, 90, 92, 138, 147; gift of God, 194, 207; nature 8, 18, 57; properties, xxin1, xxv, 4, 90–91, 130; pessimism about: 28, 126; 136, 138, 163, 210; sacrament, 1, 23, 32–44; sacramental intention, 11, 16; sacramental rite, 6–7, 9, 13; school of love, 96, 116–17; vocation to holiness, 30–49, 70, 81, 182, 224, 235, 242. *See also* Ends of marriage

May, William, 72n1

Miralles, Antonio, 72n1

Mutuum adiutorium (mutual help), 51, 55, 59, 78, 81–83, 184n1, 187, 188

Nullity, declarations of, 113, 120–24

Optatam totius, 186

Ordo Celebrandi Matrimonii, 11, 23

Pastoral issues, 103–105, 110, 113, 119–21

Paul, St: 1, 143, 145, 157, 158, 183, 225; and First Corinthians, chapter seven, 158, 193–96, 202, 206–7

Pelagians, 128, 141–47, 163

Personalism, 43, 72, 76, 106, 134–35 ; and Individualism, xxii, 73, 136n25

Personalist values in marriage, 52, 54–56, 62, 113

Pontifical Commission for the Revision of the [1917] Code, 58, 185, 187, 188n13

Pope Benedict XVI, 21n43, 114n8, 239

Pope Gregory IX, 139n28

Pope Leo XIII, 27n55

Pope Paul VI, 54, 166

Pope Pius IX, 4n4

Pope Pius XI, 34, 42, 55, 56, 57n16, 83, 165, 205

Pope Pius XII, 53, 54, 55, 83, 112

Pope John XXIII, 112, 185

Pope John Paul II, 73, 132, 167, 178, 222; *Catechesis on Human Love*, 47, 56, 206, 208, 211, 211n70, 223, 224, 226–41

Presbyterorum Ordinis, 108

Prümmer, D.M., 209n67

Remedium concupiscentiae (remedy of concupiscence), 51, 181ff.

Roman Rota, xxi, 53, 96, 112, 135, 185n5

Same-sex marriage, 46, 179–80

Self-giving, 76, 123, 179; in marriage, xxv, 44, 46, 48, 77, 85–87, 93, 94, 149, 178, 209, 217, 220, 224

Self-sufficiency, 76, 95

Sex education, 155

Sexual complementarity, 46, 65, 79, 152, 159, 172, 178, 213, 221

Sexual excitement as distinct from sexual emotion, 237–38

Sexuality: in marriage, as self-giving, self-fulfillment, self-perpetuation, 178; need for purification, 150n61, 230

Sexual shame, 227–29

Shaw, George Bernard, 221n75

Smith, Janet, 133, 178n15

Slater, Thomas, 201

Trent, Council of, 84

Vatican Council II, xxii, 2, 18, 30, 34, 35,
   39n21, 42, 50, 54, 55, 56, 57, 58, 60, 67,
   72, 76, 94, 104–109, 111, 113, 133, 134,
   150n61, 184, 185, 187, 196, 200, 204,
   206, 236; personalist, 43, 105, 111
von Hildebrand, Dietrich, 52

Waldstein, Michael, 211n70
Wojtyla Karol (John Paul II), 32n4,
   136n25, 161n89, 168n7, 177n13, 236
Wood, Susan, 14n25, 17n32, 27, 44n32
Wrenn, Lawrence, 72n1

The Theology of Marriage: Personalism, Doctrine, and Canon Law was designed in Adobe Garamond and composed by Kachergis Book Design of Pittsboro, North Carolina. It was printed on 60-pound Natures Book Natural and bound by Thomson-Shore of Dexter, Michigan.

CPSIA information can be obtained
at www.ICGtesting.com
Printed in the USA
BVHW070945100620
581102BV00002B/133

9 780813 226859